IBN AL HAMRA

Arabesque

The publisher thanks Alan Fitz-Patrick & Ibrahim Al Busafi for their assistance in creating the book.

The spellings in this book are British English.

CONTENTS

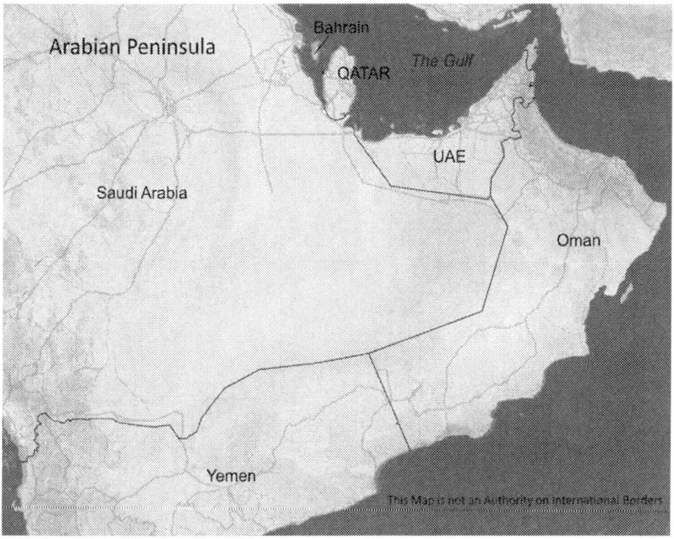

Arabian Peninsula
Bahrain
QATAR
The Gulf
UAE
Saudi Arabia
Oman
Yemen
This Map is not an Authority on International Borders

INTRODUCTION TO QATAR 2024

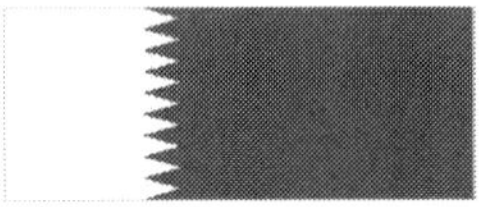

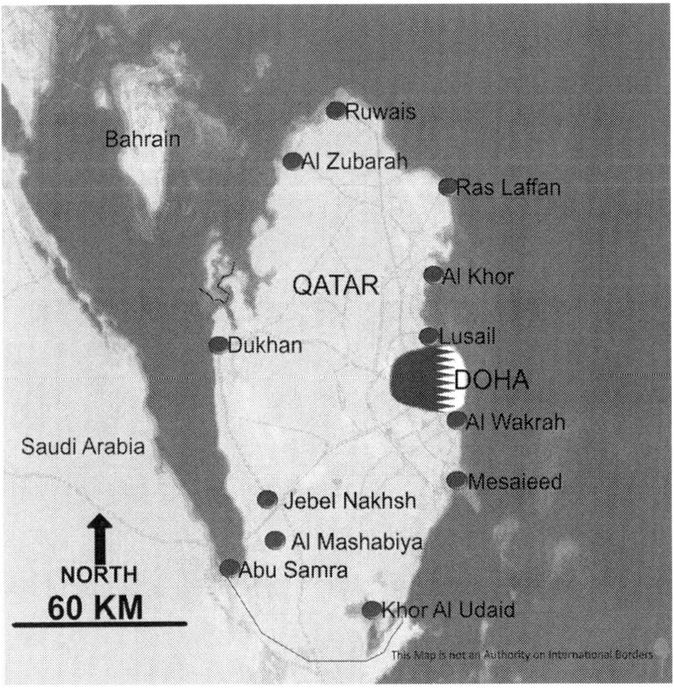

Qatar is a wonderful place to visit in 2024. The infrastructure is remarkable, and the government wants to make it easy for people to visit in 2024 and into the end of the decade. I hope this book will inspire you explore the country.

The book is organised into a short section on practicalities of getting into the country [PAGE 1]. Then places to visit [PAGE 36]– then a selection of restaurants [PAGE 145]and some hotel options [PAGE 170].

If you want to learn more about the country you will visit –

there is a section on the geography [PAGE170] & history of the country [PAGE 159]. You will then have a better idea of what has contributed to the development of the country.

CHAPTER 1
ARRIVAL INTO QATAR

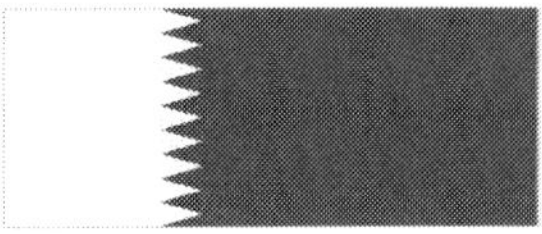

Qatar's arrival regulations have changed rapidly in the years up to 2024. They will continue to change. It's best to check the Qatari government websites below to see what the latest situation is

Key Websites

www.moph.gov.qa/english/Pages/default.aspx

www.visitqatar.qa

www.qatarairways.com/en-gb/visa-and-passport-requirements.html

dohahamadairport.com/airport-guide/at-the-airport/visas-immigration

london.embassy.qa/en

washington.embassy.qa/en

canberra.embassy.qa/en

berlin.embassy.qa/en

Nationals from 90+ countries can obtain a visa on arrival in Qatar in 2023. Passports should be valid for a minimum of 6 months from entry into Qatar. It would be prudent to have more time available in case your plans change or a flight is delayed. Citizens of some countries incl UK & USA can stay 30 days - others incl Germany & France can spend up to 90 days in Qatar – with the visa on arrival. A 30 day extension on payment of

QAR100 by credit/debit card can be obtained at the Ministry of Interior immigration office at Hamad International Airport (HIA) check-ins counter number 8. If a person does stay longer than 30 days - insurance is needed from any insurance company registered in Qatar. Qatar has a scheme 'Haya' hayya.qa/ that offers diverse benefits – such as use of eGates on arrival.

Other nationalities (including Indian sub-continent & Philippines) need to research visa options through www.qatarvisacenter.com

GENERAL ARRIVAL INFORMATION

For up-to-date information, check with your own country's foreign ministry

www.gov.uk/foreign-travel-advice/qatar/entry-requirements

travel.state.gov/content/travel/en/traveladvisories/traveladvisories/qatar-travel-advisory.html

and the Qatar government

visitqatar.com

COVID-19

During the Covid-19 pandemic the Qatari covid information could be obtained from **covid19.moph.gov.qa/** Many visitors needed to register on the Covid-19 Ehteraz App www.ehteraz.gov.qa/PER/

CUSTOMS

For customs, check the airport information **dohahamadairport.com/airport-guide/at-the-airport/security-customs**.
Prohibited items include, but are not limited to, weapons, firearms and ammunition/ alcoholic beverages/ pork products/ narcotic drugs (drugs include codeine as it contains opiates). If you take prescription drugs, consider bringing your doctor's prescription.

Tobacco allowance: 400 cigarettes.

Personal items and gifts up to a maximum value of QAR 3,000.

Imports of alcohol and narcotics are prohibited, as is anything to do with vaping, its liquid etc.

Check with the Qatar embassy in your country for official details.

Qatar Airways

ARRIVAL INTO HAMAD INTERNATIONAL AIRPORT (HIA)

Airlines serving HIA Doha include **British Airways** (Heathrow), Emirates (Dubai), **Pegasus Airlines** (Istanbul), Turkish Airlines (Istanbul), **Qatar Airways** (from innumerable airports including Austria - Vienna; Australia - Adelaide; Canberra; Melbourne; Sydney; Perth; Belgium - Brussels; Canada - Montréal–Trudeau; China - Hong Kong; Shanghai–Pudong; Denmark - Copenhagen; Finland - Helsinki; France - Nice; Paris–Charles de Gaulle; Germany - Berlin–Tegel; Frankfurt; Munich; Greece - Athens; India - Mumbai; Ireland - Dublin; Italy - Milan–Malpensa; Pisa; Venice; Rome–Fiumicino; Japan - Tokyo–Haneda; Tokyo–Narita; Netherlands - Amsterdam; Norway -

Oslo–Gardermoen; Poland - Warsaw–Chopin; Portugal - Lisbon; Singapore - Singapore; South Africa - Durban; Cape Town; Spain - Barcelona; Madrid; Sweden - Gothenburg; Stockholm–Arlanda; Switzerland - Geneva; Zürich; UK - Birmingham; Cardiff; Edinburgh; London–Heathrow; London–Gatwick; Manchester; USA - Boston; Chicago–O'Hare; Dallas/Fort Worth; Houston–Intercontinental; Los Angeles; Miami; New York–JFK; Washington–Dulles.

Allow plenty of time for immigration procedures and especially for emigration – signage is not especially good. You should also ensure that you have ample time when using transfer services.

Many airlines Apps offer flight information and, very usefully, update your checked baggage information, including what luggage carousel you should find it on. An App is helpful as in the unfortunate event that your luggage is delayed, you should know about it, shortly after landing, if you have internet access. Lost property HIA: Phone +974 4010 6666/4462 6531 - Airport hialostproperty@hamadairport.com.qa/ llqas@qataraviation.com haqiba.qatarairways.com.qa/ReportInquiry

Flight status dohahamadairport.com/airlines/flight-status

Inside the luggage area is an information area, **ATM machines** (ideal to use here as this area is less busy than outside in the arrival meeting hall), **currency exchange** operated by www.Travelex.qa (rates are not as reasonable as those fro money changers in the city). After immigration and customs, exit immediately into the arrivals hall, which has toilets, ATM machines, currency exchange, lost property and coffee shops.

In the airport look for **Bear Lamp** (HIA) - This giant sculpture of a Teddy Bear and lamp by Swiss artist Urs Fischer acts as a mascot for the airport and serves as a focus in the Duty-Free area.

Small Lie (HIA) - Small Lie, the oversize wooden marionette by Brian Donnelly, is in HIA departures area E (below the moving walkway).

Inter-Terminal Transfer

There is an automatic shuttle internal train within HIA, connecting the north & south nodes of the airport.

SIM Cards

Consider buying a Qatar SIM card. Ooredoo, the Qatari communications company, has kiosks after immigration at the airport. Pre-paid SIM cards (Hala card) with a value of QAR35 are also available, with top-ups available throughout the country. Ooredoo offers good coverage. Qatar also has a Vodafone mobile network. Often staff in the official shops can set up the SIM for you, if you wish. WhatsApp may not function without a VPN.

Getting to and from Hamed International Airport

Metro

The Doha Metro system's Red Line, also known as the Coast Line, has three termini. The Hamad International Airport (HIA) is one of these. The Metro connects the Airport with Msheireb interchange near Souq Waqif and onward to other stations, including West Bay, Legtaifiya near The Pearl (about a 30 minute journey) and the Lusail terminal. Al Wakrah is the southern terminal.

The Metro runs from 06:00 to 23:00 from Saturday to Wednesday, 06:00 to 23:59 on Thursday, and 14:00 to 23:59 on Friday.

The HIA Metro station (not the automatic shuttle internal train) is found outside the terminal.

To reach it on arrival, turn right after exiting immigration, take the lifts and follow the signs. The route through essentially straight changes floor level several times. Access directly to/from the Metro is via travellator & lift/escalator. Metro Tickets (Metro & also Tram at Lusail) cost QAR2 for a single journey & QAR6 for a single day pass. Buy a card only and top it up with a maximum charge of QAR6 per day (a Gold Car cost QAR30 and maximum charge QAR10 per day). Machines are inside the stations – the day card is probably best – unless the minute taken to buy it is important to save. The modern, clean trains usually leave at least every 10 minutes. There are helpful staff at stations - who will help with tickets.

For more information on the Metro, see [PAGE 30].

Bus Services Mowasalat (Karwa)

The Mowasalat Bus Station 25.259, 51.612 at HIA is signed; turn right after exiting immigration. Karwa is increasingly used for the Mowasalat brand name of their transport bus/taxi service.

From the Airport, bus services operate

Route 787 to Souq Waqif early morning only, 533 southeast Doha 24hours, 757 to Doha Umm Ghuwailina 24hours .

Fares are payable only with Karwa Smartcard, available from Karwa smart-card ticket machines at HIA – and in city and numerous places including supermarkets. The Karwa app is good, the seperate journey planner is poor. Fares are between QAR3 and QAR6, with most services run between 04:00 and 23:00 and running at least every hour. You tap in & tap out. For more details about bus transport, see [PAGE 33] or their App.

Taxi

The Taxi Kiosk is the easiest way to get a taxi from the Airport. This is signed at the end of the arrivals on the left side (east). The **Karwa taxi service** (run by Mowasalat) with turquoise colour cars from the Airport is metered with a minimum fare QAR25 and QAR1.20 per kilometre between 05:00 & 21:00 and QAR1.80 from 21:00-05:00. Bank card or cash payment only in Qatari Rials (get cash from the arrivals ATMs). It's possible to flag a taxi down in the street. Bookings in other locations 800-TAXI (8294) or by App. Some taxis have options for reduced mobility passengers; call 800-TAXI (8294), providing as much advance notice as possible.

Karwa Taxi

Uber also operates a taxi service in Doha. From the airport to West Bay, Sheraton/W Hotel area, a UberX may cost QAR36 and UberXL QAR46.

HIA has free **WiFi** - and free internet kiosks and desks around the Airport – and reasonable help to connect.

For more details about taxis, see [PAGE 29].

Car Hire

About 20 car rental services are available at the Airport exit, south of arrivals. They are straight ahead on the other side of the road using pedestrian crossings. Companies include - Europcar www.europcarqatar.com/; Avis www.avisqatar.com/ ; Hertz www.hertz.com/rentacar/reservation/ ; and local including Al Mana (a major Qatari group) http://www.almanaleasing.com/; Mustafawi http://www.mustafawi.qa/; Strong http://www.strongrentacar.com Rates are from QAR100 per day. If you use an international car-hire company, consider downloading their App, making any booking a better experience.

To rent a car for up to 7 days, a full current licence from various countries, including the UK/USA/EU, should be acceptable. It's ideal to have an International Driving Permit 1968 version-

For more car hire information see [PAGE 26]

SEA ARRIVAL - CRUISE

Cruise Lines call into Doha – principally on a circular cruise of The Gulf, similar to a Mediterranean or Caribbean cruise, usually with Dubai as the terminus. AIDA, MSC and TUI (Mein Schiff) have called variously into Abu Dhabi/Dubai/Oman/Bahrain/Doha in the winter months. Other cruise lines which visit Doha are on around the world cruises. The Houthi shipping attacks in the Red Sea may alter schedules.

Doha Port is less than 15 minutes' drive from either the National Museum [PAGE 46] or Museum of Islamic Art [PAGE 50]. Typically, a complimentary shuttle bus will connect the port with at least the nearby Museum of Islamic Art. It's a 1.5km walk from there to Souq Waqif [PAGE 56] or use the Metro or Karwa Taxi (app) to get around town. From the Museum of Islamic Art its less than 2km walk to the National Museum (or take a Taxi). Check with your cruise ship regarding a shuttle serivce.

The port has a village style shopping area and a small hotel. Look for foreign exchange services, taxi and bus stands, and a Duty-Free shop.

In Doha, shore excursions include a short city tour and a sand-dune safari. A 96-hour complimentary visa is generally available to cruise passengers (check with your cruise line). Your ship will liaise with the authorities regarding entry formalities (the ship will use your passport details).

Mina village Doha Port

LAND arrival - ROAD THROUGH SAUDI ARABIA

The border crossing into Saudi Arabia is at Abu Samra, in the southwest of Qatar. The name of the Saudi side is Salma. This is the only land border into Qatar. You should ensure that the documentation for all people in the car is up-to-date, including any exit/entry health requirements. Vehicle documentation also needs to be current, and in the vehicle. The insurance policy should include Qatar, the vehicle's registration country and any transit countries (such as Saudi Arabia). At the border there are immigration kiosks for GCC nationals and different ones for other nationalities – though officials may direct traffic into any kiosk. Exit requirements from Saudi Arabia need to be met, including any exit visa, if needed. If travelling from outside Saudi Arabia, you also need to consider the need for a Saudi visa and as mentioned vehicle insurance. Though there are petrol stations either side of the border – do fill up when you can. SAPTCO, the Saudi bus company, previously had a Riyadh-Doha service, though currently this does not operate. However, it is worth checking – as improved relations may mean the service is re-introduced after the publication of this book.

EMBASSIES

Many countries have embassies in Qatar, including Britain and the United States. Details are here hukoomi.gov.qa/en/ embassies . Qatar's embassies in other countries are detailed here www.mofa.gov.qa/en#The-World

Check your government's travel advice to Qatar. This advice will update periodically and impact areas such as holidays booked through travel agents and insurance validity.

www.gov.uk/foreign-travel-advice/qatar travel.state.gov/content/travel/en/traveladvisories/traveladvisories/qatar-travel-advisory.html

smartraveller.gov.au/countries/middle-east/pages/qatar.aspx

Children

Qataris love children, so if you travel as a family with young children, you will get a warm welcome. Hotels and many restaurants are usually pleased to have children; however, high chairs are a rarity, so factor this into your choice if needed. A critical issue for everyone, especially children, will be sunburn and heat. If you intend to hire a car or use a chauffeur drive type, inquire in advance about the availability of child car seats for your children. With any service request in Qatar, follow up before you arrive.

Clothing to consider wearing

What to wear in town is a bit more than personal choice, as the government, public places such as shopping malls, and occasionally Qatari individuals do impose their thoughts. If you are on holiday – you are in Qatar for enjoyment, but as in all countries its best to consider what is the official viewpoint to make for a hassle free time.

The Qatar Tourism Authority www.qatartourism.com/ says "visitors (men as well as women) are expected to show respect for local culture by avoiding excessively revealing clothes in public. It is generally recommended for men and women to ensure their shoulders and knees are covered."

The law in Qatar allows the police to act against people wearing, what is considered to be revealing or indecent clothes. As your version of "respect for local culture" and "excessively revealing clothes" may be a bit different from the police view in Qatar here are a few suggestions.

The cover-all garments worn by Qatari men and women, show the local cover-all style is prevelant with the local national citizen. Qatar's social media hashtag about clothing campaign is #Reflect_Your_Respect (check for the latest version).

It's best to try and be more conservative than you would normally. Inevitably there will be people in malls who don't follow the hashtag, but as a visitor its best to try and avoid any issues. Local people have a support network that can use if issues arise - and of course do know the current dress code (it can change). Shorts for men should be avoided in town, except for playing sports, and ideally a looser fit for trousers and shirts (not sleeveless). Women should avoid revealing strappy tops, short sleeves, crop-tops and low-cut tops; skirts or trousers should reach below the knee. Leggings for either sex should not be worn in place of only trousers. Shirts or T-Shirt without a design that includes text are ideal. Clothing with seemingly innocuous text such as 'I Love Dubai', or sports team's clothing whose sponsor is an airline of countries who boycotted Qatar for many years, including Emirates and Etihad, is best avoided given the previous political situation. Avoid bikini or speedo type swim-wear on public beaches. When not swimming, consider a loose 'cover-all'.

In general, loose-fitting non-transparent clothing is an ideal choice. The relatively high humidity in Qatar does reduce how quickly sweat evaporates. A polycotton mix is an excellent choice of material as the cotton will absorb sweat, and the man-made fibre helps keep the shape. If you have 'breathable' or fast-dry, that's also a good choice.

For most occasions, when eating out, 'smart casual' is all you will need, it's only in the more formal 5* hotels that you may need to 'button-up' – check with the specific hotel regarding this.

Doha has a largely well-paved street network so shoes that you find comfortable to walk around town should be ok. However, out of Doha, you will need shoes that can manage with rough, loose surfaces in the stony desert. Here, sandals are not ideal because they do not protect toes from stones, thorns and bites. In a sandy desert sandals can, however, help as they can avoid sand filling up inside a shoe.

Other

Qatar will have all the little things you need, such as pharmacies, good doctors, toiletries, personal care, and sanitary towels for women. Prices are broadly comparable to European prices.

Power

Qatar runs on 240v, and 50Hz electricity supply with sockets a mix of mainly square 3 Pin British style with some round 3-Pin (this was the old British style until the late 1940s); some electrical equipment is sold with a 2-pin plug. The UK is 230v and 50Hz, so Qatar power is usually compatible with UK standards though you may need a socket adaptor. The USA and Canada run on 120v and 60Hz; therefore, you need an adaptor for power and plug sockets. Australia runs on 230v and 50Hz so though you may not need a power adaptor but will need an adaptor for plug sockets. Your hotel may have adaptors for your devices; they certainly are widely available in Doha at low cost in larger supermarkets (Lulu etc)

CHAPTER 2
HEALTH AND ACCESSIBILITY

The quality of healthcare in Qatar is generally remarkably high. According to QPSA, there are 19 major hospitals with 3,134 beds. With about 890 persons per bed, this is roughly double the UK's 460 persons per bed and the USA's 410 persons per bed.

There are pharmacies, with English speaking staff, throughout Doha city and beyond, including some that open 24 hours. Larger pharmacies in Qatar are well stocked and these include the UK Boots brand franchise. Many of your requirements or a suitable substitute should be available at these pharmacies if you run out for any reason.

If you travel with medicines, bring the original prescription. Should you need more medicine, it's also helpful to show the prescription to a local Qatar healthcare provider. The medicine should remain in original packaging with enclosed use literature. Narcotics or psychotropic substances are on banned import lists. Codeine is, as are many Herbal medicines. For the UK government's take on this, read more www.gov.uk/foreign-travel-advice/qatar/health.

Ensure you have insurance to cover you for medical treatment, making sure you are covered for existing conditions, as you will have to pay for medical treatment in Qatar. Emergency evacuation in case of serious accidents needs to be considered.

Typical travel health threats, such as deep vein thrombosis (DVT), need to be considered.

The temperature and effect of the sun may well be the primary health issue that most visitors will need to consider. In mid-summer, the sun's angle in London is lower than in spring or autumn in Qatar. Therefore, protection against sunburn should be taken throughout the year; most especially for children. Drinking rehydrating liquids is essential. Outside air-conditioned buildings, the heat causes water loss. Inside, the drying effect of air-conditioning will also affect the body's water content. Consider the impact of heat exhaustion and heatstroke if you hike outside. Symptoms include red, dry or damp skin, headache, and dizziness. Water from the tap in Qatar is likely to be safe, certainly to brush teeth etc. In Doha, the water is desalinated seawater that leaves the Water Desalination Station safe to drink, though with a noticeable taste. However, the water-pipe system and any storage tank, may alter its safety.

You should review your own government's travel advice to Qatar, as they are experts in their specific field.

www.fitfortravel.nhs.uk/destinations/middle-east/qatar

wwwnc.cdc.gov/travel/destinations/traveler/none/qatar
(note the unique prefix)

It is essential to consult with your health care provider about your own personal health needs and precautions to take. That is the only way to ensure you get the correct advice.

Health care providers may review hepatitis A; hepatitis B; Rabies, tetanus vaccines as options. A health care provider may also discuss how the heat may affect a body and how you can be aware of symptoms, especially in younger and older people such as dry or damp skin, muscle cramps, nausea, headaches and confusion, mainly as some medications may increase the effect. Other areas they may discuss, might include preventing Leishmaniosis, which is spread by sand flies. This can cause itchy bumps, rashes, lesions and gland swelling. Other insect-spread issues they may discuss are Malaria, Dengue fever and West Nile virus. Mosquitos spread these. Ask your healthcare provider about their recommendation to repel insects. If you will travel outside towns in Qatar, Deet and Permethrin may be suggested. Some health providers may mention MERS-CoV virus (a Camel spread infection, including through drinking un-pasteurised Camel milk) that is related to SARS pneumonia and Crimean-Congo haemorrhagic fever (a tick-spread disease), though the incidence of these is incredibly low.

Check the latest COVID-19 situation covid19.moph.gov.qa/EN/Pages/Default.aspx

www.qatarairways.com/en-gb/travel-alerts/requirements.html

Check also with your government's website (as above) and with www.masta-travel-health.com or www.passporthealthusa.com for vaccinations that are suggested.

Special Needs Travellers

Though a modern country, Qatar does not have the range of facilities required by many travellers with special needs. Speak with your healthcare provider and specialised organisation for their knowledgeable advice in your particular instance. There are low floor buses in Doha with designated seating for people with special needs. Major shopping malls and 5* hotels will have the best facilities; many have lifts and broad corridors and, critically, special needs toilets. Souq Waqif has reasonable accessibility and special needs toilets; however, the uneven 'ancient' streets might cause problems. There are wide corridors and special needs toilets in the Museum of Islamic Art [PAGE 50]. The National Museum [PAGE 46] is very much worthwhile visiting and again has good access and wide corridors in galleries and special needs toilets. There are some steps at Mathaf Museum, but it does have special needs toilets. Most other museums have limited facilities. The wide pedestrian access and paved surface should add to the appeal of visiting the Corniche. Camel race tracks and other sports facilities have limited access. In short, Qatar may not be ideal but for many special needs travellers it should provide little real difficulty.

CHAPTER 3
SAFETY

For most visitors and residents, Qatar is a safe country, with few physical assaults or robberies. Although crime rates are low, crimes do happen in Qatar, though they are rarely reported. Use the same care about your personal safety, credit card, passport and personal possessions as you would at home.

Passive health and safety features in public places are often missing, these can be as basic as hand rails. It pays to pay more attention to your immediate environment and the impact it may have on your safety.

Having insurance when you visit Qatar is important as third-party liability within Qatar is decided under a vastly different legal system to many western countries. Any claims made in Qatar that are successful may attract a very much smaller monetary compensation than in most western countries.

Check out your own government's travel advice to Qatar [PAGE 2/10/22/238]

Alcohol & Drugs

Alcohol is sold in authorised places, including more expensive restaurants and hotel bars. Drinking alcohol in non-authorised places is prohibited. Alcohol may not be carried into Qatar. There is, however, a Duty-Free at the airport departures, which does sell alcohol for consumption once you have left Qatar (the shop will pack it in a sealed bag). Drinking alcohol in a public place or before driving etc, is well within a zero-tolerance area of Qatar's law enforcement – attracting, perhaps, a jail term of 3-years and large fines

Severe penalties are carried out for possession & use of prohibited drugs, as does trafficking in them. If a person is convicted, capital punishment is used in Qatar.

Avoid public **display of affection** with adults of the opposite sex. Even holding hands with your spouse or older children may be considered affectionate. Police action can result, if a complaint is made.

LGBT+

Homosexuality is absolutely prohibited in Qatar. Article 296 of the Qatar Penal Code details "One is convicted to no less than a year and no more than three years in prison in case of: 3- Leading, instigating or seducing a male anyhow for sodomy or dissipation. 4- Inducing or seducing a male or a female anyhow to commit illegal or immoral actions."

Qatar also made an issue of Rainbow coloured clothing and accessories during the World Cup – avoid wearing clothing that include Rainbow colouring. Penalties, if caught in sexual activity, can include imprisonment, physical lashing and potentially death. Do review your own government's advice [PAGE 2/10/238].

Language that might be considered abusive, or gestures that can be construed as offensive can attract police action. This is even if they are made within the 'privacy' of your car, towards another road user. Penalties include prison and fines.

Road Safety

The roads in Qatar, especially Doha, are in good to excellent condition. Major roads are 3 or 4 lanes in each direction – with good entry and exit roads. Signage is in Arabia and clear English.

Speed is in kilometres. With a young, wealthy population and powerful cars Qatar's most obvious safety issue might be driving. Sometimes there is little consideration to pedestrians or other road users, both within urban areas and out-of-town. If you drive, adopt a mode of 'defensive driving', especially staying alert to other road users' actions or potential actions. Ensure you and all your passengers wear seat belts.

Radar – the most up-to-date equipment will send traffic violations, real-time, to most car hire companies. The fines are attached to passport information and payable before exiting the country.

Outside Doha, straying animals may be met on roads, and these add to dangers when driving.

Off-road driving does increase the risk of accidents in all respects, especially at speed.

If walking on a roadside pavement, remain alert to the general traffic and, if possible, walk facing the traffic so that awareness of oncoming vehicles is possible. Drivers can be inconsiderate, as well as considerate, but it's the inconsiderate drivers you should remain alert for.

In some areas away from Doha, on the edge of small settlements, there may be feral dogs which can be intimidating when walking.

Media

Pornography is banned, and the internet is very effectively monitored and censored for what is considered offensive or subversive.

Your own government is unlikely to be able to offer more than basic advice about lawyers who can act for you if you are arrested, prosecuted or jailed.

Photography & Video

Doha's West Bay skyline is stunning – very Instagrammable. Around dusk is the ideal time as the skyscrapers lighting comes on – a terrific location to take photos from is the Dhow Harbour or Museum of Islamic Art [PAGE 50] park. Both this museum and the National Museum are also photogenic, though the Museum of Islamic Art offers a better variety of angles that can include the dhows in the harbour. Souq Waqif has a great deal to offer, from the buildings, shops, crowds and usually the Arabs on horseback and less often camels; don't forget the falcon souq. If you are into exotic cars there are plenty in Doha. The Pearl is often a good place to grab a photo of several cars - afternoons onwards especially at weekends are ideal times. The general scenery is more difficult to capture in a good photo as its a monotone and flat landscape. However in the late afternoon Khor Al Udaid [PAGE 81] is good along with the west coast for sunsets.

Do be a bit cautious of where you take photographs. Any government building, palace or military and security (police etc) location are protected areas and not to be photographed.

The focus by western media on the working conditions of labourers in Qatar does mean that construction sites should not be photographed.

Its best to avoid photography of individual people without their permission, especially women.

Your own country's foreign ministry's advice regarding Qatari culture is worth reading for an official perspective

www.gov.uk/foreign-travel-advice/qatar/local-laws-and-customs

travel.state.gov/content/travel/en/international-travel/International-Travel-Country-Information-Pages/Qatar.html

CHAPTER 4
GETTING AROUND & INTERNAL TRANSPORT

WALKING IN DOHA IS POSSIBLE IN MANY AREAS, especially closer to the sea. The heat & humidity is a factor in you deciding whether to walk – or use transport. There are extensive parks from near the Museum of Islamic Art through to The Pearl [PAGE 107]. Al Bidda Park [PAGE 68] is the largest, and cycles are available to hire here at Saikl [PAGE 71]. There is plenty of underground parking here, and the Al Bidda Metro station and buses offer public transport. Around the Corniche Metro station are a couple of small gardens. North of West Bay is 5/6 Park, with its maze. As well as its beach, Katara has Katara Green Hills, served by Katara Metro station on the Red Line.

The main Corniche in Doha is very walkable, with metro stations and bus routes giving easy access. The park behind the Museum of Islamic Art could be a good finish, as it has a few coffee shops near. A walk from Souq Waqif [PAGE 56] through to Msheireb [PAGE 66] has lots of interest, making it a pleasant slow experience. South of Doha, the beachfront at Al Wakrah [PAGE 78] is an excellent choice for a stroll.

The heat may be a deciding factor in how far you choose to walk.

In Doha, public transport gives reasonable access to many areas of interest. The Metro is supported by a MetroLink bus service, where individual bus routes feed to and from a Metro station. The bus network spreads throughout the city. It concentrates on main roads, especially towards Doha's southwest, where there is a light industrial, and there is accommodation for construction workers. App-based taxi services offer a way to augment public transport, for example from a Metro station to a final destination. They can be flagged down on the road. All transportation is air-conditioned.

Note that the **Metro is closed on Friday morning** through to 14:30 (Friday afternoon) and does not operate between midnight-06:00 most days – though Karwa bus and taxis services do work.

Qatar road

Driving

Qatar drives on the right-hand side of the road (the driver sits on the left of the vehicle as in Europe and much of the world). There is a mix of traffic light controlled road junctions, roundabouts *(rotary)* and flyovers (overpass) and underpass. Signage's text is in Arabic and English with speed and distance signs in kilometres with numbers only in the Hindu/Arabic number system (as used in the west). Vehicles are typically automatic, with air-conditioning. In essence, driving regulations are comparable to most western countries. These include not leaving the scene of an accident (see below), fines for illegal parking, penalties for not wearing seat belts, using phones etc. The maximum speed is 120kmph, with lower speeds down to 60kmph. There are some 100 petrol stations in Qatar, offering various services, including shops and car wash. Petrol (gasoline/fuel) prices are set by Qatar Petroleum (based on oil prices) and recently have varied between QAR 1.20 – 2.10 per litre. Service is by an attendant who is low paid. A small tip/rounding up helps, especially if your windscreen was cleaned while the vehicle is refuelled.

A road network of five, four and three-lane motorways serve Doha, which, despite the 120kmph speed limit, encourage speeding by being broad and relatively traffic-free out of town. Fixed location and mobile speed radar with still and video cameras include sophisticated recognition systems including the number plate & face; allow the imposition of fines including phone use. There is no regulation requiring any warning of a specific speed-trap camera. Speed bumps and 'speed tables', which often have little notice or visibility, attempt to slow traffic. If you hit one at speed, damage may occur to your chassis. Trucks are prohibited from using roads in Doha from 06:00 -08:00 / midday - 15:00; 17:00 p.m. - 22:00. Due to the traffic volume, you will find roads especially heavily congested during these hours.

The original core of Doha, which is focused on Souq Waqif, is now surrounded by a series of ring-roads. The inner ring road is now named Al Diwan St. Moving outward is B Ring Road, C, D, E (D & E combine to the west and become the Doha Expressway), F and G (which leads to the Salwa/Lusail Route. A less easily oriented series of roads form a network north and west of West Bay.

For many short-term visitors, there will be a crucial couple of roads. Firstly, the Corniche, which follows Doha Bay and gives immediate access to The National Museum, Museum of Islam Arts, Souq Waqif and West Bay. The Corniche is a very scenic drive or a 7km walk. It is also a direct route for public transport connecting many of Qatar's principal tourist attractions. This route is also used by taxis coming from the airport.

The second key route is a driving route leading from the port around the city. This route is formed by the Ras Abu Abboud Expressway, B Ring Rd, Al Khaleej St, Al Istiqlal St and Lusail Expressway, which acts as an inner ring road skirting south of Souq Waqif and leading to Katara and The Pearl.

Car Hire

Renting a car in Qatar is possible for visiting nationals of many countries (including UK, EU, USA etc.). There is mostly a minimum age of 25years & older (some companies have an age limit of 21+) holding a full licence for over a year.

The licence of your home country is valid for 7 days and if supported by an International Driving Permit (1968 variety) this can be valid for up to 6 months. A temporary driving licence is available in Qatar and is legal for up to 3 more months. Passport & photocopies and 3 colour passport-style photos are required to apply. Applications at Traffic Department Headquarters, Omar Bin Abdul Aziz St, Doha, Qatar, must be made in person (cost QAR160). The licence may be issued after 5 days.

A license issued from a GCC (Gulf Cooperation Council) country is also valid.

These requirements vary with the car hire company - some may be unaware of new regulations - and others may simply be more cautious.

Also required will be your credit card - with several months validity and your Passport for photocopies. Fines must be paid before departure. They can also be automatically debited from your credit card from the security deposit you gave.

Remember to check the car for dents, scratches, marks and the mileage - photographs should be taken before you accept the vehicle. Do not forget to do the same for the interior. Make certain there is a functioning spare tyre, jack and tools.

Also ask the hire company to check for any fines that the vehicle might still have outstanding. Consider whether to accept that car - as its quite possible for the police to stop the car and expect you, the driver, to pay the fines incurred by previous drivers (who may be living in Qatar and therefor not have passed through the airport).

Keep all the paperwork for the hire in the vehicle. Ensure you have the car hire company's emergency number; make sure whether the car should be returned with a full or (near) empty tank. Know the number of included kilometres allowed per day, the charge per extra kilometre and how much 'deposit' is held against your credit card.

Driving without a suitable licence is a crime in Qatar and also voids any insurance. Other crimes include - allowing children under 10 years old to occupy a front seat; driving over the speed limit; driving under the influence of alcohol or drugs; leaving an accident you are involved in; not wearing a seatbelt; illegal parking; jumping a red light, carrying a greater number of people in a vehicle than there are available seat belts; using a mobile phone while driving – including checking it for any purpose. The speed limit on most in Doha roads is between 60-100 kilometres per hour. The maximum speed on highways is 120 kilometres per hour. As the express routes are in such good condition - and out of the city have low traffic densities - use cruise control to keep within the speed limit. Radar – with the most up-to-date equipment (car number plate recognition/face/use of phone etc) will send traffic violations, real-time, to most car hire companies. Fines are attached to your passport information and must be paid before departure.

Always check in advance with a car hire company for their specific requirements.

If needed check if a car hire company offers a booster seat for children, Sat-Nav, camera and parking assist sensors.

Qatar has numerous car hire companies, including

Europcar www.europcarqatar.com/; Avis www.avisqatar.com ;Hertz www.hertz.com/rentacar/reservation ;And local including Al Mana http://www.almanaleasing.com/; Mustafawi http://www.mustafawi.qa/; Strong http://www.strongrentacar.com .

Rates are from QAR120 per day for a small car to around from QAR500 for a 4x4.

If you use an international car-hire company, consider downloading their App that may make any booking a better experience.

Accident Reporting

To register a minor road accident, you can use Metrash2 App. You may obtain and activate Metrash2 Service through SMS or Self Service Kiosk, or helpdesk@moi.gov.qa. Speak with the car hire company while receiving the vehicle about this App and accident regulations as requirements can change. It is not essential to hire a car.

In case of an accident, speak with the car hire company at once to seek their updated advice as they may handle the below for you.

Irrespective of the circumstances or blame remain calm and polite to others involved.

In case of injury

1/ Phone 999 – Ambulance

2/ Advise your location

3/ Answer any questions from the emergency service

4/ Follow their advice

For minor accidents, you can (after speaking with the car hire company - always do this as regulations can change and they will know exactly what you should do).

1/ Supply no more than four pictures of each vehicle. One photograph should show the vehicle's number plates clearly.

2/ Move your vehicles from the scene and park away from the road.

3/ Ensure the location services of your phone are enabled.

4/ Sign in to Metrash2, select 'Traffic Services', and open the 'Accident Report' option.

5/ Enter details of both vehicles and note the Vehicle number plate, driver's identification card number & driving licence (all residents of Qatar have an identification card), and mobile phone number – dial it to ensure it is correct.

6/ Attach photos of both vehicles and click on the agreement on the validity of the data.

7/ Send the report to the traffic investigation police.

8/ A notification SMS (text message) will be sent to you asking to wait for another text to complete the procedures.

9/ After reviewing the accident photos by traffic investigators, an SMS will be sent to both parties with instructions to go to your insurance company for vehicle repair approval. The vehicle repair police report can be printed from the Ministry of Interior's official website, or the insurance company concerned.

These regulations can change. It's ideal to contact the car rental company and request that they deal with everything; it's a bureaucratic process, and they are used to it. Ensure you are kept informed by text or email so that you have a record and can also respond if needed.

Taxi

There are various taxi services available, including the turquoise coloured Karwa taxi service (run by Mowasalat / Karwa), which is metered with a minimum city fare QAR7 and QAR 1.60 per kilometre (these charges have been changed frequently so do check) between 05:00 & 21:00 and QAR1.90 from 21:00-05:00. It's possible to flag a taxi down in the street or use Bookings 800-TAXI (8294) or by Karwa App. Some taxis have options for reduced mobility passengers; call +974 4458 8888, providing as much advance notice as possible, or download the Karwa app. Pay by Cash/Card etc.

Uber also runs a taxi service in Doha. From the airport to West Bay, Sheraton/W Hotel area, an UberX may cost QAR36 and UberXL QAR46. Cashless payment is used.

Irrespective of the type of taxi you use, always check how the fare is calculated and never accept a ride where the driver says that 'you decide' on the fare. When the journey stops – almost certainly he will then decide the fare. Agree the fare in advance making sure it's the total with no 'waiting' charges etc – preferably when you have an idea of a reasonable rate.

If using Karwa to get to a Metro station - use the code 'Rail' to receive a 20% discount (see also the MetroLink bus).

Metro

For many visitors a combination of the Metro, the feeder bus service MetroLink and Tram service in Lusail is all thats needed for transport.

At the Metro passengers will find helpful staff near the ticket machines.

The Metro uses on a travel card pass system; for standard carriage & each person above 5 years needs a valid travel card. There are standard carriages, 'Gold' carriages (specific card) and family/female carriage (no men unaccompanied by a female).

A single journey is QAR2. A full day travel pass is capped at QAR6/- A standard travel pass costs QAR10/-, and credit must be added for valid travel. The cards are also used on the Lusail Tram (but not Karwa buses). Other values, and Gold Club carriage services (a card costs QAR100 and needs credit added, and charges are capped at QAR30 daily), are available and obtainable at Metro stations. Journeys are timed for charging. The maxim time given per journey is 90mins.

The Metro works from 06:00 to 23:00 from Saturday to Wednesday, 06:00 to 23:59 on Thursday, and 14:00 to 23:59 on Friday. The **Metro is closed on Friday morning** through to 14:30 (Friday afternoon) and does not operate between midnight-06:00 most days.

The Doha metro system has three lines (Red, Gold, and Green) and 37 stations open (more stations and an additional line may open after this). They are part underground in central Doha and part elevated overground elsewhere.

Doha Metro

The **Red Line**, also known as the Coast Line, has three termini including **Hamad International Airport**. The line travels through West Bay and onto Lusail. Two interchanges, Al Bidda and especially Msheireb, are within walking distance (1.5 km) to Souq Waqif.

The east-west **Gold Line** (Historic Line) stretches from Ras Bu Aboud to Al Aziziya. It includes the interchange at Msheireb and the stations at Souq Waqif also for the Museum of Islamic Art) and National Museum.

The **Green Line** from Al Mansoura, in southern Doha, also passes through the two interchanges, Al Bidda and Msheireb and on west to Al Riffa. Use www.qr.com.qa/qrgis/PlanMyJourney/ for planning.

The **Mowasalat MetroLink** bus service is intended to supply a last kilometre service to and from a Metro station. This runs from around 05:30 through to around 23:00 Sunday to Wednesday and finishing later on Thursday & Saturday and starting later and finishing later on Friday. The services, which operate several times an hour, are circular routes from outside most metro stations (ask station staff as the stop is not always next to the Metro station's doors).

Use the Karwa App for more information.

MetroLink bus at Al Qadeem Metro

A **MetroExpress** passenger van service is available 'on-demand' to registered Metro passengers to/from 6 central stations. It is requested on Karwa App.

Tram

Within the Msheireb area is a circular tram system with 9 stops (Sahat Al Nakheel: Wadi Msheireb – for the Metro: Galleria – for Souq Waqif: Msheireb Prayer Ground: Heritage Quarter – for the museums: Al Baraha: Sahat Al-Masjid: Al Kahraba Street: Al Mariah Street Station). It runs between 06:00 and midnight. It's a popular complimentary service.

There is a tram service in Lusail town, with a terminal at Lusail & Legtaifiya metros also in Al Seef (Lusail coast) a new development). The Metro Travelcard is valid on the Lusail tram (there is no Gold Club on the trams)

Bus

Mowasalat's Karwa buses (a distinctive turquoise colour) in Qatar have a Karwa payment card system, with a tap on entry and exit charge system. Fares range from QAR2.50 to QAR9 for longer journeys out of Doha. The cards are available in two 24hour options (QAR10 for 2 journeys within 24 hours of purchase and QAR20 for unlimited travel within 24 hours of purchase). A long term rechargeable card is QAR30. Ticket Vending Machines are available at HIA - they are also available from Karwa Bus Stations, and Ooredoo (mobile phone network provider). Larger supermarkets such as Lulu and Carrefour also sell them.

Karwa bus

Obvious Red Boxes on the Road usually mark bus stops – and a small sign.

The '**Doha Bus**', a private tourist service, offers a Hop on – Hop off type service [PAGE 140].

Bicycle & Scooter

Using a bicycle is unusual as daily transport for western expats in Doha.

However leisure cycling is increasing in popularity. Carbon Wheels [PAGE 93] offers products and repair services. Residents of Doha cycle on the expressway road routes; however, for a visitor, it would be prudent to ride with more locally experienced riders.

There are some short leisure cycling options in Aspire Park or Al Bidda Park. A longer distance route runs from near Doha Sports Park GPS 25.378, 51.498 - north through Lusail to near Al Bayt Stadium, Al Khor GPS 25.654, 51.495 (about 32km one way).

Cycle track Lusail

The earlier annual cycle Race, the Tour of Qatar, by Tour de France since 2002, was dropped after 2016. It was held in early February over 5 days - perhaps it will run again.

For short trips **E-Scooters** can be rented on-demand in Doha. Loop Mobility (App) http://www.loopmobility.co/ and more companies incl Falcon Ride, Fenix. Check for latest conditions if renting. Look for where you can use them (things like cycle lane etc) - and where to return/leave them. This is a relatively new form of transport and regulations change - and use enforcement will be imposed.

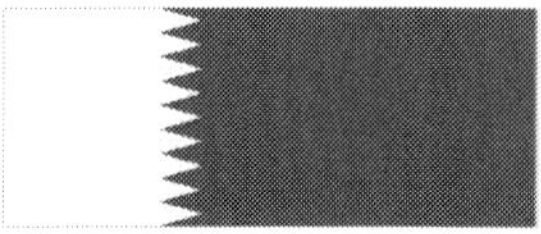

CHAPTER 5
PUBLIC HOLIDAYS AND RELIGIOUS PERIODS

2024/2025/2026 - JANUARY 1 **NEW YEAR'S DAY** (BANKS only, not official government holiday)

2025/2026 - February second Tuesday in February **National Sports Day**.

2025/2026 - March the first Sunday in March **Holiday for banks only.**

2024 March 10/ 2025 February 28 / 2026 February 17 **Ramadhan** [PAGE 245] dates depend on the lunar new moon sighting. The start is officially announced, possibly the day before. The end of Ramadhan is dependent on the beginning of Eid Al Fitr

2024 April 10 / 2025 March 30 / 2026 March 19 **Eid Al Fitr** an Islamic holiday. The dates are dependent on the lunar new moon sighting, and the start is officially announced, possibly only the day before. The number of days' holiday are around 5. These may start before that actual date of Eid – and with a weekend, this means government and business are closed for a week+.

2024 June 18 / 2025 June 6 / 2026 March 26 **Eid Al Adha** is an Islamic Holiday. Announcements as with Eid Al Fitr.

2024/2025/2026 December 18 **Qatar National Day** – (Founder's Day - public holiday). This is an official holiday on the same date each year. Typically, a celebratory parade is held on the Corniche (which as a result is closed around this date) and activities are organised elsewhere such as Souq Al Waqif, Al Wakrah Old Souq, Aspire Park, Al Rami Sports Club, Katara Cultural Village and Qatar Foundation.

CHAPTER 6
EASY QATAR

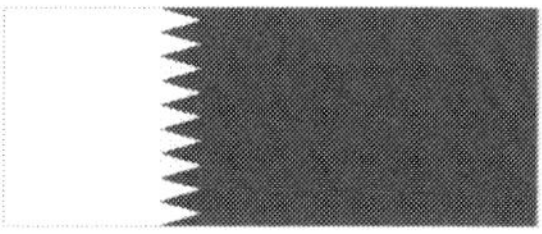

Culture vultures half-day in Doha

If all you have is a few hours free in Doha - this is for you. Transport links are good using either the Metro (Msheireb or Souq Waqif) or Taxi. Start with visiting the impressive Museum of Islamic Art [PAGE 50]. This visually imposing building is built on a man-made island, accessed by an avenue of Date Palms. To the east is a park and the rear overlooks the harbour in Doha. The five floors hold an impressive collection of, as it says, Islamic art.

From the museum, take a 1.5-kilometre walk west along the Corniche into Souq Waqif [PAGE 56]. About halfway is the dhow harbour, which is worth a detour if you have time. Souq Waqif was the original trading hub of Doha. Today it is a labyrinth of small shops and cultural sites. Restaurants [PAGE 147], where you can refuel after your walk. Prices range from budget to luxuriously expensive.

Museum full day in Doha

This is for you if you have a full day free in Doha and want to immerse yourself in history and culture. The National Museum Metro gives quick access to begin the day.

The National Museum [PAGE 46] is an ideal place to begin. This was opened in 2019, and its focus is, in general, on the history and culture of Qatar. The building's design is based on the crystal 'desert rose' formation, though it could also be likened to a jumble of flying saucers. The interior is spacious and surprisingly immersive.

Museum of Islamic Art & Doha skyline

Walk, or call a taxi for the 2km journey to the Museum of Islamic Art [PAGE 50]. The route cuts west and then north past the Movenpick hotel on Ali bin Amur Al Attiya St. This museum is spread over five floors, with specially collected exhibits. The museum includes various temporary exhibitions and dining choices.

Stroll along the Corniche, where a superb choice of options is available for lunch in Souq Waqif [PAGE 147]. After lunch, explore Souq Waqif [PAGE 56] which is an intriguing maze of shops and sights, including the Falcon Souq.

From Souq Waqif, its less than 800metres to the Msheireb Museum's complex [PAGE 66] in the west. The museum's four buildings offer insight into Doha's cultural and social changes over its recent history. Use the free tram to see what the Msheireb area is then take the Metro from Msheireb Station at the end of the day.

Dune bashing and a stroll through Katara full day.

South of Doha are the dunes bordering The Gulf. To experience these, make an advance booking with your choice of tour operator [PAGE 139]. Check with your operator about any lunch options by the sea.

The drive south from Doha is initially along expressways before arriving at powder-like white dunes, spread like a carelessly tossed blanket. It's quite an experience to drift through these dunes in the care of a skilled 4x4 driver.

Returning to Doha, organize for you to be taken to Katara [PAGE 99], where your paid tour can end. Here within a distance of only 500metres is the Postal Stamp Museum [PAGE 103], a centre devoted to Falcons and hunting [PAGE 100], some great restaurants [PAGE 159] and a plethora of sights. The Katara Metro station is easy an easy walk at the end of the day.

Beach Day Pass

Most of the beach front hotels have day pass options to use their beach. The cost might range from QAR250-500 - there are lots of things that change the price such as day of the week or if it's in a holiday period. Alternatively, the beach at Katara is much lower in cost **www.katara.net/Visiting/Visting-Katara-Beach**

Alternatives are B12 Beach Club, Doha, in the West Bay area. Day pass for QAR 200 at the weekend and QAR 150 during the week - under 18 free. +97459996122

Doha Sands, a day pass for QAR 100 at the weekend and QAR 75 during the week - those under 18 enter for free.

West Bay Beach westbay-beach.com/, day pass for QAR 50 - under 12 enter for free. Extra charges for equipment. Hours 08:00 – 02:00 all on Dafna Street.

CHAPTER 7
GUIDE

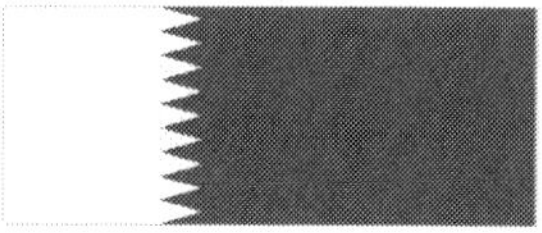

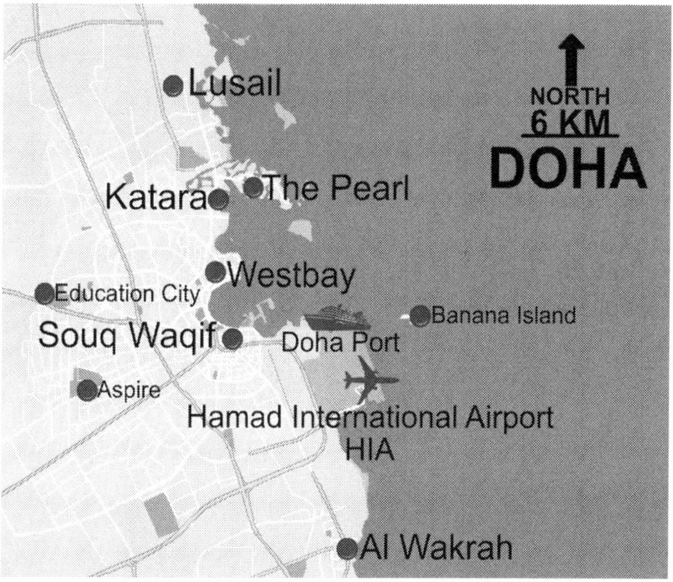

DOHA HAS AN INCREASING NUMBER OF ATTRACTIONS, mostly grouped in easy to get locations. This guide lists the places to visit in geographical order rather than by type.

In Doha, for instance, they are detailed below in their order if you chose to walk. This means that starting, for example, at the

National Museum and going towards Souq Waqif, the next entry in the book is also the next tourist place to its west; the Fish Market, then the Islamic Art Museum, Riwaq Gallery and so on. From Doha, the guide heads to different areas in Qatar. You can visit these places in the order listed or select those that interest you; check the index for their entry.

Restaurants and hotels cover these briefly. The guide would be vast - and in any case so many open weekly - that it would be impossible to keep up. Use these as a start for your own research, they are worth considering.

When visiting, you need to consider your own fitness, general health, heat and humidity on the day you visit and decide whether to walk or take transport. Only you or your health advisor can choose this. Always have drinking water to hand, and also when losing electrolytes, their replacement may be needed. GPS details are a general reference, not for exact location or navigation by, as your own device may record details differently. Anomalies in satellite transmission may also change accuracy.

Public transport in Doha is excellent, modern, well maintained and integrated. For a visitor the Metro, feeder buses and trams may be all the transport needed.

CHAPTER 8
PLACES TO VISIT

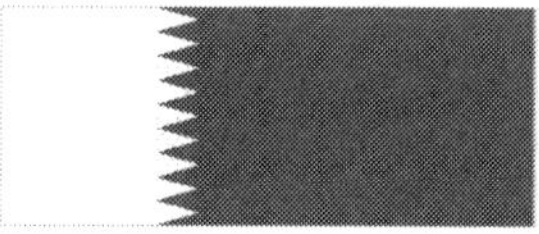

CORNICHE, SOUQ WAQIF & CENTRAL DOHA

Dhow Building Yards / مصنع السفن - Easily reached on the eastern part of the Al Corniche is a small Dhow Building Yard. This is a private operation; however, a smile and a request to look is usually answered with a 'welcome'. However as this is prime real estate it may disappear in favour of a boutique hotel, sooner rather than later.

Typical hours - appx 08:00-17:00 Sun-Thurs Entry charge – no charge

Rough GPS - 25.285, 51.560 Street - Ras Al Aboud

Expressway just east of Oasis Hotel. - Al Corniche / الكورنيش Public Transport - Bus 109,777 Metro Gold Line National Museum

National Museum

NATIONAL MUSEUM OF QATAR

- متحف قطر الوطني /

The National Museum of Qatar is intended to bring to life the story of Qatar. The modern museum, which opened in 2019, is a multi-level building, with the collections held on what amounts to a single floor, which weaves around the structure for around 1,500m. The exterior structure is fibre-reinforced concrete discs, 539 in all, supported by a steel structure.

Jean Nouvel drew his inspiration for the exterior appearance from the 'desert rose'. These are evaporative crystals of mineral-rich sands in a previously saline environment. With little imagination, it also looks like a crash-landing of UFOs. Scattered around the grounds are small gardens and an activity area for children. Artwork by Jean-Michel Othoniel of 114 fountains representing Arabic calligraphy fronts the building.

The entrance is tucked in a middle area, below the overlapping discs rather than on an obvious pathway.

Payments are made in the lobby. Take the escalator up from

the entrance into the gallery area past near the giant silver-coloured sculpture Motherland, a '*baṭṭulah*' face mask by Hassan bin Mohammed Al Thani. The museum's interior has dim lighting and is probably without right-angles, flat surfaces, or vertical walling. It gives the slightly uncomfortable sensation of being in a boat. An immersive, multi-dimensional sound and video system gives a really engaging experience throughout the galleries.

The zigzag route takes you through all the galleries as you gently descend.

The first gallery illustrates the Formation of Qatar from a geological viewpoint. Starting 700million years ago, it includes meteorites and fossils with an audio-visual backdrop to show the evolving natural environment.

National Museum

Qatar's Natural Environment today is covered with an ecological focus in the second gallery. Taxidermied animals in realistic settings are set against a very engaging audio-visual screening of Qatar's nature.

Following on is the Archaeology of Qatar, with displays from the Stone Age through Iron Age and Islamic Period. The galley has a broad-based viewpoint of archaeology and includes more modern exhibits, not just prehistoric. Explanatory videos support understanding the skills involved in producing stone tools and pottery.

The People of Qatar are the focus of Gallery 4 and 5. The Cirebon Wreck, a 10th-century ship that sank off Java, is used to illustrate trade links available to Qatar into the far east during that period. This was probably built in the Straits of Malacca and sank carrying Chinese and Asian finished goods, thought to have been intended for delivery into Basra, the port for Baghdad. Nomadic life on sea and land is illustrated. Naturally, the use of camels in Qatar is portrayed, along with equipment and accessories and their '*wasms*', brands to show the owner and their Tribe. Traditional weaving is shown, including floor coverings and tent equipment. The world of Pearls is covered in Gallery 7. A unique item is the Pearl Carpet of Baroda. This was commissioned by the Maharaja of Baroda (to hang in the Prophets Tomb in Medina.). Auctioned in 2009 for US$5.5 million, it is intended to display the luxurious use of Gulf pearls. However, it also shows the flow of wealth between Qatar and India (and beyond) during the 19th & 20th centuries & with its purchase into the 21st century.

The final galleries cover Qatar in the Modern Period, with the essential impact of oil on the country, and give a perspective of the wealth it brings.

Finishing the visit to the new National Museum, a visit to the old National Museum, which was the Palace of Sheikh Abdullah bin Jassim Al Thani. This is an early 20th c structure, which was enlarged and recreated over the century. Inside is a range of buildings refurbished in the style of the early 20th c.

It's worth dropping into the gift shop, with its remarkable ceiling and see if there is a souvenir for you. On the roof is the excellent Jiwan restaurant, serving a modern take on Qatari and Gulf cuisine in a French style.

Hours - Sat–Thurs: 09:00–19:00 / Fri:13:30–19:00 Sun closed. Entry charge - QAR 100 (all ticket prices here are for non-residents of Qatar) Online booking through nmoq.org.qa/.

Rough GPS - 25.287, 51.548 Street - On Museum Park St near the east Al Corniche extension - Al Corniche / الكورنيش Public Transport - Metro Gold Line National Museum - Contacts - +974 4452 5555 infonmoq@qm.org.qa www.nmoq.org.qa

Fish Market / سوق السمك - On the eastern end of the Corniche, this small open-air market is a great stop early in the morning to see fresh fish being landed directly off small boats. Later it is deserted. Typical hours - best in morning Public Transport - Bus 76, 109 Metro Gold Line National Museum

Rough GPS - 25.291, 51.548 Street - Al Corniche / الكورنيش Public Transport - Bus 76, 109 Metro Gold Line National Museum

Council of Ministers Secretariat General / الامانة العامة لمجلس الوزراء - In the exterior atrium between the two sections of the Council of Ministers Secretariat General building (west side of road) is the '**Reflective Flow**' chandelier, designed by Beau McClellan. At 18 tons, the chandelier is listed by Guinness World Records as the most enormous chandelier in the world. It's difficult to see during the day, but the lights come on at night so you can enjoy them.

Typical hours - not open to the public -

Rough GPS - 25.291, 51.544 Street - Al Corniche / الكورنيش Public Transport - Metro Gold Line National Museum

Museum of Islamic Art & West Bay skyline

MUSEUM OF ISLAMIC ART

- متحف الفن الإسلامي /

The Museum of Islamic Art is an important centre for the collection, display and study of Islamic art from around the world. The museum opened in 2008 and reopened after refurbishment in late 2022. It is a five-story, purpose-built building on a man-made island for the collection, with a geometric exterior design and spacious interior. A public park surrounds it to the north, east and south, while the dhow harbour is to the west. I.M. Pei, the architect, drew his inspiration for the exterior from the '*sabil*', an ablution and drinking water fountain within the courtyard of the Ibn Tulun Mosque in Cairo.

That *sabil,* with its angular façade, is the focus of the mosque's large courtyard.

In Doha, an avenue of date palms leads visitors up towards the museum's entrance.

The Sabil Ibn Tulun Mosque in Cairo.

There is an enforced dress code of conservative dress for both men and women. After security checks at the entrance, to the right is the publicly accessible library. The library's focus is on Islamic Art, with books in both Arabic and English. The library does not lend books.

This is a traditional museum, with pieces set in display cases. Its focus is only on objects from the Islamic world, bought explicitly for the museum. With their excellent lighting and cases, the spacious rooms display each piece in a way that older museums struggle to do.

In the central atrium, an imperial style staircase leads up to floor 2 and the exhibits. Elevators are available. There are two floors with permanent galleries arranged as horse-shoe shape around the atrium, which extends up through the entire building.

The galleries follow naturally one after the other as a linear flow from the glass wall overlooking the harbour and continuing around to the gallery opposite the starting point.

Floor 2 focuses on the Beginnings and Spread of Islam, with astrological devices, navigation equipment, and a substantial collection of calligraphic material, including illuminated pages. Repeating geometric patterns are a staple of Islamic decoration from the 14th century; on this floor are several examples. Navigation equipment includes astrolabes, from the 10th c. Ceramic tilework pieces from central Asia feature decorative calligraphy. Calligraphy is also a feature in illuminated books. The museum has a fine example; the Shahnameh, an epic about Persia. This is by the acclaimed Persian poet Ferdowsi, and this example is beautifully illuminated with fine calligraphy.

Floor 3 is a Journey through the core of the original Islamic World including Central Asia, Persia, Syria, Egypt, India and Turkey, rather than its geographical wider span that might include southeast Asia. This floor is best viewed starting from the eastern side (left of the glass wall), as there is a rough chronological order from early to late Islamic art. Mamluk glass shows the skills of a whole group of craftspeople needed to create a glass vase, decorated and also inscribed with calligraphy. Look for a 19th c gold devotional necklace from Tamil Nadu. Although the necklace has gold, with silver and rubies, nuts are also a feature of this piece; value has many forms.

Floor 4 holds temporary exhibitions in two non-connected galleries which. Concerts of diverse types are held here with information & some ticket sales from www.qatarphilharmoni-corchestra.org. Before you leave - there is a gift shop, perhaps something for you or your friends and MIA café, a spacious place to enjoy some snacks or lunch with a great view across the harbour. In the east of the museum, on the ground floor, is a small library.

Museum of Islamic Art - Indian Dagger - AD1800

The exterior of the museum has the Museum of Islamic Art Park. It's a superb place to stroll through – with the museum and West Bay as remarkable backdrops. Cultural events are held occasionally – adding to the park's appeal. The park can be accessed from the museum's entrance door after a short walk and an elevator down. The walk from the museum to the 7 sculpture by Richard Serra is about 1 kilometre; golf-style buggies offer a complimentary shuttle service. Along the route are coffee shops and landscaped gardens. The walk's terminus includes another metal sheet sculpture by Richard Serra. He also made a sculpture East-West in Zekreet, western Qatar.

Sitara (door covering) of Kaaba in Makkah

Hours - Sat-Wed 09:00-19:00 Thurs 09:19:00 Fri 13:30:19:00 Entry charge - QAR 100 (non-residents) - or bundled Qatar Museums Pass - qm.org.qa/tickets/select-tickets/

Rough GPS - 25.295, 51.539 Street - Eastern end of Al Corniche - Al Corniche / الكورنيش Public Transport - Metro Gold Line Souq Waqif - Contacts - +974 4422 4444 www.mia.org.qa

IDAM by the French restauranteur/chef Alain Ducasse is on the Museum of Islamic Art fifth floor. He has many Michelin stars across the world, doubtless the Museum of Islamic Art hopes one or more will be awarded here – even though he is not the chef. With views over the museum's atrium & outdoor dining for sunset views along the Corniche there is a great ambiance. This is nouvelle cuisine French-style fine dining - as you would expect with a slight Arabic twist. 12:30-14:00 PM/19:00-21:00 idam.com/ *****

Al Riwaq Gallery / متحف الفن الإسلامي Just southeast of the Museum of Islamic Art, Al Riwaq Gallery holds temporary exhibitions. In the past, artists such as Takashi Murakami and Damien Hirst have had events here. Check the website for current shows.

Typical hours - 09:00-18:00 Sat-Thurs - Fri 14:00-19:00

Rough GPS - 25.293, 51.543 Street - Eastern end of Al Corniche - Al Corniche / الكورنيش Public Transport - Metro Gold Line Souq Waqif - Contacts - qm.org.qa/en/visit/museums-and-galleries/

7 (Seven) - 7 by Richard Serra stands for the multiplicity of meanings the number 7 has in Islam. It also makes a fitting terminus to the park behind the Islamic Museum and an ideal location to watch the skyscrapers light up at dusk.

Rough GPS - 25.298, 51.540 Street - Museum of Islamic Art - Al Corniche / الكورنيش Public Transport - Metro Gold Line Souq Waqif

Corniche / الكورنيش - Possibly the most seen 'tourist attraction' in Doha, simply because it's not only incredibly scenic, but a route between main tourist areas. The sweep of the Corniche takes in the National Museum, Museum of Islamic Art, Dhows, Souq Waqif Al Bidda Park and evening views of the almost psychedelic illuminations of West Bay. Walking from east to west follows the attractions above, ending in the Sheraton's park, and is the route suggested by this guide; it also has the best views of West Bay. There are numerous 'photo' stops on the walk of around 7km - allow a couple of hours plus for a leisurely stroll. A bottle of water in hand is ideal, along with your camera. A few cafes are along the route - with lots in Souq Waqif.

Rough GPS - 25.291, 51.534 Street - Al Corniche - Souq Waqif / سوق واقف Public Transport - Metro Gold Line Souq Waqif/ Red & Green lines Al Bidda hub/ Red Line Corniche / Red Line West Bay

Dhow harbour - and West Bay skyline

Dhow Harbour / ميناء الداو - Here are a fleet of Dhows, anchored off the jetty along with modern boats. The public jetty (locally called a harbour) offers an excellent opportunity to see Dhows close up and get a different angle (rather than the Museum of Islamic Art) photographs of Doha. Sea excursions leave from the jetty. The Anantara hotel's reception for Banana Resort Island is also here. The small island in the centre of the harbour was, until 2006, a small resort hotel. It must be waiting for a new development, possibly a water fountain.

Rough GPS - 25.295, 51.535 Street - Off Al Corniche near Souq Waqif - Al Corniche / الكورنيش Public Transport - Metro Gold Line Souq Waqif

The Pearl Monument / اللؤلؤة - On the Corniche, just after the Islamic Art Museum, is a fountain in the shape of an open Oyster shell with a Pearl inside. It's a helpful 'place mark' along the Corniche, as is the spiral minaret at the Sheikh Abdulla Bin Zaid Al Mahmoud Islamic Cultural Centre. There is a sub-way here to get to Souq Waqif.

Rough GPS - 25.291, 51.534 Street - Al Corniche - Souq Waqif / سوق واقف Public Transport - Metro Gold Line Souq Waqif

Sheikh Abdulla Bin Zaid Al Mahmoud Islamic Cultural Centre / مركز الشيخ عبد الله بن زيد ال محمود الثقافي الإسلامي - This centre, also called Al Fanar, explains and promotes Qatar's culture, the Arabic language and Islam. The building takes its design from the Malwiya Minaret of Great Mosque in Samarra, Iraq. Inside are prayer rooms and lecture halls. Arabic language lessons are offered. The centre is helpful if you wish authoritative information about Islam in Qatar - they hope you will be converted.

Pearl Monument - Corniche

Typical hours - 08:00-13:00 Sun - Thurs Rough GPS - 25.289, 51.536 Street - Junction Abdulla bin Jassim St and Hamid Al Kabir St - east of Souq Waqif. - Souq Waqif / سوق واقف Public Transport - Metro Gold Line Souq Waqif - Contacts - +974 4444 7444 binzaid@islam.gov.qa www.binzaid.gov.qa

Souq Waqif & Police with their horses

SOUQ WAQIF

- سوق واقف

Souq Waqif combines tradition with modern requirements in an excellent setting in the heart of Doha. Its core is the rectangular market area, though adjacent areas create a larger square area of commerce, dining, entertainment, and hotels of around 20 hectares (about 500x440m). At times it can be almost overwhelmingly busy – it's very popular with both locals and visitors. It must be the most visited tourist attraction in Doha.

If you have time to visit only one place in Doha, this is it.

In origin, the date for the souq must be similar to the origin date for Doha, which grew from the 1820s. The souq served Doha; as the town grew, it also served Qatar in general and the ships which anchored offshore. Souq Waqif (the standing market) was set up close to the sea, on either side of a wadi (Wadi Msheireb). This wadi route was an open space for people to walk between stalls in dry weather. Until the early 1970s, the souq was on the sea's edge, and heavy rains would cause Wadi Msheireb to flow through the souq into the sea. Conversely, seawater might also be pushed inside the souq if the wind blew in the right direction at very high tides. Both the shopkeepers and their customers had to stand - it was the standing souq, hence the name.

In 1880 the Ottomans built Al Koot Fort, which must have increased trade for the merchants in the nearby souq to its northeast. In 1927 the Amir of Qatar rebuilt the fort, making this area the centre of Doha. The growth of the oil industry after World War 2 naturally increased overall trade, especially after dramatic price increases in the early 1970s. However, new department stores (such as The Centre in 1978) and shopping malls (The Mall in 1997 and City Centre in 2001) resulted in the souq losing its dominance.

In 2003 a fire destroyed large areas of Souq Waqif, and its fate seemed sealed. However, Sheikh Hamad bin Khalifa Al Thani and his wife Sheikha Moza bint Nasser Al Missned decided that the souq would be restored. This happened in two phases; one was a general rebuilding in 2006 and 2008 when all buildings dated after 1950 were demolished. The remaining buildings were renovated to keep their traditional style with modern supporting infrastructure.

A key element in the rebuilt souq is its multi-use; retail shops sell a mix of everyday requirements for the local population, services like shoe repairs and souvenirs for visiting tourists. Cafes and restaurants encourage shoppers to linger; frequent entertainment events based on Souq Waqif Square and peripheral sites, including a cinema below the square bring people in on a regular basis. Security personnel, mounted on horse, add to the souq's picturesque appeal. Finally, the souq's original residents have been replaced by the various hotel's guests. This might be called gentrification.

Southern Souq Waqif

Today Souq Waqif is a largely pedestrianised area. To its south, the former car park has been replaced by an open public square, Souq Waqif Square, and an underground car park. The original street layout has been kept. In this guide, the route to enter is from south & the main square – where taxis drop passengers – there is the large underground car park – and 2 Metro stations (Msheireb in the west and Souq Waqif to the southeast) are within 1.5 & 600m walk. North of the square is the Falcon Souq – beyond this is the Camel and Horse Stables. Northwest of the square is the main maze of shops, the heart of Souq Waqif, there are also many restaurants here including Parisa. Southeast of the square is the landmark Golden Thumb –

a small Police Station and a mass of restaurants along the street north of the Police Station – including Parisa. To the south of the square is an underground cinema and a street – mainly lined with restaurants. Al Koot Fort is on the southwest – is not open. To the west of the square is Msheireb, with its museums, Barahat Msheireb square and more. The entire area is engaging, with interest of many types. Spend an hour or a leisurely day - they will be time well spent.

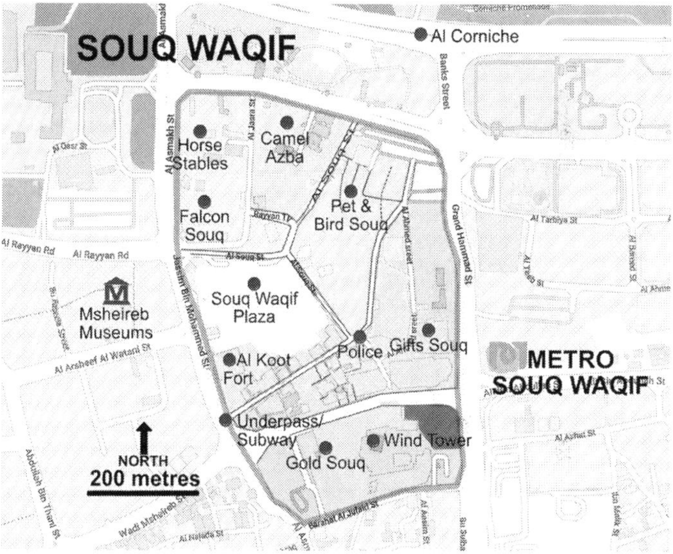

The **Falcon Souq** 25.288, 51.531 between Al Jasra St & Al Asmakh St opens roughly 09:00-12:30 /17:00-21:00 (Fridays only in the afternoon). This souq has individual shops. The best time to visit is in the afternoon, ideally Thursday, when potential buyers visit to check out the birds. However, the birds are all sitting waiting for you during regular shop hours. They wear the 'rufter', a hood that covers the eyes and ears, so they do not get too stressed by all the activity around them. Why not buy the falcons hood (locally called a *burka*) for a nice souvenir. The

Falcon Hospital is just to the north of the falcon shops. A vital element of this falcon area, it is not ordinarily open for casual visits.

Souq Waqif - Falcon Souq

To the north of the Falcon Souq is **Horse stabling** (GPS 25.289, 51.530) and going north from that – and turning right (east) along Abdullah bin Jassim St (south of a small park) is the **Camel Azba** pen area (GPS 25.289, 51.531).

Camels - Souq Waqif

The Falcons, Horses and Camels are free to view – be respectful of the people involved with them – they have work to do and are not simply part of the scenery.

If you are a football fan – the shop, "**Besht AlSalem**", that supplied the Bisht to Messi at the World Cup 2022 finals cup presentation, is in the souq. It's at the end of a passage – that starts about 20m to the left of the Police Station. Its complete with a photo of the Amir and Messi.

Besht AlSalam - Souq Waqif

The **main Souq Al Waqif** is on either side of Al Souq Street. This is a fantastic area to wander through, though it's impossible not to get disorientated as the passageways are mainly covered

The **Pet and Bird Souq** is to the east of Al Souq Street. Here are countless domestic pets, wild birds (budgerigars etc.), and wild animals. Continue walking through to get to a fantastic cafe to sit in, have a coffee and snack and enjoy the atmosphere - **Majlis Al Dama**. its hidden in the passageways east of the Pet and Bird Souq. Majlis Al Dama takes its name from Al Dama, a board game similar to draughts/checkers. With each player having 16 pieces, it has a decidedly Qatari twist. The game is often played between customers inside the coffee shop. Beyond Majlis Al Dama a turn right (south and away from the Corniche) is a street lined with restaurants – including the exotic **Parisa** (a Ritz Carlton restaurant), a Persian dining experience. In Farsi the name means 'fairy like' and the glittering interior could indeed be a home for fairies. An excellent alternative restaurant is the less glamorous Al Shurfa (the Tivoli Al Jomrok Boutique Hotel's restaurant), just to the west of the Corniche entrance to the souq. Al Shurfa's balcony has uninterrupted views over the Corniche to West Bay.

South from Parisa and the street is full of inexpensive restaurants. Your choice might depend on where there is seating. You arrive at the **Police Station** (blue signboard and white Arabic & English lettering GPS 25.286926, 51.533037) where horses might be standing and then the Golden Thumb.

To the southeast of the souq (southern end of Al Souq Street) are the **Gold and Crafts Souqs**. Opening Hours – 09:00-12:00 / 15:00-21:00 Sat-Fri. Here are gifts and gold in a colourful setting. The gold is generally ornate, in Gulf or Indian style at 19 carats plus, though you may find simpler designs if you search. Prices might be negotiated down by 5-10%. If you are buying handicrafts in the souq, bargain a lot more.

Tivoli hotels (www.tivolihotels.com/en/souq-waqif-doha) have several boutique hotels in Souq Waqif and some of the better restaurants in Souq Waqif.

The core of the souq is less than three hectares, while the larger area is under twenty hectares. To put this into context, the core area is comparable to the building space of the Palace of Versailles and the larger area, about 25% of the ornamental gardens next to Versailles. This does mean that as a location, it is not too large and is comfortable to explore and enjoy.

Typical hours: The souq comprises individual businesses with their own hours. Most shops open between 10:00-12:00/16:00-22:00, and Restaurants from 10:00-22:00 -

Ramadhan timings will vary. Entry charge - No charge to enjoy the atmosphere. – the square's Rough GPS - 25.287, 51.530

Majlis Al Dama

Public Transport - 2 Metro stations (Msheireb in the west and Souq Waqif to the southeast) are within 1.5 & 600m walk of the souq.

Wind Tower House / بيت الملاقف - An authentic Wind Tower House, now set in the rebuilt Souq Al Najada 200m south of the Golden Thumb. Wind towers are found throughout Persia and were also used on the western, coastal, side of The Gulf. Wind towers are usually four-sided structures, though they can be other shapes, which rise above and are part of a building, usually a house.

Wind Tower House

The upper part of the tower is open on each side and roofed. A barrier within the tower directs the wind down to supply a breeze that adds a cooling effect into the house. Water evaporators within these types of towers might add to the cooling effect. There is a recreated wind tower in the southwest of Souq Waqif. This Wind Tower House in Souq Al Najad is currently not open but previously was a museum. Rough GPS - 25.285, 51.533 Street - Junction of Grand Hamid St (Banks St) and Ali bin Abdullah St - inside the courtyard of Souq Al Najada Public

Transport - Bus - Metro Red/Gold/Green Lines Interchange Msheireb

Al Koot Fort / قلعة الكوت - Just to the southwest of Souq Waqif near the underground car park entrance is Al Koot Fort. This was built in 1927 on the site of an 1880 Ottoman fort on the north of Wadi Msheireb. The Ottomans abandoned their fort when they withdrew from Qatar in 1915, and it became dilapidated. The then ruler of Qatar, Sheikh Abdullah bin Jassim bin Mohammed Al Thani rebuilt it, to secure the Souq Waqif. This has been a museum for the exhibition of handicrafts; however currently it is not open.

Rough GPS - 25.287, 51.531 Street - south of Souq Waqif - Souq Waqif / سوق واقف Public Transport - Metro Red/Gold/Green Lines Interchange Msheireb

MSHEIREB MUSEUMS

- متاحف مشيرب

The Msheireb Museums hope to tell an untold aspect of Qatar's, not so long ago, history. They are set within four separate, single floor houses, each telling a different part of the story. Designed by Ralph Appelbaum, their restoration is sympathetic to their original structure. They are part of the Msheireb organisation chaired by Sheikha Moza bint Nasser Al Missned, the mother of the Amir of Qatar. The Museums are a subsidiary of the Qatar Foundation (App available).

The museums are less than 200m west of the Souq Waqif square (opposite the underground car park entrance) and make an easy add-on to a visit to Souq Waqif. The buildings are next to each other on Al Arshef Al Watani St. Therefore, a visitor can easily visit all four or just one.

The smallest of the buildings is **Radwani House**, which gives visitors insight into how family life evolved in Qatar. The house was occupied until 1971 and is an attractive single-story courtyard house. The building highlights how its use changed over time and how domestic family life was transformed in Doha. Almost as an illustration into the changes in Doha, Radwani

House is enveloped by office blocks, those of the Qatar National Archive and the Amiri Guard. As with all this museum's houses, Radwani House was home to the more affluent people in Doha.

Msheireb Company House

Company House Set within a house once used as the headquarters for Qatar's first oil company, this museum tells the story of the Qatari petroleum industry workers and their families. They helped the flow of wealth that transformed Qatar into a modern society. There are displays of equipment that look antiquated, even of only a few decades old.

The **Bin Jelmood House** is space for reflection on the story of slavery and its trade in Qatar and the broader Gulf, which still is little acknowledged within the region. It comments about slavery in Islam, that Islam 'regulated the institution of slavery, improving the lives of the enslaved through the Quran's teachings...'. It also has a section on modern slavery. It is unique in The Gulf Region and unusual in the world (Liverpool in the UK and Wallace, Louisiana USA also have museums about slavery). This is a concept for a museum that many capital cities lack - presumably others will offer a different perspective.

Mohammed bin Jassim House is on the other side of the road (next to Msheireb Mosque). Built by Sheikh Mohammed Bin Jassim Al-Thani, son of the founder of modern Qatar, this heritage house addresses Msheireb's past, its present and what it hopes is a sustainable future.

Typical hours - Sunday: Closed Monday to Thursday: 09:00 – 17:00 Friday: 15:00pm – 21:00 Saturday: 09:00 –17:00

Rough GPS - 25.287, 51.529 Street - East side of Al Asmakh St - Msheireb / مشيرب Public Transport - Metro Msheireb (Hub) - Contacts - +974 40065555 museums@msheireb.com www.msheireb.com

While in Msheireb hop on the complementary **tram**. It stops outside the museums – and loops past Harrods (restaurant only) Barahat Msheireb square – which as occasional events, Msheireb Galleria shopping and near Msheireb Metro station (stop1&9).

Al Bidda, Al Rumaila, Wadi Al Sail Parks' Doha Grand Park' / الحدائق البدع و الرميلة و وادي السيل - Al Bidda Park is a large landscaped park on the Al Corniche in central Doha, divided into sections by streets. The total area is around 1.7sq km (slightly larger than Hyde Park London) and includes a water feature, cafes, a children's park 25.303, 51.514 and a maze. There are designated sports areas, cycle paths, an outdoor gym and tennis courts. Specific barbeque areas need to be used for cooking, while several small cafes spread through the park. Walkways give access over roads from one area to the next. Underground car parks (with space for 6,000 vehicles!) are approached from the Corniche (southbound) and Uhud St. This is busiest at the weekend and after 16:00hrs. Toilets and first aid are available.

Rough GPS - 25.298, 51.516 Street - West of the Al Corniche-Al Bidda Park area / حديقة البدع Public Transport -, Metro Red Line/Green Line Al Bidda

Imam Muhammad Bin Abdulwahhab Mosque

جامع الإمام مُحمَّد بن عبد الوهاب

- This is the largest mosque in Doha and is open to non-Muslims. The mosque is named after the Islamic theologian from the 18th c in Riyadh, Saudi Arabia and was opened in 2011. The mosque is simply decorated in keeping with the austere version of Islam in Qatar. Inside there are separate prayer rooms for men and women and the library, with some books in English. The floor space for the men's room is 7,400m, and the entire building has three floors. The 93 domes refer to the multi-dome mosques in Makkah and Al Madinah.

Visiting a mosque in The Gulf The below checkpoints may help your planning. Guided tours may be available through www.binzaid.gov.qa (Sheikh Abdulla Bin Zaid Al Mahmoud Islamic Cultural Centre - Al Fanar). Children under 8 are not permitted. Photography is only possible with mobile-phone and is excluded in the ladies' prayer rooms. Men should wear long trousers and long-sleeved shirts, avoiding text on them. Women should wear clothing that only shows their face, hands and feet. The mosque issues returnable headscarf and Abaya to wear if needed. Footwear must be removed before entering. Each sex can only visit the appropriate area in the mosque. When the tour is finished, you can then enjoy the panorama to the east over the city as the skyscrapers are illuminated, and the call to prayer is made. An ideal time to visit for photography only, from the car park, is before the sunset prayers. As the mosque is relatively isolated from main routes, a Uber-style taxi is the easiest transport. Metrolink M107 bus does go from Red Line West Bay (ask station staff for correct station exit – it's the north side).

Typical hours - Open to non-Muslims during non-prayer times. 08:00-11:00 (not Friday). Other times that are not prayer times (except Friday) are possible but less certain. Always check newspapers for each days prayer times. Entry charge - No Charge -

Rough GPS - 25.318, 51.507 Street - Junction Khalifa St and Al Istiqlal St - Al Jebailat / الجبيلات Public Transport Red Line West Bay & MetroLink Bus - Contacts - + 974 4470 0000 binzaid@islam.gov.qa www.binzaid.gov.qa

Imam Muhammad Bin Abdulwahhab Mosque

Qatar National Theatre / المسرح الوطني – With its easy to get to location and has a well-designed interior, it offers a good venue in Doha for performers. Unfortunately, it is without a dedicated website to find out about performances.

Typical hours - Entry charge - as per event -

Rough GPS - 25.305, 51.516 Street - off Al Corniche - Al Corniche / الكورنيش Public Transport - Metro Red Line Corniche - Contacts - +974 4483 6118 www.dohafilminstitute.-com/venues/qatar-national-theatre

Saikl Bike Rental / سيكل للدراجات الهوائية - Bikes rented for adults and children by the Hour (with helmets) also bike repair service. Branch in Sheraton grounds

Typical hours - 15:00-midnight daily

Rough GPS - 25.298, 51.513 Street - Off Al Khaleej St-Al Bidda Park area / حديقة البدع Public Transport –

Metro Red Line/Green Line Al Bidda - Contacts - +974 5028 0404 info@saiklqtr.com www.saiklqtr.com

Khalifa International Tennis and Squash Complex / مجمع خليفة الدولي للتنس والإسكواش - With over 20 courts plus a central court of 7,000 seats this is a major hard-court outdoor tennis complex. It has held WTA & ITF events. Courts are available to book, STA.

Typical hours - as per event Entry charge - as per event -

Rough GPS - 25.312, 51.515 Street - Majlis Al Taaawon St-Al Bidda Park area / حديقة البدع Public Transport - Metro Red Line Corniche (1500metres) - Contacts - +974 4440 9666 admin@qatartennis.org www.qatartennis.org/

Fire Station / الدفاع المدني - Just west of the Corniche is the old Fire Station, converted into an art centre in 2014 with a gallery and material shop by Cass Art +974 4452 5625. This, at its heart, is a small incubator to develop artists from Qatar to develop their talent. Some 20 artists are supported every year with a finishing exhibition held. Rotating exhibitions of other art is held. An artists supply shop retails art materials. There is a small theatre for public events, and a cafe #999 is open to relax in, next to Al Bidda Park.

Typical hours - Sat-Thurs 09:00-19:00 Fri 13:30-19:00 Entry charge - no charge (QAR50 non-residents of Qatar) check on qm.org.qa/en/visit/visitor-guidelines/

Rough GPS - 25.303, 51.507 Street - junction Mohammed bin Thani St and Al Istiqlal St-Al Bidda Park area / حديقة البدع Public Transport - Metro Red Line Corniche (1500metres) -

Contacts - +974 4422-4222 contact@firestation.org.qa www.firestation.org.qa

Qatar Bowling Centre / مركز قطر للبولينج - With a World Champion Bowling Team - this is the bowling centre in Doha. There are 32 lanes, Billiards, Table Tennis and Cafe. They hold international events, which may affect opening schedules.

Typical hours - Sat-Wed 09:00-24:00 Thurs 09:00-02:00(night) Fri 09:00-01:00(night) Entry charge - from QAR 8 per game - shoes included

Rough GPS - 25.292, 51.516 Street - off Khaleej St - Al Corniche / الكورنيش Public Transport - Metro Red Line/Green Line Al Bidda - Contacts - +974 4432 9178 qatarbowlingfederation@gmail.com www.qatarbowlingfederation.com

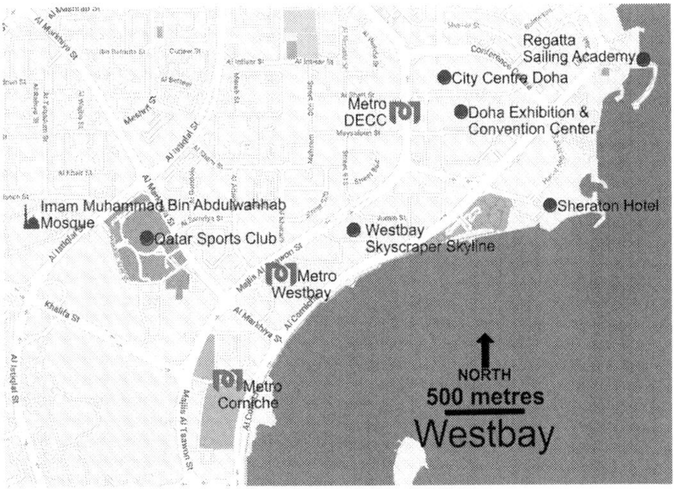

WEST BAY

Qatar Sports Club, Suheim Bin Hamad Stadium, Qatar Handball Federation / نادي قطر الرياضي - This is a sports complex focused on one of Qatar's more successful football league teams (Qatar Sports Club). Regular local football matches are held; check for a detailed schedule in the media. Parking is minimal, so if the game is a major event, a taxi, bus, or Corniche Metro Station (Red Line) are good choices.

Typical hours - 08:00-22:00

Rough GPS - 25.317, 51.514 Street - Junction Al Istiqlal St and Al Markhiya St - Al Dafna / الدفنة Public Transport - Metro Red Line 1500metres walk - Contacts - +974 4483 1777 info@qatarsc.com www.qatarsc.com/

City Centre Doha / سيتي سنتر الدوحة - With Carrefour, Debenhams department store, banks & money changer numerous shops including jewellery, footwear, discount shops, fashion, electronics and restaurants - City Centre is probably the most convenient mall for visitors in Qatar. Unfortunately, this mall's customers are drifting to newer malls.

Typical hours - 10:00-midnight daily

Rough GPS - 25.326, 51.530

Street - Conference Centre, Omar Al Mukhtar - West Bay / الخليج الغربي Public Transport - Metro Doha Exhibition and Convention Center (DECC) - Contacts - +974 4493 3355 info@citycenterdoha.com www.citycenterdoha.com/

Doha Exhibition & Convention Center (DECC) / مركز الدوحة للمعارض والمؤتمرات this is the main exhibition centre in the heart of Doha. With hotels, shopping mall and metro - it's probably the best location for exhibitions and conferences in Doha. From 1 up to 5 halls can be configured.

Typical hours - as per event

Rough GPS - 25.323, 51.529

Street - Conference Centre, Omar Al Mukhtar West Bay / الخليج الغربي Public Transport - Metro Doha Exhibition and Convention Center (DECC) - Contacts - +974 4033 1111 www.decc.qa/visitors/ info@decc.qa

Ice Skating Rink / ساحة التزلج - Ice Skating within the atrium of a shopping mall. It's a peripheral service for the mall; maintenance and management are below similar facilities in other major cities.

Typical hours - 10:00-21:00 Daily (Fri 13:00-23:00) Entry charge - from QAR35 -

Rough GPS - 25.326, 51.530 Street - Junction of Omar Al

Mukhtar Rd and Conference Centre Rd - West Bay / الخليج الغربي Public Transport - Bus 57 Metro Doha Exhibition and Convention Centre (DECC)

Landmark Mall - The Landmark Mall doesn't have the glitz so many of Qatar's other malls. It does, however, have a good supermarket, Carrefour. Though a franchise, isn't a clone of those in France. The buying is locally made, and the products include the brands of Qatar and the region. The Marks & Spencer however has exactly the clothes you would expect.

Typical hours - 09:00-22:00

Rough GPS - 25.334, 51.467 Street - Doha Expressway / Al Markhiya St - Al Duhail / الدحيل Public Transport - Bus 100, 101 - Contacts - +974 4487 5222 info@landmarkdoha.com www.landmarkdoha.com

DOHA SOUTH AND EAST

Al Arabi Club / النادي العربي الرياضي - Here at Al Arabi Club, in the south of Doha are several sports facilities, most notably a football stadium, where Al Arabi, which is one of Qatar's most successful clubs, has its home ground. There is a lot more, including basketball and a swimming pool. The club is also home to Qatar's Volleyball Assn.

Typical hours - 08:00-22:00

Rough GPS - 25.259, 51.519 Street - west of Rawdat Al Khail St - As Salatah al Jadeeda / اسلطة الجديدة Public Transport - Bus 603 from Msheireb Bus Station - Contacts - +974 4467 3666 info@alarabi.qa www.alarabi.qa

Al Thumama Stadium / استاد الثمامة - In the south of Doha, this World Cup Stadium is not well served by public transport outside sporting events.

Rough GPS - 25.235, 51.531 Street - E Ring Road - Al Thumama / الثمامة No easy Public Transport connections at normal times

Al Thumama Stadium

Dragon Mart and China Mall / سوق التنين - The Dragon Mart / China Mall is more of an alleyway rather than a modern shopping mall in the southwest of Doha, but is an indoor shopping experience and focused in its appeal. This is a pile it high - sell it cheap area with Building materials, Fabrics, Electronics and more from East Asia.

Typical hours - Numerous independent shops have individual times around 10:00-22:00

Rough GPS - 25.194, 51.455 Street - Junction of Industrial Area Rd and East Industrial Street north - Industrial Area / منطقة صناعية Public Transport - Bus 701 from AlGreen Line Al Shaqab Metro

Asian Town / المدينة الاسيويه – South of Dragon Mart (across the highway) his is the general leisure area that serves a large area of ex-pat labour, chiefly from the Indian Subcontinent. Here is a Cricket Stadium Rough GPS 25.190, 51.461, an open-air concert theatre, Cinemas, Supermarkets, and low-cost restaurants. These offer low-cost services and products focused on the vast accommodation 'township' residents to its east.

Typical hours - Various Leisure, Retail and Dining options have different but awfully long hours.

Rough GPS - 25.189, 51.461 Street - Junction of Industrial Area Rd and East Industrial St - Industrial Area / منطقة صناعية Public Transport - Bus 610 from Red Line West Bay Metro

Qatar Racing Club / نادي سباق قطر - A track for Motor Bike and Car racing & timed circuits. Events are held mainly Thursday/Friday/Saturday from 18:00 during winter October-April.

Typical hours - as per schedule Entry charge - as per event

Rough GPS - 25.175, 51.481 Street - north of G Ring Road - Khawr Al Udaid / Mesaieed / خور العديد / مسيعيد Public Transport – no public transport - Contacts - +974-40286000 qatarracingclub.business.site

Al Ahli Sports Club / النادي الأهلي الرياض - Qatar's oldest football club is south of the town centre. Al Ahli's football ground is the Hamed bin Khalifa Stadium with a capacity of 12,000; it held the Asian Cup Final in 1988. A variety of public facilities, including a swimming pool, make it worth checking out for your leisure.

Typical hours - 08:00-22:00

Rough GPS - 25.252, 51.534 Street - Junction Najma St and D Ring Rd. - Nuaija / نعيجة Public Transport - Bus 609 from Red Line West Bay Metro - Contacts - + 974 4032 7777 info@al-ahliclub.com www.al-ahliclub.com

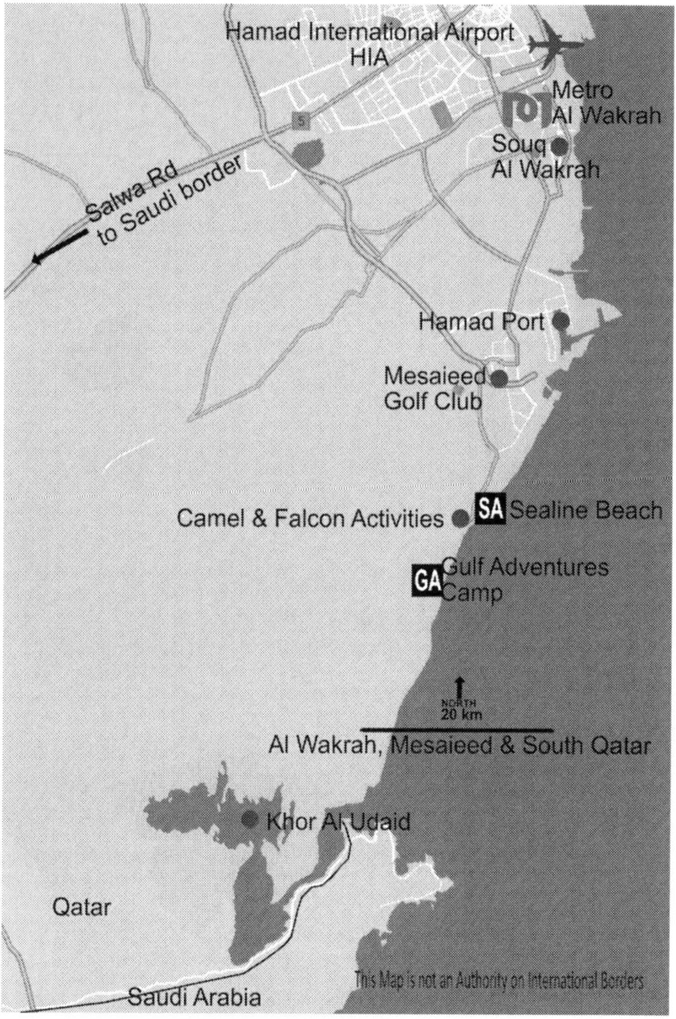

AL WAKRAH, MESAIEED & SOUTH QATAR

Al Janoub Stadium Al Wakrah / إستاد الجنوب في الوكر - Designed by the late Zahra Hadid in her sweeping style of building, Al Janoub Stadium has 40,000 seats for the 2022 World Cup.

Rough GPS - 25.159, 51.575 Street - Khat Al Wakrah Rd - Al

Wakrah / الوكرة Public Transport - The closest Metro is Al Wakrah which is 7km away; however, the MetroLink bus service may offer a service from Metro to the stadium.

Gulf Youth Bicycle - Selling bikes, mainly lower cost makes and those aimed at children. Possibly the largest selection in Doha.

Typical hours - 09:00-21:00 (Friday 16:00-22:00)

Rough GPS - 25.214, 51.580 Street - off Al Wakrah Rd - Barwa Village / قرية بروة Public Transport - Bus MetroLink 126 from Red Line Ras Abu Fontas - Contacts - +974 4455 1092

Souq Al Wakrah

/ سوق الوكرة - Souq Al Wakrah

is a heritage style development a 19km drive south of Doha's centre. At the parking area, golf-style buggies are available in the busier evening times to take you into Souq Al Wakrah.

Souq Al Wakrah is a seaside version of Souq Waqif and is far less busy. The seafront is nice stroll especially in the hotter months as sea breezes are slightly cooler.

The concept of Souq Al Wakrah is of a residential village, rather than a commercial souq, with 'homes' in the 'heritage area' working as retail shops and restaurants. Here there are perfume shops, gifts, dried fruit & nuts and sweet shop, cultural shops with things like carpets and swords. A small fish market opens daily but is best early in the morning. A grouping of restaurants on the beachfront, appx GPS 25.169, 51.610, offers a variety of Middle East cuisines. A seafood restaurant is 100m north of the main restaurant area. As they do in Souq Waqif, Tivoli Hotels have a property, Souq Al Wakrah Hotel; with five dining outlets this is worth considering rather than hotels in Doha. It's a 20-minute drive south of HIA. A small grouping of restaurants is west of the sea, near the car park's southern end and the small fish souq. These are lower cost - with sea-food options.

South of the heritage area is the small port, which usually has dozens of Dhows tied up. Offshore there might be authentic sailing Dhows at anchor. The jetty is 1,200m long, creating a good evening walk from the beach area.

West of the Souq Al Wakrah heritage area is Abdulrahman bin Jassim Fort – see below.

Typical hours - The souq comprises individual businesses with their own hours. Most shops open between 10:00-12:00/16:00-22:00, and Restaurants from 10:00-22:00 - Ramadhan timings will vary. Entry charge - free to enjoy the atmosphere.

Rough GPS - 25.173, 51.609 Street - east of Al Wakrah Main St - Al Wakrah / الوكرة. Public Transport Bus MetroLink 127 or Karwa 613 from Red Line Al WakrahMetro.

Al Wakrah Park / حديقة الوكرة - This is 500m north of Al Wakrah Souq. The beach area that runs a kilometre north of the park is used for swimming and barbeques, often by bachelor groups - it's unusual for single women to use the beach. It has no lifeguard, safety equipment or other facilities. The bottom is a bit muddy around the mangrove.

Rough GPS - 25.179, 51.612 Street - Mesaieed Rd - Al Wakrah / الوكرة Public Transport – as Souq Wakrah.

Sheikh Abdulrahman bin Jassim Fort 'Al Wakrah Fort'/ قلعة الوكرة was probably built in the early 20th century. It is on the site of an earlier fort, used when Sheikh Abdulrahman was made governor of Al Wakrah. It has been remodelled with the corner towers reduced in height and more buildings inside. Currently, it is not open, however if the gates are open, why not ask if it is possible to look inside.

Rough GPS - 25.172, 51.606 Street - Al Wakrah / الوكرة Public Transport Bus MetroLink 128 or Karwa 613 from Red Line Al WakrahMetro.

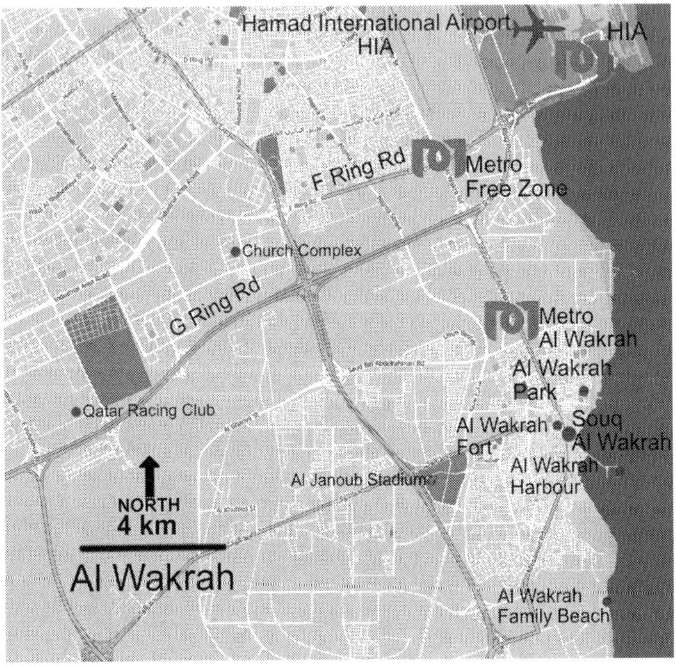

Al Wakrah Family Beach / شاطئ الوكرة العائلي

5km south of Al Wakrah is a beach for women and families only. Unaccompanied men are liable for arrest. The water here is shallow, especially at low tide. Swimming is likely to be difficult because of lack of depth, and only possible a long way out from the land. However, it's a fun place for families, and undulations in the exposed sandy sea bed trap fish, making for an exciting place to explore for children. Unlike hotel beaches, maintenance and cleaning is sporadic. There are toilets. Between the family beach and Al Wakrah Souq is a general beach. There are no lifeguards, safety equipment or facilities.

Rough GPS - 25.131, 51.616 Street - Mesaieed Rd - Al Wakrah / الوكرة Public Transport – no public transport

Camel & Falcon Activities / أنشطة الجمال والصقور - Arabia doesn't get more Arab than a ride on a camel. Here, opposite the Sealine Hotel, and a bit south along the road near the Sarab Camp (tented accommodation about 500m from a beach +974

6657 3448) are casual Camel Rides and usually Falcon handlers, negotiate the charge for a camel ride etc. If, however, you are going to a camp-site near Khor Al Udaid, Camels are available at most of the camps (check about this when booking)

Rough GPS - 24.862, 51.512 Street - Sealine Beach Rd - Khawr Al Udaid / Mesaieed / خور العديد / مسيعيد Public Transport - No public transport.

KHOR AL UDAID

خور العديد

In Qatar's southeast is Khor Al Udaid, here are 'The Inland Sea' and the sand dunes which surround it. The area is on the border of Qatar and Saudi Arabia. Across the Khor Duweihin (part of The Gulf) is Abu Dhabi.

Khor Al Udaid was chosen as a land and sea nature reserve in 2007 and stretches over around 1833 square kilometres. The khor (creek/inlet) itself is an inlet of The Gulf. It was part of the estuary of the pre-historic river, Wadi Sahba, which flowed into The Gulf from the central Arabian plateau. Cascading into the khor are the powder white dunes created from corals and shells. Several sections are locally called '*naqiyat*' نقيان meaning pure, a reference to their colour.

In the northwest, the dunes are scattered, while in the south, they are continuous, forming a sea of sand. If you can find undisturbed Sabkha here and elsewhere (it's unlikely), look for the gypsum crystal formation called a 'Desert Rose'. This small formation, usually a few centimetres across, is caused by the evaporated deposits of gypsum or baryte (sulphates), which include some sand. The National Museum's architecture was inspired by this formation. The steeper slopes, most especially undisturbed isolated barchan dunes, might become 'Singing Sands'. When the slope collapses, the vibration of sand passing over a static area of sand causes an audible and physical vibration to the dune. This is not a completely empty landscape; there are small camps that have meals available.

Dunes near Khor Al Udaid

The dunes are used as a recreational area by 4x4 vehicles. The powder-like nature of the sand does mean that driving on them is particularly challenging. The sand is an extremely soft base for vehicles, so careless driving can cause a car to bog down.

Most local tour operators supply excursions into the dunes. Part of the Qatari / Saudi border is just south of the water of Khor Al Udaid, less than 1km from the southern edge. The new border was agreed in November 2021. Though where the border line is not obvious – security concerns mean its best, for your own interests, not to step onto the southern shore & if in the water remain close to the northern shore.

Rough GPS - 24.615, 51.365 Street - Khor Al Udaid / خور العديد Public Transport – no public transport & 4x4 required.

Khor Al Udaid - dune driving

Gulf Adventures Camp Beach Camp - On the edge of relatively shallow seas and powdery white sand dunes, this camp is run by Gulf Adventures. It offers a getaway from Doha - ideal if you don't like self-catering camping. The set-up allows dozens of people to enjoy the combination of sun, sea and sand - camels are on call. The only missing ingredient to the Instagram perfect setting is a few coconut palms. There are several alternative beach camps run by other companies.

Rough GPS - 24.805, 51.491 Street - On the East Coast south of Mesaieed مسيعيد - Khawr Al Udaid / Mesaieed / خور / مسيعيد العديد Public Transport - No public transport - Contacts - +974 4436 1461 www.gulf-adventures.com

Jebel Nakhsh / جبل نخش - Set on the stone desert of southern Qatar, with electricity pylons marching towards the horizon. One of the more distinctive hills in Qatar due to it rising sharply about 100m above the surrounding plain. Remains of fossil sea creatures from the Miocene period can be seen embedded in the rock. The site is 1km off the road, so it's a 4x4 journey.

Rough GPS - 24.875, 50.907 Street - West of the Salwa Rd

near the Saudi Arabian border. - Salwa / سلوى Public Transport - No public transport

Camel ride - Khor Al Udaid

Al Mashabiya and Al Eraiq reserves. / محميه لعريق المسحبيه - The Al Mashabiya Reserve opened in 1997 as a 54sq km animal breeding facility. It has native ungulates, especially Arabian oryx and Sand gazelle, and also Ostrich. The Al Eraiq Reserve was set up later to prevent overgrazing. The area is gravel plain, sand sheets, wadis, mesa, etc. The vegetation consists of *Acacia tortilis, A. ehrenbergiana, Lycium shawii, Ziziphus spina christi*, etc. Other species include the Arabian hare and Spiny-tailed lizard; many bird species can also be seen.

Typical hours - NOT OPEN OFFICIALLY

Rough GPS - 24.837, 50.876 Street - east of Junction 5 on the Salwa Rd close to Salwa Beach - Salwa / سلوى Public Transport - No public transport

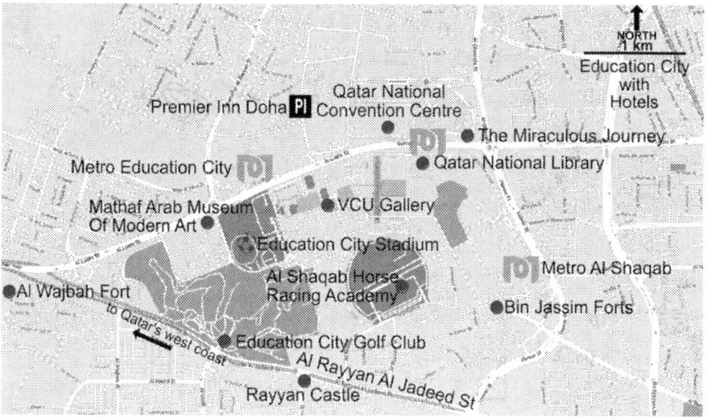

EDUCATION CITY AND WEST DOHA

British Council Qatar / المجلس البريطاني في قطر - The British Council is an educational and cultural organisation. A semi-government conduit for British services

Typical hours - 08:00-20:00 Sunday-Thursday Entry charge - Rough GPS - 25.280, 51.490 Street - Al Saad / السد Public Transport - No public transport - Contacts - +974 800 5501 general.enquiries@qa.britishcouncil.org www.britishcouncil.qa

In **Education City** there is a **tram network** that runs from Gold Line Al Shaqab Metro. The Yellow Line goes from the station and links up with the Blue Line and then Grey Line.

The Miraculous Journey - This series of 14 sculptures by Damien Hurst portrays the development of a baby in the uterus, from conception to birth. These are true to life and unmissable. In any city they would attract controversy, as they have done in Doha. The cost is reported to have been US$20 million.

Rough GPS - 25.321, 51.444 Street - Sidra Medical and Research Centre exterior - Education City / المدينة التعليمية Public Transport - Metro Green Line Qatar National Library and then a 5-minute walk northeast

Qatar National Convention Centre / مركز قطر الوطني للمؤتمرات - This is a substantial modern convention centre, home to the spider sculpture Maman by Louise Bourgeois. Exhibition halls, modern auditoriums for conferences as well as entertainment events with smaller halls and rooms offer space for smaller events such as board meetings. Concerts of several types are held in the convention centre, often in the smaller halls. For information and tickets, check out qatarphilharmoni-corchestra.org. Parking availability is substantial with a quoted 2,800 spaces (many of which are used by staff); also, there are direct Metro links, good Bus options and of course Taxis offer flexible options.

Typical hours - as per events Entry charge -

Rough GPS - 25.321, 51.437 Street - Al Luqta St/ Dukhan Highway - Education City / المدينة التعليمية Public Transport - Metro Green Line Qatar National Library - Contacts - +974 4470 7000 sales@qncc.qa www.qncc.qa

Qatar National Library

متاحف مشيرب

- A massive, several stories, ultramodern library; the Qatar National Library functions not only as a regular public library but as a research facility and also as the state repository. The building is in a modern deconstructionist style with an extraordinarily bright interior rather than a dim style favoured by so many libraries. There is plenty of space to sit and research; it's a vast space. Hidden beneath the floor is a state-of-art book delivery system, where borrowers can deposit a returned book (at ground level) in a receptacle. The book is automatically delivered to the correct book shelving using RFID chips.

Qatar National Library

Typical hours - Saturday – Thursday: 8:00 AM - 8:00 PM Fridays: 4:00 PM - 8:00 PM

Rough GPS - 25.319, 51.442 Street - Al Luqta St - Education City / المدينة التعليمية Public Transport - Metro Green Line Qatar

National Library - Contacts - +974 4454 6039 qnl@qnl.qa www.qnl.qa

VCU Gallery (Virginia Commonwealth University School of The Arts in Qatar) / جامعة فرجينيا كومنولث للفنون في قطر - If you are in Education City, drop in here for a changing exhibition of student's art.

Typical hours - 09:00-12:00 Sun-Thurs Entry charge - No Charge -

Rough GPS - 25.314, 51.434 Street - south of Al Luqta St - Education City / المدينة التعليمية Public Transport - Metro Green Line Qatar National Library or Education City - Contacts - +974 4402 0555 www.qatar.vcu.edu

Education City Stadium (Qatar Foundation Stadium) - This sports stadium is near Education City. It has good Metro services and a Premier Inn not far away.

Rough GPS - 25.311, 51.426 Street - Al Rayyan Al Jadeed St - Education City / المدينة التعليمية Public Transport - The closest Metro is Green Line Education City, about 600m walk away or use the tram network. - Contacts +97450826700

Al Shaqab Horse Racing Academy & Arena

أكاديمية الشقب لسباق الخيل

Dressage and show jumping area with periodic events (see media or website). This is a state of the art academy for riding with extensive and expensive stabling for Arabian and Thoroughbred horses. Tours are available against booking. Consider staying in Al Shaqab Hotel, within the grounds, a small hotel with comfortable accommodation and a restaurant - a walk from the hotel block. www.amlak.com.qa/en/portfolio/al-shaqab-hotel/

Endurance horse racing is also held based from Qatar Endurance Village 24.967, 51.506 at Mesaieed south of Doha. Events are usually on Saturdays with a start in the early morning. The events are 100km+, so they last much of the day (with physical checks during a race). 4x4 vehicle is essential to view much of the action. If you contact the event organisers, they may be able to offer options to view.

Typical hours - Events as per schedule - regular working hours 07:30-15:30 Sun-Thurs

Rough GPS - 25.306, 51.440 Street - Al Shaqab St - Al Shaqab / الشقب Public Transport - Bus 526 from Metro Green Line Al Shaqab & Green Line Metro Al Shaqab or National Library- Contacts - (+974) 4454 1992 alshaqabtours@qf.org.qa www.alshaqab.com

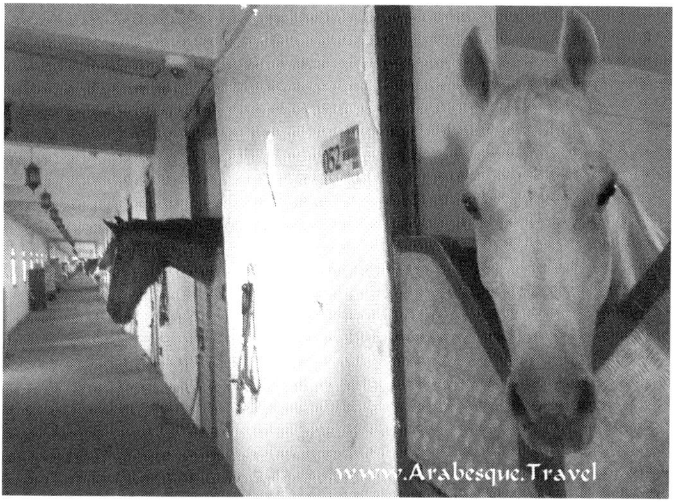

Horse stables -Doha

Education City Golf Club / نادي مدينة التعليمي للجولف - New course 18 hole (+ short course)

Typical hours - 07:00-17:00 Entry charge - membership -

Rough GPS - 25.303, 51.422 Street - Al Rayyan Al Jadeed St - Education City / المدينة التعليمية Public Transport – Bus 616 from Green Line Metro Al Shaqab - Contacts - +974 7773 7973 Info@ecgolf.com www.ecgolf.com

Mathaf Arab Museum of Modern Art / متحف: المتحف العربي للفن الحديث - Mathaf Museum of Modern Art occupies a re-purposed school building and was opened in 2010. Part of the Qatar Foundation, it is based around the collection of Sheikh Hassan bin Mohamed bin Ali Al Thani, who created the sculpture Motherland in the National Museum. The museum organises frequent exhibitions, principally of local artists. A broad range of learning opportunities and resources and periodically holds shows by students are part of the experience. A substantial area of outdoor sculptures adds interest to a visit, as does a choice from its permanent collection. A small gift shop and cafe add to the options on a visit.

Typical hours – Sat-Thurs 09:00-19:00 Fri 13:30-19:00 Entry charge – QAR100 (non-residents of Qatar) or bundled ticket on-line booking qm.org.qa/tickets/select-tickets/ -

Rough GPS - 25.310, 51.419 Street - Al Luqta St, just before the start of Dukhan Highway via Gate 1 entrance (or from Al Rayyan Al Jadeed St) - Education City / المدينة التعليمية Public Transport – Grey & Blue Line Education City Tram. From Green Line Metro stations, a 15 min (appx) walk - Contacts - +974 4402 8855 mathaf_info@qma.org.qa www.mathaf.org.qa

Bin Jassim Fort To the east of Al Shaqab are a couple of fenced off forts next to each other, known as Bin Jassim Fort. These probably date from the early 20th century & are not open.

Rough GPS - 25.305, 51.449 Street – Al Athar St - Al Rayyan / الريان Public Transport - Bus 526 from Metro Green Line Al Shaqab.

Rayyan Castle / قلعة الريان - Rayyan Castle is also known as Sheikh Ali bin Abdullah Fort. Sheikh Ali was the Emir of Qatar from 1949-1960. The fort is essentially a fortified residence, which then was built outside Doha in the early 20thc.

The large wall, 180m long on each side, enclosed several other buildings, including a mosque. North of the fort is a secondary fortified building. A nice touch is the roofline over the entrance door with detailing in the colour and form of the serrations on the Qatari flag. Currently, Rayyan Fort is not open.

Rough GPS - 25.301, 51.431 Street - Al Rayyan Al Jadeed St - Al Rayyan / الريان Public Transport - Bus 526 from Metro Green Line Al Shaqab

Al Wajbah Fort / قلعة الوجبة - Built in the 19th c this small

Al Rayyan early 20thc

fort is to the west of Doha's centre. The fort is a courtyard type with a range of rooms opening directly onto the open space. It has been substantially restored and, therefore, might be open in the future. Currently not open, and it is set to the east of very high-security buildings, do ensure you adhere to non-photography of these and any prohibited notifications.

Rough GPS - 25.302, 51.393 Street - south of Dukhan Rd. - Al Wajbah / الوجبة Public Transport - Bus 512 (then 2km walk) from Green Line Metro Education City

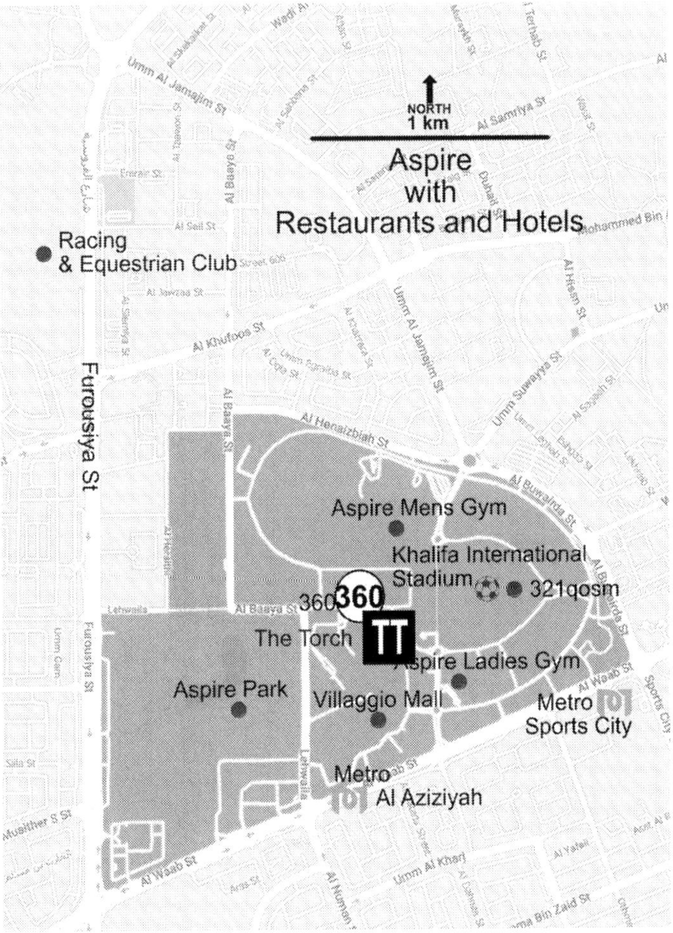

Racing & Equestrian Club

مضمار السباق والفروسية

This is a superb complex with race track and stables.

The stables can be visited; organise this through a tour operator.

The impressive Horse Race Track and Show Jumping Arena have world-class facilities and viewing options. The programs are weekend oriented. Major events spread over the several months from Oct-May.

The grandstand can accommodate 3,000 spectators, which is good as it's a free-to-enter track. The parade ring and winners enclosure are beautifully laid out. Of course, the perfect day to visit is for the Amir Sword Festival - held on over 3 days on a weekend in late February. There are various prestigious events - the newspapers will have details or the website below.

Typical hours - as per event Entry charge - usually no charge - dress as suitable for the event - especially when the Amir is attending, much as in Royal Ascott there is a dress code.

Rough GPS - 25.278, 51.428 Street - Furousiya St - Muaither / معيذر Public Transport - Bus 701 from Green Line Al Shaqab Metro - Contacts - +974 44197722 info@qrec.gov.qa qrec.gov.qa/

Aspire Park / حديقة اسباير - Aspire is a public family only park with large grassed areas and relatively mature trees. A lake is a principal feature - beside this is the statue/sculpture Percival. A jogging track of about 3km runs around it. Like many areas in Qatar, there is free wi-fi. Some small cafes offer snacks. There is minimal car parking for its size. Though the park is open 24 hours a day, the facilities themselves have a shorter opening time.

Typical hours - 08:00-22:00

In the park is a sculpture by Sarah Lucas, a British artist who often uses humour in her work. Perceval is a Bronze life-size English Shire Horse and Cart (with cement vegetable Marrows), on the western side of the lake in Aspire Park. This sculpture is representative of the small ceramic ornaments found in British homes of the mid-20th century.

Rough GPS - 25.260, 51.436

Aspire Park - Baaya / Aspire / اسباير / بعيا Public Transport - Bus 701 Green Line Metro Al Shaqab or Gold Line Metro Al Aziziyah

Carbon Wheels - Bike sale and service

Typical hours - 12:00-21:00

Rough GPS - 25.259, 51.439 Street – Off Al Waab St, in

Aspire Park Public Transport – Gold Line Al Aziziyah - Contacts - +97440064342 info@carbonwheels.qa www.carbonwheels.qa

Khalifa International Stadium / استاد خليفة الدولي - In the Aspire zone, with excellent public transport and a couple of hotels, including The Torch.

Rough GPS - 25.264, 51.447 Street - Al Waab St - Baaya / Aspire / اسباير / بعيا Public Transport - Metro Gold Line Sports City

321 Qatar Olympic & Sports Museum

This of course is devoted to sports. It's a beautifully laid out museum, guiding you in on a track. Full of sports history – from ancient times through of course to the 2022 World Cup. Well worth a visit. Smart dress required by all museums under the Qatar Museums organisation. Photography permitted – without tripos/selfie stick. Typical Hours Sat-Thurs 09:00-19:00 Fri 13:30-19:00 321qosm.org.qa/ Ticket (online booking) QAR100 (or bundled Qatar Museums Pass) on-line booking qm.org.qa/tickets/select-tickets/ -

Aspire Ladies Gym Comprehensive fitness centre with swimming pool, gym and exercise classes. Ladies only.

Typical hours - 07:00-20:00 Sat-Thurs Entry charge - from QAR150 monthly -

Rough GPS - 25.261, 51.447 Street - Junction Al Waab St and Aspire Park Rd Public Transport – Gold Line Sports City or Al Aziziya (Villaggio) - Contacts - +974 4413 6430 http://aspire-activeqa.com/ladies-gym-doha/

Villaggio Mall - Perhaps the most interesting mall in Qatar for visitors. With a boating canal (a short trip QAR15), ice skating & more and a good range of retail outlets including Virgin MegaStore, Carrefour, and high to mid-price brands.

Typical hours - 09:00-22:00 (Friday closed 11:00-12:30 prayer time) Cinema Qatar - Within the Villaggio Mall shopping mall are several screens, including iMax. Though prices are slightly lower than European prices, the downside is that films may be censored to local requirements, affecting a storyline.

Audiences behave as if at home, talking and using phones during screenings.

Typical hours - Check film screenings Entry charge – from around QAR75 - Contacts - info@cinemaqatar.com support@cinemaqatar.com

Villaggio Mall

Gondolania Ice Rink & Leisure / جوندولينيا للتزلج - Found inside Villaggio Mall, this is an extensive indoor leisure area focused on children. Given its name, there have to be Gondolas, add in Go Karts from QAR70, Ice Skating QAR35 upwards, Laser Games from QAR40, 10-Pin Bowling, Roller Coaster and so on.

Typical hours - 09:00-23:00 Daily Entry charge - from QAR 30 up to QAR150

- Contacts - +974 4403 9800 info@gondolania.com www.gondolania.com

Rough GPS - 25.259, 51.445 Street - Junction Al Waab St and Aspire Park Rd - Baaya / Aspire / اسباير / بعيا Public Transport – Gold Line Metro Al Aziziya (Villaggio) - Contacts - +974 4422 7400 info@villaggioqatar.com www. www.villaggioqatar.com

Al Saad Sports / نادي السد الرياضي - Local sports club (football-based) with swimming pool adjacent

Typical hours - 08:00-22:00

Rough GPS - 25.266, 51.483 Street - off Al Nadi St - Fereej Al Soudan / فريج السودان Public Transport – Gold Line Metro Al Sudan - Contacts - +974 4444 8080 alsadd@mcs.gov.qa www.al-saddclub.com

Ali Bin Hamad Al Attiyah Arena / ملعب علي بن حمد العطية - A multi-purpose indoor arena for Handball, Badminton, Boxing, Wrestling

Typical hours - 08:00-23:30 Entry charge – per some events

Rough GPS - 25.270, 51.490 Street - Al Nadi St - Fereej Al Soudan / فريج السودان Public Transport - Gold Line Metro Al Sudan - Contacts - +974 4032 5529 www.abha-arena.com

Central Market Area / السوق المركزي - Until the mid-1990s, the Central Markets area was on the edge of the urban area of Doha, an ideal location for a significant 75-hectare wholesale market. Today urban sprawl has included towns 8km and more west of these markets within Doha's built up metropolis. The markets spread south for 2km along Wholesale Market Rd. They include (from the north at Salwa Rd to the south) a general market, the 'Omani' Souq (named because of the large number of Omani merchants who set up business there in the 1950s). Other markets sell Dates, Fish, Sheep & Goats, Birds, Camels and separately, a slaughterhouse. The Doha Municipal plant nursery finishes this row of flora and fauna oriented establishments. This area is oriented towards a wholesale/bulk buy customer, and the surroundings match the low cost of the produce. For a visitor, this is a remarkable insight into shopping for many of Qatar's residents, low paid workers. Typical hours - 07:00-21:00 daily.

Rough GPS - 25.248, 51.476 Street - at the junction of Wholesale Market St and Salwa Rd - Abu Hamour (Bu Hamour) / بوهامور Public Transport - Bus 604 from Msheireb Bus Station

Katara boulevard

NORTH AND WEST FROM DOHA

The Pearl & Katara

Doha Golf Club / نادي الدوحة للغولف - West of The Pearl, this popular and well established 72par 18 hole course holds the Qatar Masters in March. The course is large enough to almost make you think it's in the depths of lush green countryside in Arabia, then skyscrapers of West Bay loom into view. It is one of the more remarkably city located golf courses. As expected, the clubhouse's restaurant is good; it's an Intercontinental hotel operated one. Guests of members who are experienced players are able to play (proof of handicap required) – check current options & dress code.

Typical hours - 06:00-21:00 Rough GPS - 25.380, 51.505 Street - off Al Jamia St - West Bay / الخليج الغربي Public Transport - Metro Red Line Qatar University (a short taxi ride) - Contacts - +974 4496 0777 info@dohagolfclub.com www.dohagolfclub.com

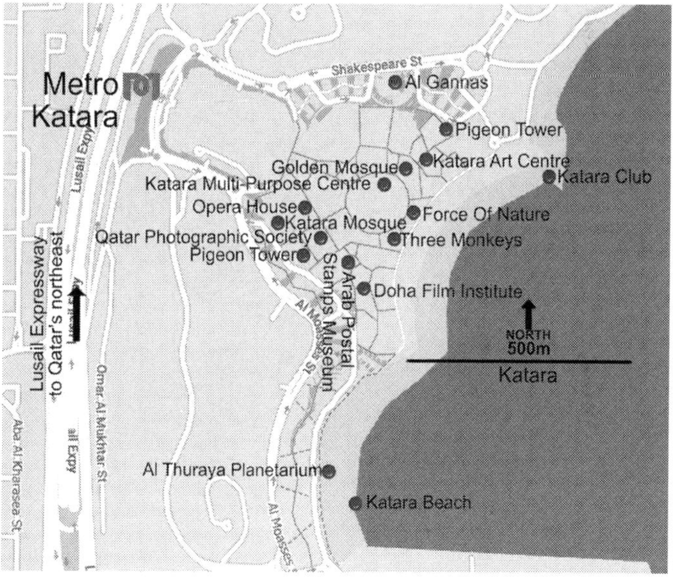

KATARA

كتارا

Katara is a modern cultural/leisure area about 10km north of the Cornice and Souq Waqif area. Although entirely modern in creation, it is a take on an Arab town, with its narrow, winding, car-free streets shaded from the sun.

From Katara Metro – a boulevard leads east into Katara. This

boulevard is an opulent take on a European city. Enjoy some people watching at the popular **Cioccolat Italiani** cafe on the right.

North of this boulevard is Doha's **Children's Museum by OliOli**. It's a hands on experience for children from 1 year-16 and its wrapped in a fantastic enclosure. http://olioli.qa . Pre-booking is needed prices from QAR45-135 – hours as per-booking.

Children's Museum by OliOli

East of the museum is the Falcon Club, **Al Gannas** / القناص - Al Gannas (The Hunter) is an organisation that promotes the tradition of Falconry or Saluki hunting. Their headquarters in Katara is in the shape of a Falcons' *Bur*ka' (Rufter). They hold an annual **Marmi Festival** during most of January in the sand desert southwest of Mesaieed (very appx location 24.894, 51.465) with Falcon hunting and Saluki races. (They start at 06:00 & 12:45 appx). Free 4x4 transport may be available from the 'Sealine Roundabout' 24.863, 51.513. For this event, it is essential to check with organisers and ideally take their complimentary transport offer.

Typical hours - 07:00-14:00 Sun - Thurs

Rough GPS - 25.362, 51.527 - Contacts - + 974-4408 1366 algannas-qtr@katara.net http://algannas.website (also http://algannas.net)

Street Cafes - Katara

Beyond this area is a large number of **street cafes** selling all manner of snacks and drinks. Unfortunately, like Souq Waqif – it's a standing experience – there are no chairs/tables.

Overlooking this area is a couple of Pigeon Towers – others are next to the Karata Mosque.

Katara Pigeon Towers / برج الحمام - كتار – These towers take their inspiration from Pigeon Towers found in much of the greater Fertile Crescent of antiquity; most especially, for this design, a group of towers southeast of Riyadh and farther afield those of the Nile Delta. The original antique towers were specifically built to house pigeons to collect their Guano for nitrogen-rich soil fertiliser or a supply of birds for Pigeon Pie. Pigeon towers in Iran may incorporate a Wind Tower design to cool the interior. These Doha ones with their White Doves seem to be ornamental rather than as used originally.

South of the Pigeon Towers near the street cafes (above) is the main area of Katara – that overlooks the sea. Here in a rough order are places running in a clockwise direction.

Katara Club / نادي كتارا- Karata Club is an upmarket Spa & gym directly on the northern section of the beach at Katara. The setting is matched by its ambience and general club service; the restaurants let down the experience slightly.

Typical hours - Sun - Thurs 06:00-22:00 - Fri & Sat 09:00-21:00 Entry charge - membership -

Rough GPS - 25.361, 51.529 Street - off Shakespeare St - Contacts - +974 4408 1580 info@katara.club www.katara.club/

Katara Art Centre (KAC) / مركز كتارا للفنون - An art gallery, workshop, artists' incubator', retail outlet for art and interior design. Katara Art Centre is a hub for cultural communities to create a critical grassroots base in Doha for contemporary life. Weekends have popular events, adding vibrancy to Katara, though Katara is vibrant without this addition.

Typical hours - Sat-Thurs 10:00-22:00 Friday 14:00-22:00 (departments do work shorter hours) Rough GPS - 25.361, 51.528 - Contacts - +974 4408 0244 hello@dohakac.com www.dohakac.com

The **Golden Mosque** on the opposite (north) side of the outdoor theatre-in-the-round is traditional in design but very unusual in its surface treatment - of gold. If you, as a non-Muslim, wish to visit – do so Sat-Thurs 09:00-11:00 (non-prayer times). Before entering, it is polite to ask, *'mumkin a shoof?'* (may I look) in case of a regulation change. Dress as in the Imam Muhammad Bin Abdulwahhab Mosque [PAGE 69]. Rough GPS 25.360, 51.526

Katara Multi-Purpose Centre / مركز كتارا متعدد الأغراض - A modern multi-purpose function centre for events, exhibitions, meetings and even weddings. On its 'roof' is an outdoor theatre-in-the-round, almost a Roman amphitheatre with 5,000 seats. Check media for upcoming events here.

Typical hours - as per event Rough GPS - 25.360, 51.526

Force of Nature

The Force of Nature This statue by Italian artist Lorenzo Quinn is precisely what it says, a tribute to the force of nature, specifically hurricanes. It is made of bronze, iron, and stainless steel and overlooks the sea east of the Amphitheatre. Similar statues to this Katara one can be seen in Berkley Square London, Avenue of the Americas New York and China. A variant is at Reston USA.

Rough GPS - 25.360, 51.527

Three Monkeys - Gandhi's Three Monkeys (a somewhat sarcastic title) by Subodh Gupta is based on See no Evil, hear no Evil, Speak no Evil. These have a military twist and are just outside Saffron Restaurant in Katara.

Rough GPS - 25.359, 51.527

Arab Postal Stamps Museum / متحف الطوابع البريدية العربية - The Arab world's philatelic history, with stamps from 22 countries. The stamps offer an insight into what each country wants to project about itself. The displays are traditional rather than an immersive insight; this is a set up by Katara. There is an online ordering service for stamp collectors from Qatar Post store.qatarpost.qa/webstore/.

Typical hours - 09:00-21:00 Sun-Thurs / 09:00 midday / 17:00-20:00 Sat on Friday closed

Rough GPS - 25.359, 51.525 - Contacts - azayan@hotmail.com www.katara.net/en/communities/arab-postal-stamp-museum

Doha Film Institute - Doha Film Institute funds and supports the production of local, regional and international films with an Arab focus. It hosts film screenings (check local media or website - most are at the weekend), educational programmes and workshops. As with so much in Qatar - this is a hub of the Qatar Foundation and its chairperson Sheikha Al-Mayassa bint Hamad bin Khalifa Al Thani.

Typical hours - 08:00-16:00 Sun - Thurs Entry charge - as per event -

Rough GPS - 25.359, 51.526 - Contacts - +974 4420 0505 info@dohafilminstitute.com www.dohafilminstitute.com

Opera House / دار الأوبرا - This is a traditional-looking Opera House that wouldn't look out of place in Milan or Paris. The building is the home of the Qatar Philharmonic Orchestra qatarphilharmonicorchestra.org, which held its first performance in October 2008. As with so much in Qatar, the Orchestra's performances are focused on the new. They support rising new Arab performers and composers with performances in Qatar and worldwide. Performances are principally during the winter, including classical western and other cultures concerts.

Typical hours - as per performance Entry charge - as per event

Rough GPS - 25.360, 51.525 - Contacts - +974 4454 8185 events@katara.net www.katara.net

Katara Mosque

Southwest of the Katara Multi-Purpose Centre is **Katara Mosque**. This is a Turkish influenced mosque with Iznik style tilework - though the overall style seems closer to Iraqi mosques. Designed by Zeynep Fadillioglu, who created the interior of the acclaimed Sakirin Mosque in Istanbul, the craftsmen were restorers from Istanbul's Dolmabahce Palace. Entrance as in Golden Mosque.

Three traditional **Pigeon Towers** are next to the mosque – which must, as a result, need frequent cleaning.

There are many small retail outlets for art, fashion and more in Katara. Katara also has innumerable restaurants, including those small takeaways east of Al Gannas. The outdoor theatre-in-the-round with its workshops is at the centre of an increasingly attractive location. Events and exhibitions create a dynamic environment with annual events. These include a falconry festival in September and an Arabian horse show in early February kiahf.qa. The **beachfront** adds to its appeal, all-be-it pay to enter. There is an excellent choice of water sports activities here, including Jet-Ski, Dhow Ride, Kayak, etc. Parallel to the beach area is a promenade that runs south.

Pigeon Towers - Katara

To the north and south of the entrance boulevard are small **grassed-over hills**. Each is little used – and are a quiet area to set and relax.

Rough GPS - 25.361, 51.525 Street - off Lusail Expressway - Katara / كتارا Public Transport - Metro Red Line Katara at the main entrance. www.katara.net

The Pearl

is an upmarket housing area, set on artificial islands surrounding a lagoon type marina. The principal attraction is its water taxi.

The Pearl

Water Taxi / العبارة - Within The Pearl, this public 'water taxi' cruises around the enclosed bay area. It's almost quicker to walk. However, this taxi is a bit unexpected in Doha; it's almost, but not quite, La Serenissima. There are several landing gates - including 25.364, 51.541 (organise tickets here) & 25.366, 51.545. Private hire is possible, against advance booking and charge QAR200/- +. A more extended trip that includes the 'Qanat Quarter' (which is reminiscent of Venice) to The Pearl's north has a charge of QAR50/- for around 40 minutes.

Typical hours - 14:00-00:00 (Public service) Sun - Thurs Entry charge - QAR25/- - Contacts - +974 4409 5279 hmo@ronauticame.com www.ronauticame.com

Lagoona Mall / لاجونا مول - Lagoona Mall is a modern mall operation within The Pearl. Apart from the expected outlets like McDonald's and Carrefour, it does have a reasonable selection of shops not found in other malls. This is where Doha's Zigzag Towers are found. Also, a few major 5* hotels.

Typical hours - 10:00-22:00 (Fri 14:00-12:00)

Rough GPS - 25.376, 51.525 - Contacts - +974 4433 5555 Lagoona@darwishholding.com www.lagoonamall.com/

The Pearl Rough GPS - 25.364, 51.541 Street - Porto Arabia Avenue - The Pearl / اللولو Public Transport – Red Line Metro Legtaifiya and MetroLink bus.

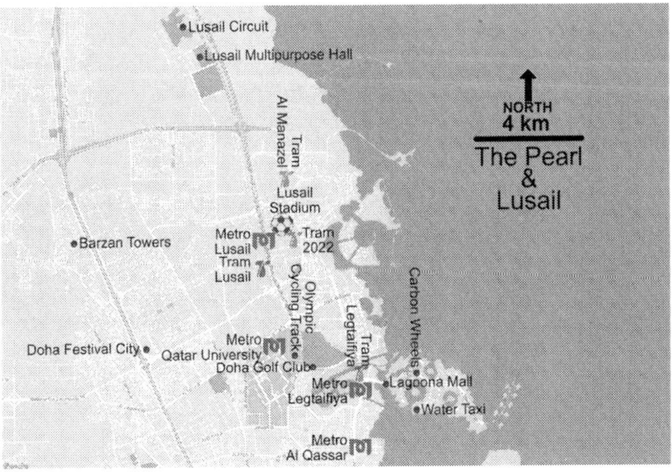

LUSAIL

This area is still under development - though key infrastructure is in place. From the Lusail Metro (Red Line - hub at Msheireb 30 min journey) a walk or tram (Purple Line goes the entire length - Orange Line turns south) along the **Lusail Boulevard** (a good choice of places to eat including Tayo and Ivy) leads to the sea. The Boulevard has periodic events and is lit at night. South of this is perhaps the most developed area in Lusail. The Orange Line Tram - has a stop Tarfat South, at **Place Vendome**. This is a large, upmarket, 3 floor shopping mall with shops and currently an emphasis on places to eat. This is a European style of architecture and does have an open courtyard 'a la' the original

Place Vendome. Farther south on the Orange Line, stop Marina Central is near the **Katara Towers**. This is a crescent shaped hotel complex. Hotels in Lusail can offer good value if you dont mind being away from the original core of Doha & having a longer journey from the airport.

Lusail Stadium / إستاد لوسيل - The inauguration and final stadium for the 2022 World Cup with 80,000 seats designed by Foster & Partners. From Lusail Metro on the Red Line, it's a 700m walk – use shuttle buses for events.

Rough GPS - 25.421, 51.492 Street - Al Khor Coastal Rd - Lusail (Losail) / لوسيل Public Transport – Lusail Metro.

Lusail Multipurpose Sports Arena / ملعب لوسيل الرياضي - Operated by Qatar's Olympic organisation, this is a modern 15,000 seat venue to host indoor sporting and entertainment events. Handball, volleyball, wrestling, badminton and more have a home here, as do musical events and professional wrestling (WWE etc.). South of this arena is the Qatar Shooting and Archery complex www.qatarshooting.qa.

Rough GPS - 25.482, 51.462 Street - Al Khor Coastal Rd - Lusail (Losail) / لوسيل Public Transport – Bus 702 & 722 from Lusail Bus Station - Contacts - +974 4494 4777 qoc@olympic.qa www.olympic.qa

Lusail Stadium & Cycle Track

The Challenge 2015 - The Challenge 2015, a sculpture by Ahmed al-Bahrani, the Iraqi artist, are 5 giant hands reaching for a Basketball. This is outside the Lusail Multipurpose Hall. Ahmed has several other sculptures in Qatar, including the Flag of Glory within the National Museum, a bronze sculpture, again of hands supporting a flagpole with the Qatari flag.

Lusail Circuit Sports Club / حلبة لوسيل للسباقات - Motor race track (5.3km) with track days at least once a month for car, bike, go-carts & MotoGP and from 2023, Formula 1. It's a floodlit circuit - so it also holds spectacular night time events. You should check directly with the track for a schedule. Various dining and hospitality options are available.

Lusail Circuit

Typical hours - 24 Hours Entry charge - per event

Rough GPS - 25.488 , 51.449 Street - Al Khor Coastal Rd - Lusail (Losail) / لوسيل Public Transport – Bus 702 & 722 from Lusail Bus Station - Contacts - +974 4472 9151 info@lcsc.qa www.lcsc.qa/

Doha Festival City / دوحة فيستيفال ستي - Large shopping mall with indoor snow toboggan slope. Midprice retail outlets include IKEA, Riva, Next, Debenhams, Old Navy and an extensive range of Restaurants. Doha Festival City is one of the newest of Doha's large malls. It is owned by Al Futtaim, who also run the gulf-wide City Centres. These are managed to a high standard, though many are almost indistinguishable from each other.

Vox Cinema - Multiplex cinema with 3D. Though prices are perhaps slightly lower than European prices, the downside is that films may be censored to local requirements, changing a storyline. Audiences often behave as if at home, talking and using phones during screenings. Screenings include English language, Arabic & Hindi films; occasionally Tamil films are shown.

Typical hours - check film schedule Entry charge - around QAR75 -

Contacts - qat.voxcinemas.com/contact-us qat.voxcinemas.com

Doha Festival City Typical hours - 10:00-22:00 Sat-Thurs (Friday closed 11:30-13:00) Rough GPS - 25.386, 51.443 Street - Junction Al Shamal Rd and - Al Daayen / الضعاين Public Transport - Bus 517 Lusail Bus Station, 701 Al Shaqab Metro - Contacts - info@dohafestivalcity.com www.dohafestivalcity.com- +974 4035 4444

Barzan Towers

Barzan Towers / ابراج برزان - Barzan Towers are a late 19th century/early 20th c couple of fortified towers of lime rubble and coral. Like many other buildings of the period in Qatar, Sheikh Mohammed bin Jassim Al Thani builds these. Though restored 20 years ago, the impact is authentic, including resident pigeons!

Rough GPS - 25.418, 51.413 Street - west of Al Shamal Rd - Umm Salal / أم صلال Public Transport - Bus 528 Green Line Al Shaqab Metro (1200metres)

North of the Lusail Circuit, on the Khor Coastal Rd, is the private Lusail Palace of Sheikh Tamim.

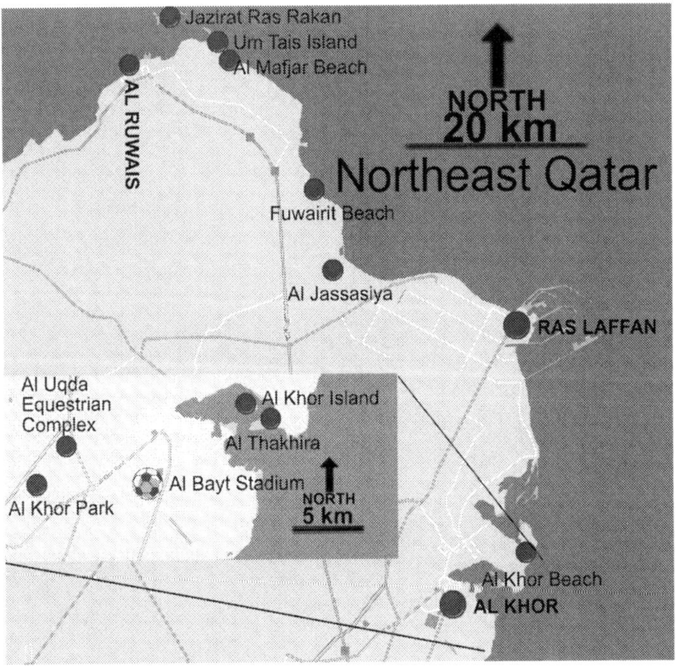

NORTH-EAST QATAR

Al Bayt Stadium / استاد البيت - Designed to look like an Arab tent with 60,000 seats, this football stadium is a 60km drive from Doha. There are minimal hotels in the area; the Sultan Beach Resort is the best choice 7km away.

Rough GPS - 25.652, 51.484 Street - Al Khor Coastal Rd - Al Khor / الخور Public Transport - Bus 701 from Al Shaqab Metro and service during matches from Lusail Metro.

Al Uqda, Equestrian Complex / اسطبلات العقدة - Al Uqda Equestrian Complex is a multipurpose facility with a grass race track, jumping arena and riding school. It periodically holds public events, over a dozen race days (from Nov-Feb), and Arab horse shows and auctions. As with most sporting events in Qatar, winter is the best time to see these.

Typical hours - open to suite events Entry charge -

Rough GPS - 25.672, 51.438 Street - off Dukhan Highway -

Al Khor / الخور Public Transport - No public transport - Contacts - +974 4482 5708 info@QARec.gov.qa QARec.gov.qa/

Al Khor Beach / شاطئ الخور - North-east of Al Khor and east of Al Thakhira, after a rough unmarked drive of 4km, are a series of small beaches with shallow water - and areas of seaweed and seagrass. Turtles and Dugong feed off seagrass - here and in similar environments below.

Rough GPS - 25.717, 51.593 Street - off Al Khor Coastal Rd - Al Khor / الخور Public Transport - No public transport

Al Khor Park / منتزة الخور - Around 9km southwest of Al Khor is a 20-hectare family only (except Sundays), reasonably well-maintained park that is extremely busy at weekends.

Next to the park (with separate ticket & entrance) is a purpose built **Panda House for two Pandas Suhail & Soraya**. These animals arrived in October 2022 & will live there for 15 years in an enclosure over 100m long. Online timed booking only on day of entry with **'Oun' App** QAR50. Daily 10:00-15:00.

Al Khor Park Typical hours - 08:00-22:00 General Park Entry charge - QAR15/- -

Rough GPS - 25.649, 51.420 Street - Al Shamal Rd - Al Khor / الخور Public Transport – no Public Transport

Al Thakhira

Al Dakhera / الذخيره -

This is the largest area of Mangrove in Qatar. Coral reefs, seagrass beds, etc., with Hawksbill turtle offshore. The mangroves of Al Thakhira lie opposite Al Thakhira village and near Al Khor town. Flora includes *Avicenna marina* (Mangrove), *Anabis setifera, Salsola imbricate, Lycium shawii* etc. The fauna includes over 130 species of birds and reptiles, including Hooded malpolon, Spiny-tailed lizard and numerous insects. Kayaking can be done through the Mangrove (see operators [PAGE 139])

Rough GPS - 25.748, 51.540 Street - Al Thakhira - Al Khor / الخور Public Transport - Bus 722 from Lusail – then a 2km walk.

Bin Ghannam mangroves

Possibly more accessible for a casual visit to mangroves is at **Bin Ghannam Island** /also called Al Khor Island. Here a walkway takes you through the mangroves onto the island. A small hide can help bird watching. Rough GPS - 25.686, 51.554 No Public Transport.

Al Jassasiya (Al Gasasia) Rock Art

الجساسية

The petroglyphs at Jebel Al Jassasiya are promoted by the Qatari government to illustrate Qatar's history and maritime heritage. Petroglyphs were first noted in Qatar by non-locals in the 1950s. These at Jebel Al Jassasiya were pointed out in the 1960s and recorded in detail in 1974. Quarrying in the area has since reduced the number of these at Jebel Al Jassasiya. However, still, the site consists of 12 low outcrops of rock with several hundred examples of petroglyphs. They are on either side of the tarmac road, enclosed by a fence – with open gate. Both line art and 'cupules' (small circular round depressions arranged in clusters) are represented. The cupules are probably a version of mancala, the board game played by moving a small object over the board to defeat an opponent. The small objects were perhaps made of stone or a shell. Other petroglyphs include line drawings, typically of various types of dhows. Many have been stylistically interpreted to date between the 11th and early 16th centuries. Other line drawings include *wasms* (tribal markings), human figures and animals.

Al Jassasiya rock art

Rough GPS - 25.952, 51.406 Street - A few kilometres to the

east of route 1 - Ash Shamal / الشمال Public Transport - No public transport

Fuwairit Beach / شاطئ فويريت - Fuwairit Beach is public and relatively busy at the weekend. Its popular for Kitesurfing. Access is via the Al Shamel Rd and then off-road. Attached to the mainland (north of the palaces and abandoned ruins) is a sand spit, an important location for Hawksbill Turtle nesting. As a result, this beach is closed during peak nesting season 1 April to 31 July). Mangroves line the silted khor (creek).

Rough GPS - 26.059, 51.354 Street - East of Al Shamel Rd north of Doha - Ash Shamal / الشمال Public Transport – no public transport

Al Mafjar Beach / شاطئ المفجر - Opposite the small ruined village of Al Mafjar, an isolated beach area and sand spit extend to Qatar's most northerly point. The sand is very loose, and a 4x4 is essential. As on many other beaches in Qatar, there is no lifeguard, safety equipment or facilities. There are a surprising number of semi-permanent caravans along the northeast coast.

Rough GPS - 26.136, 51.301 Street - off Al Shamal Rd - Ash Shamal / الشمال Public Transport - No public transport

Um Tais Island / جزيرة ام تيس - Um Tais Island (Um means mother and Tais is a male goat – so this is the 'Mother of the Male Goat Island') is a sand bar off Qatar's northern coast. It's just separated from the mainland and a relatively undisturbed place. Um Tais's attraction is enhanced by substantial areas of Mangrove. This sand bar is so low lying that parts are destroyed and rebuilt during storms.

Rough GPS - 26.156, 51.276 Street - off Al Shamal Rd - Al Ruwais / الرويس Public Transport - No public transport

Jazirat Ras Rakan (Island) / جزيرة ام تيس This small sandy offshore island is more easily accessed than Um Tais Island. Seagrass can be seen in the sea off its beaches. Opposite both these islands, on the mainland, is the only hotel in northern Qatar, Zulal Wellness Resort.

Rough GPS - 26.178, 51.226 Street - off Al Shamal Rd - Al Ruwais / الرويس Public Transport - No public transport

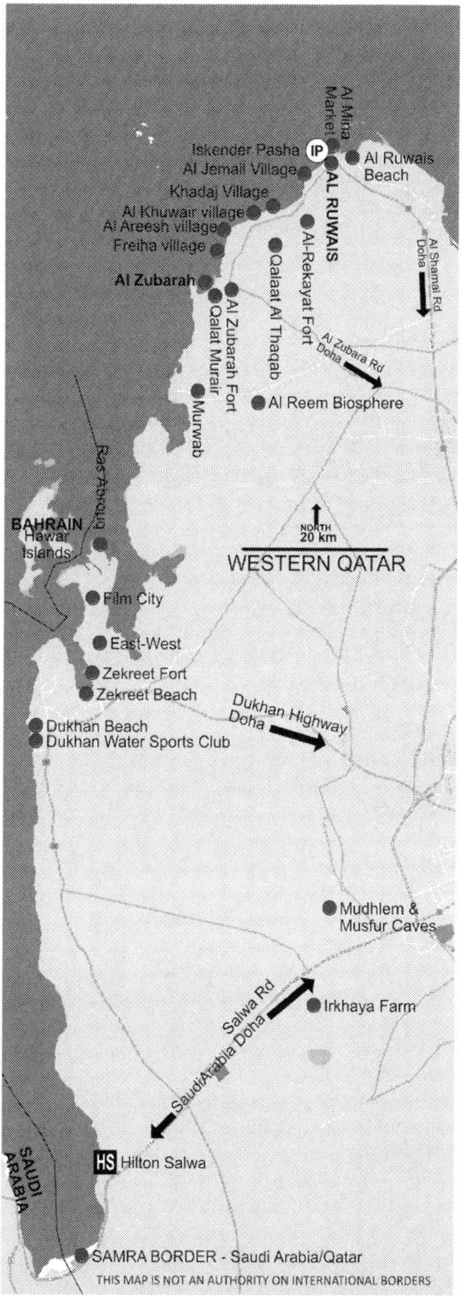
Al Mina Market
Iskender Pasha
IP
Al Ruwais Beach
Al Jemail Village
Khadaj Village
AL RUWAIS
Al Khuwair village
Al Areesh village
Freiha village
Al-Rekayat Fort
Qalaat Al Thaqab
Al Shamal Rd Doha
Al Zubarah
Al Zubarah Fort
Qalat Murair
Al Zubara Rd Doha
Murwab
Al Reem Biosphere
Ras Abroug
BAHRAIN
Hawar Islands
NORTH
20 km
WESTERN QATAR
Film City
East-West
Zekreet Fort
Zekreet Beach
Dukhan Highway Doha
Dukhan Beach
Dukhan Water Sports Club
Mudhlem & Musfur Caves
Salwa Rd
Irkhaya Farm
SaudiArabia Doha
HS
Hilton Salwa
SAUDI ARABIA
SAMRA BORDER - Saudi Arabia/Qatar
THIS MAP IS NOT AN AUTHORITY ON INTERNATIONAL BORDERS

AL RUWAIS & NORTH COAST, WEST COAST, CENTRAL QATAR

The west of Qatar has an extended coastline, at some distance from roads. Note that the Qatar / Bahrain / Saudi International Border runs in the sea along parts of the coastline. Each country does arrest any person who enters their territory illegally.

Al Ruwais town has a reasonable range of services including petrol. GPS 26.127, 51.208

Al Ruwais Beach / شاطىء الرويس - A small beach, not really for swimming (or sunbathing).

Rough GPS - 26.144, 51.216 Street - off Al Kasooma St - Al Ruwais / الرويس Public Transport – no public transport

Al Mina Market / سوق الميناء - Here in Al Ruwais Port in northern Qatar is a retail market offering a wide range of products, mainly from Iran. They include inexpensive carpets, handicrafts, cheap manufactured products and dried fruit and nuts. In short, this is a modern Iranian bazar.

Typical hours - 08:00-18:00 / 08:00-20:00 Sun-Weds / Thurs-Sat Entry charge -

Rough GPS - 26.141, 51.207 Street - Al Ruwais Port - Al Ruwais / الرويس

Ghost Villages of western Qatar

Over less than 30km along the coast to the south of Al Ruwais are a series of settlements that range from pirate lairs to a UNESCO World Heritage Site. The landscape is bleak – with little vegetation, Unspectacular in themselves, certainly compared to the glitz on the other side of the peninsula, they offer up a mournful impression of the hard life in Qatar before oil. As there are no shops in any – all are little more than ruins, bring water to drink and as they have very dusty or damp ground come in shoes to protect you that you do not mind getting filthy. As all face west over the sea, sunsets are an atmospheric time to visit. This area is one to use a 4x4 vehicle to reach.

Al Jemail Village / قرية الجميل - The ruined village of Al Jemail has signed east access off the tarmac road southwest of Al Ruwais. This is one of several similar abandoned villages on the west coast road, to the south of Al Ruwais. Dating from the mid 19thc-mid 20thc the houses are mostly dilapidated, with crumbling walls, which are a mix of lime and coral stones. Some buildings still have ceilings, which show timber beams, matting and mud/gypsum roofs. The least derelict building is the mosque, which still has its old minaret standing. The old doorway in the minaret was to allow access to the minaret's internal stairs for the call to prayer from its top. The village is just above high tide. At low tide, vast areas of sand are exposed - making for a good walk.

There are innumerable low stone walls in the shallows of the sea from Al Jemail south to Al Zubarah. These are **inter-tidal fish traps**, *'al maskar'*, which trap fish as the tide goes out. Clearly, this opportunity to capture fish must have been a critical reason all these small villages grew up along the coast.

Al Jemail mosque

Rough GPS - 26.094, 51.152 Street - about 8km by road southwest of Al Ruwais (the last few hundred meters are on a rough track) - / No Public Transport

Khadaj village / قريه خداج - Possibly the smallest of these abandoned ruined fishermen's settlements on the northwest coast. Here there are perhaps the remains of four houses.

Rough GPS - 26.081, 51.112 Street - Off the tarmac west coastal Rd, the last 2km is a rough track. - / No Public Transport

Al Areesh / العريش - Much of the housing, which is late 19th century and early & mid-20th c, is ruined; it was a settlement of the Al Kabesi Tribe. The old school is the small, more modern building on the eastern edge. The mosque's minaret is still standing as at Al Jemail. To the west is the village's cemetery.

Rough GPS - 26.051, 51.057 Street - Off the tarmac west coastal Rd, near the Coast Guard station; the last 2km is a rough track. - / Public Transport - Bus route 100 and a walk on rough ground from the tarmac.

Qalaat Al Thaqab (fort) / قلعة الثقب - This small abandoned fort 11km north-east of Zubarah has three towers and a few rooms. It served to protect the water wells next to the fort. The agricultural area clearly suffers from a lack of water, making the fort's purpose obsolete many years ago. It was restored in 2005 and awaits a purpose. The floral shaped structure next to the fort was built in 2015, presumably referring to the wells. Stick to the tracks leading off the tarmac road as the soil is like powder, and rain might cause vehicles to lose traction. 4x4 is ideal for all the areas of western Qatar.

Rough GPS - 26.033, 51.117 Street - About 3km south on a rough track, off the tarmac west coast coastal road to the south of Al Ruwais. No Public Transport.

Al Khuwair / الخوير - The abandoned 18th-century village of Al Khuwair sits on the edge of a desolate area in northwest Qatar. The village was a base for Rahmah ibn Jabir Al Jalahimi known to Britain as a pirate. He was a style icon as, having lost one eye, he introduced a vital part of the 'pirate' dress, the eye patch. Rahmah was previously a partner with the Al Khalifa sheikhs of Bahrain, but feeling he lost out on the benefit of the spoils when they occupied Bahrain became their enemy. He co-operated with the Al Saud in Riyadh, who periodically raided and occupied the east coast of Arabia in the late 18th century. He somehow avoided conflict with Britain, despite attacking shipping in The Gulf. Clearly, he was an excellent tactician and perhaps diplomat. Rahmah ibn Jabir died in battle in 1826 after deliberately using his own ship as a floating bomb to destroy a Bahraini ship that had one of the Al Khalifa sheikhs on board.

The sandbanks and coral off the coast, which protected the village from attack, must have been a fundamental reason for settling here. Much of the housing, which seems to be late 19th or early 20th century, is ruined; the mosque's minaret is the tallest structure. It has a doorway leading to the stairs up to the minaret's upper platform, from where the call to prayer could be made. Al Khuwair village relied on water from the wells at Al Thaqab about 5km southeast. A few modern houses are set to the east of Al Khuwair. Al Ruwais to the north of Al Khuwair has petrol and shops.

When driving off the tarmac, stay on tracks as the general area is Sabkha and soft mud when wet. This can easily cause a vehicle to become stuck.

Rough GPS - 26.068, 51.083 Street - Off the tarmac west coastal Rd, marked with four radio masts; the last 1500m is a rough track. No Public Transport.

Al-Rekayat Fort / قلعة ركيات - Al-Rekayat Fort is a small, square structure. Like most forts in Qatar, this is a single-story building. Al-Rekayat Fort has a single round tower on one corner, and the other corners are square towers made from rooms that project beyond the main wall. This fort dates to the 19th century. It was renovated about 30 years ago with some work undertaken more recently. Inside, a series of rooms abut onto the exterior walls. When writing this guide, there are some collapsed walls within the fort. As with all these old forts, take suitable precautions when entering. Within the fort, there is a water well & presumably others in the adjacent farm.

Typical hours - a free to access open area next to a private farm. Entry charge - no charge -

Rough GPS - 26.051, 51.130 Street - about 13km by road southwest of Al Ruwais (the last 1.5km to the south of the tarmac road are on a rough track). No Public Transport

Freiha / فريحة - Freiha is possibly the oldest of the abandoned villages in northwest Qatar. Judging from ceramic finds by the University of Copenhagen, it is believed to date from the 16thc, bringing it to the period when the Portuguese arrived in The Gulf. Carsten Niebuhr, the German explorer, must have visited the settlement in 1765 as it was included in his map of The Gulf. A hypostyle mosque (the walls are only a few levels of stone high) is almost on the beach, with a courtyard and an ablution well in the southern corner. The settlement's cemetery is just 100m to the mosque's south. A larger building of about 40m on each side is to the mosque's east. This was probably a fort with a series of rooms on the exterior walling, as is usual in Qatari forts. Courtyard type housing - the classic Arab style - is typical in Freiha. Stone and coral are the primary walling materials, with the walls mud-plastered. However, the fort and mosque were of better construction with a simple lime plaster. Freiha's water was obtained from a well in the higher ground to the east of the settlement.

To the north of Freiha, just south of the modern house, is a secondary settlement. Its cemetery is walled, making it seem as if it is a more recent one. Waste middens, set back 100+m from the beach area, are between these two sections of Freiha. Another small satellite settlement is to the south of Freiha. Beyond the tarmac road is another abandoned settlement, Ain Mohammed, from the mid 19thc to the 20thc. Freiha shows every sign of having an ebb and flow of population and occupancy. The three satellite settlements might have grown if Freiha's population had moved elsewhere.

Rough GPS - 26.014, 51.040 Street - About 22km drive south from Al Ruwais on the west coast road - and about 4km north of Al Zubarah Fort. The final 1km to the west of the road is across open ground - Al Zubarah / الزبارة No Public Transport

AL ZUBARAH

For the site at Al Zubarah entry charge is QAR35 (or ticket bundle) – with last entrance into the archaeological site around 15:30. Turn up well before 15:30 to allow time to organise tickets. The fort (below) is open until 17:00appx – so view this after the archaeological site if needed.

More information on the site's history sees [PAGE 249].

Al Zubarah Fort

Al Zubarah Fort / قلعة الزبارة – more details [PAGE 249] This small mid-20thc military fort stands for a pivotal period in Qatar's history. It was built in response to Bahrain's building of an outpost on the Hawar Islands to the southwest. The fort is a single-story, with three circular towers and a fourth square tower. Arranged against the exterior wall are the interior rooms – all of which open onto the courtyard. Climb up the rear left tower for a view over the area. Inside the rooms have displays about the history of the site. Outside, some relatively ordinary buildings have a museum about Al Zubarah. Exhibits include explanations about pearling. A rusting ship's canon, and perhaps a couple of camels complete the scene. As this fort symbolises Qatar's history, periodic unique events are held here - some may close the building. For more information, see the Al Zubarah section below.

Typical hours - 09:00-17:00 daily Entry charge QAR35

Rough GPS - 25.977, 51.046 Al Zubarah / الزبارة No Public Transport

Qalat Murair / قلعة مرير - Built in around 1768, the largely invisible remains of Qalat Murair fort is 300m southwest of Al Zubarah Fort. The Qalat Murair fort was approximately 160m on each four sides. The fort, which is contemporary to Al

Zubarah town, protected the numerous shallow water well around it. Around Qalat Murair fort were several courtyard houses and a mosque. Qalat Murair was destroyed in the 1960s, a period when Al Zubarah Fort was improved, and a rough track was made to the peninsula of Ras Ushairiq to Al Zubarah's west. The material of the fort may have been used for the construction of Al Zubarah Fort.

Rough GPS - 25.974, 51.043 Street - /

Al Zubarah Town / الآثار الزبارة – More details [PAGE 249] The abandoned town of Al Zubarah sits as a walled 61-hectare site that extends about 1.5km along a shallow, sheltered bay. The UNESCO area is larger and extends beyond the fort and includes part of the sea shallows. A visit offers a partially excavated 200 years old town in a beach setting. There is white sand from coral and rocky outcrops and offshore, a few inter-tidal fish-traps, *'al maskar'* المسكر. The town has had some excavations by the University of Copenhagen.

Several species of land mammals can be found near Al Zubarah, Dromedaries and very occasionally, Sand Gazelle might be seen, along with fox. Dugongs feed on seagrass, and Common Bottlenose Dolphin hunt for fish in the sea.

Socotra Cormorants

Many birds can be found throughout the year, including Socotra Cormorant, which might be seen on Umm Jatila Island off the north of Al Zubarah. Osprey might be seen hunting for fish in the lagoon. In winter, Greater Flamingo gather on the mud-flats offshore. *Uromastyx aegyptia*, Yellow Spotted Agama and Sand Vipers are reptiles found inland. In the sea, other reptiles are found, including Green Turtle and Hawksbill Turtles.

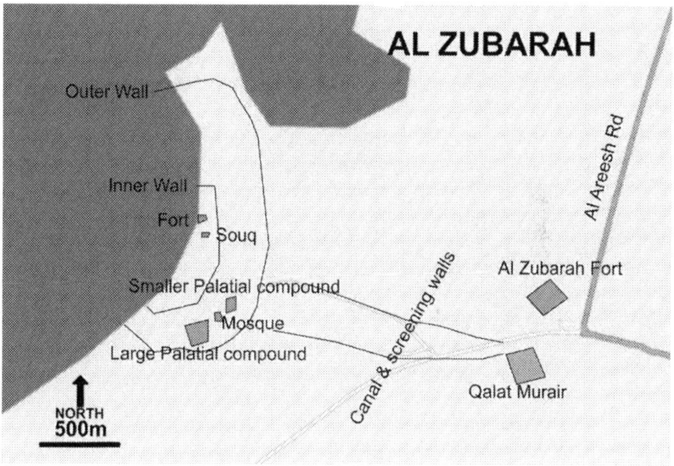

South of the fort and archaeological site south is an old canal of some 1.8km, and two screening walls. These are believed to have served Qalat Al Murair, the ruined fort south of Al Zubarah Fort, on the southern side of the road. Much of the southern area outside the walls is Sabkha, which will be wet and, in places, slippery after rain or very high tide.

To reach Al Zubarah's archaeological site – you have go in a small coach – and take the escorted tour of the site along a slightly elevated walkway. The walk is around an hour and of about 2kms.

This description is of the entire site – in case the walkway is extended from its current focus on a small section of the site.

Al Zubarah has two town walls. The inner wall, of about 1km in length with 11 towers, dates after the 1811 destruction of the town and is built over earlier buildings, as the later population occupied a smaller footprint. The original outer wall was presumably much higher than its current height. Generally, now it's between 0.5 & 1 meter in width and is about 2.5km long with 22 towers.

Northern House - Al Zubarah

A 'northern house' is on the walk in the northern area of Al Zubarah. This is believed to be a merchants house. Originally it was a two story building with a multitude of rooms and several staircases. This was normal for merchants who typically would have private family accommodation on the upper floor – and public rooms and warehousing on the ground level. Possibly after the town was attacked – this house was repurposed into a smaller footprint.

The souq is next to the beach. It would allow for goods to be taken off and onto boats. Dates were stored here – and trade as far away as Japan took place as shown by ceramics from this location. Though whether this was direct or, more probably, indirect is unknown.

Just northwest of the souq is what is assumed to be a small fort. This overlooks deeper water to its southwest, which may have been an open harbour. It was probably in the area between the fort and the peninsula of Ras Ushairiq to Al Zubarah's west that British warships sank many dhows in 1895. These were believed to be massed for an attack on Bahrain. In the north of the town is possibly another mosque. Farther north, the outer town wall extends into the sea for about 50m. This supplied a barrier against ships grounding on the shallow offshore reefs in the northern area of Al Zubarah.

The walk continues and unfortunately currently exits the site before the 'palatial compounds'.

In the southeast of Al Zubarah are fortified 'palatial compounds', each square in outline. The larger is set against the southern part of the outer wall. This large building of over 100m on each side, with a corner tower on each corner, was practically self-contained with date fruit stores and a hammam. Plaster on the walls included standard Arabic decorative features, unsurprisingly with a hint of Persian and India. A smaller square palatial compound is to the northeast of the larger palatial compound. The smaller palatial compound was only 60m along each wall, with square towers on the corner. A mosque that collapsed only in 1965 is between the two palatial compounds. Photos taken before its collapse show it with columns and arches between them.

Around the palatial compound area is a residential section. Unlike older Arab towns, it has a regular grid-like street layout perpendicular to the outer wall; it was a planned settlement. Most of the housing was of a courtyard type.

Though Al Zubarah is a UNESCO site and Al Zubarah Fort is an iconic building in Qatar, they are far from touristy. It's quite possible you will be the only visitor at this UNESCO site.

Rough GPS - 25.977, 51.029 Street - On the Al Shamal Rd northwest of Doha - Al Zubarah / الزبارة No Public Transport

Under the Law of Antiquities of Qatar, it is a criminal offence to excavate or remove any antiquities without permission from Qatar Museums or deface or otherwise damage any parts of a historical site.

Al Reem Biosphere Reserve

Rawdat Al Numan / منطقة الريم المحمية - The overall Al Reem Biosphere Reserve extends from Al Zubarah to the north, east to Al Ghuwaitiya and southwest to Zekreet. The terrestrial site includes limestone cliffs, mesas, wadis, sabkhas, and gravel plains. Coastal swampy mudflats and shallow sea waters rich in seagrass beds complete the reserve. It's an open desolate area with a surprising amount of human development within its designated area. The most vegetated land area is at Al Numan, where there is scattered acacia and farms.

Rough GPS - 25.860, 51.080 Street - Much of the northwest region of Qatar. There are fenced areas such as Rawdat Al Numan روضة نعمان that protect vegetated areas. The word روضة /Rawdha / Rawdat means meadow which occurs after rain. The area south of film city is also included in the reserve. - Ash Shamal / الشمال No public transport

Ras Abrouq / رأس أبروق - In west Qatar, a peninsula with not only Film City but a remarkable variety of archaeology. Flint working and scattered tools might be seen on some limestone Mesas. Ubaid pottery of a similar period has been found. The beaches here are overlooked by low limestone cliffs. The most northerly point is a small coastguard station, Bahrain's waters are only a few hundred metres off the beaches.

Rough GPS - 25.622, 50.832 Street - Al Jamiliyah / الجميلية - No public transport

Film City

Film City / مدينة السينما - In a desolate area devoid of trees and most other plants and wildlife is Film City. This is a 3,000sqm reimagined Qatari village created for a Qatari TV series in 2000. At only a few thousand sq meters, it's not large, so easy to walk around. The style suggests Souq Waqif's rebuild may have been inspired by it. There is a caretaker who usually welcomes visitors. A stone's throw away is a small Oasis that has had roaming Ostrich,

Oryx, and Gazelle. If seen – remember these are not tame, so care should be taken, especially if you have children. A 4x4 is needed as with all off-road locations in the west of Qatar - it's best to have a full petrol tank and at least 2 vehicles. If one has a problem, there is another car and driver to help. Continuing through the wilderness, about a kilometre further north, on the same track, are several modern stone 'huts' built on a low escarpment and one created on a 'yardang'. These huts are not far from the sea and a few beaches. The beaches are about 25km from the tarmac, so it's at least a 50km round-trip. Note that the northern area of this peninsula is a couple of hundred meters from Bahrain's territorial waters, in which you would be an illegal visitor. Arrests by both Qatar and Bahrain are made for unlawful entry into their territorial waters. If an arrest is made, few Embassies will be of any help.

Typical hours - 24 Hours Entry charge - no charge -

Rough GPS - 25.578, 50.847 Street - off route 30 / Dukhan Highway the West Coast Rd taking the track north with your 4x4 from 25.460376, 50.894989 opposite a parking area. The track is about 16kms, and do not leave it as the wet areas are Sabkha, where you may get bogged down very quickly especially after rain. After almost 7.4kms, a track west leads to 4 steel 'planks'– the modern art **East West** - 'East West' is a sculpture installation in the west of Qatar by artist Richard Serra. Spread over a distance of 850m East West are 4 massive steel boards, in the middle of a stone desert. Kilroy may never have made it here, but plenty of others have ensured people know they have been.

Rough GPS - 25.517, 50.871 Street - Abrouq nature reserve - Zekreet / زكريت No public transport

Close to these (1.5km northwest) is a low cliff face used for rock climbing 25.519947, 50.847781. This track west eventually reaches Zekreet. - Zekreet / زكريت No public transport

Zekreet Fort / زكريت - Northwest of the modern village at Zekreet are the ruins of Zekreet Fort. The fort was built around the start of the 19th c. It may have been associated with Rahmah ibn Jabir Al Jalahimi (see Al Khuwair [PAGE 120]). Like Al Zubarah, the fort seems to have been abandoned around 1811.

Yardangs - Zekreet

The archaeologist Beatrice de Cardi researched the fort in 1974 as part of the Qatar government's initial research into its history. This fort is a plain design of 1,800sqm with three round towers and a square tower, very typical of other Qatari forts. Traces of rooms can be seen against the interior walls.

Typical hours – 24 hours Entry charge – no charge

Rough GPS - 25.490, 50.844 Street - From the Dukhan Highway, take the exit north to Zekreet. Drive through the village (you will be on a dirt-track road) and onto the fort about 500m north of the village. - Zekreet / زكريت No public transport

Zekreet Beach / شاطئ زكريت - About 300m west of the Zekreet Rd, this shallow, sheltered lagoon is relatively quiet. Kitesurfing is done here, and the shallow waters are relatively calm. The sand is very loose, and a 4x4 is essential. There is no lifeguard, safety equipment or facilities, as elsewhere in Qatar. The Qatar / Bahrain International Border runs in the sea on the edge of the coastline.

Rough GPS - 25.471, 50.849 Street - off Zekreet Rd - Zekreet / زكريت No Public Transport

Dukhan Beach / شاطئ دخان - Near Dukhan with some shelters next to the beach and Date palm. Easy access from the tarmac road. Other stretches of public beach lie along the next few kilometres north and south.

Rough GPS - 25.414, 50.759 Street - Corniche Dukhan - Dukhan / دخان Public Transport - only buses 707 & 727 from Industrial Area Bus Station.

Dukhan Water Sports Club / نادي دخان للرياضات المائية - This is a small well established club with access to the sea with lots of activities, including a swimming pool and Jet Skies. This is a membership Club for employees of companies associated with Dukhan. If you are in Qatar for some time, it's worth visiting if you have friends who have a pass.

Typical hours - 08:00-18:00 Entry charge - by invitation only -

Rough GPS - 25.411, 50.760 Street - off the Dukhan Highway west of Dukhan. - Dukhan / دخان Public Transport - only buses 707 & 727 from Industrial Area Bus Station.

Aqua Park / أكوا بارك - A water park, some 45mins drive southwest of Doha. It's only 10 years old, yet it's showing age, with below-expected maintenance standards and hygiene. At just over 3 hectares with about a dozen activities, most of which are relatively small, the drive out may be as long as is spent enjoying the activities.

Typical hours - 11:00-20:00 Mon-Weds (Tues Ladies 14:00-22:00) / 10:00-22:00 Thurs-Fri (Fri Family Day) / Sat 10:00-20:00 closed Sunday Entry charge - QAR120 entrance / Child QAR100 (plus some rides are extra) -

Rough GPS - 25.155, 51.294 Street - South of Salwa Rd Rawdath Rashid Interchange - Abu Nakhla / ابو نخلة - no public transport - Contacts - +974 4490 5878 www.aquaparkqatar.com

Heenat Salma Farm / مزرعة هينة سلمة - An organic farm in central Qatar. Here there is an opportunity to take part in farm life, harvest dates (in season), milk livestock, and enjoy natural food. There is a small farm shop. Holistic treatments are also available, and for a lucky few, there are comfortable tents to stay in overnight.

Typical hours - as per activity Entry charge - from QAR250

Rough GPS - 25.387, 51.257 Street - Ash Shahaniyah / الشحانية - no public transport - Contacts - +974 5096 0007 heenatsalma.earth

Mudhlem & Musfur Caves / كهف مظلم / كهف دحل المصفر - Mudhlem and Musfur caves are small sinkholes with a potentially dangerous scree slope to down to the bottom. The area has several small or potential sinkholes that many people gain access to, though they are fenced off. Mudhlem cave is roughly at - GPS 25.123, 51.228 and Musfur cave is at 25.174, 51.211 both near Salwa Rd Mekainis Interchange - Mekainis / مكينيس No public transport.

Irkhaya Farm

مزرعة ارخايا

Here, to Doha's southwest, is a mix of habitats, primarily man-made, that offer good birdwatching opportunities. The natural environment is a scrubby stony desert. However, here there are also several dozen pivot fields for fodder. Also, to the west of the fields is a substantial settling pond for treated sewage water, with rush (*Phragmites australis*). This vegetation and water attract insects, such as grasshoppers and flies. These attract lizards and birds all year round. Occasionally people may be seen hawking as there is plenty of prey for their falcons. Irkhaya Farm is about an hour's drive from Doha (4x4 is needed as the final few kilometres is a rough track). The track off the Salwa Rd south of Junction 5, leads past a couple of farms to aggregate plants and heavy equipment yard - you will be in a dusty environment. You will need to navigate past aggregate trucks. The main settling pond is about 4 kilometres west of the truck yard.

Typical hours - 08:00-16:00 (Fridays 08:00-11:00) Entry charge - no charge -

Rough GPS - 25.013, 51.163 Street - south of Salwa Rd - / Public Transport - No public transport

WEST DOHA

Ahmed bin Ali Stadium / **Al Rayyan Stadium** - West of Doha on the Dukhan Highway. One of the World Cup 2022 stadiums

Rough GPS - 25.330, 51.341 Street - Dukhan Highway - Al Rayyan / الريان Public Transport - Green Line Metro Al Riffa

Mall of Qatar - A vast shopping mall, far from other attractions, the Mall of Qatar is on the road to the Camel Race Tracks and the west coast. It's full of franchise shops with a few local brands – however, is it different enough to make the drive worthwhile if you need to do some shopping.

Typical hours - 10:00-23:00 Entry charge -

Rough GPS - 25.324, 51.350 Street - off Dukhan Highway / National Day Ceremonial Rd - Al Rayyan / الريان Public

Transport Green Line Metro – Al Riffa Contacts - +974 4034 6000 www.mallofqatar.com.qa

Robot Jockeys

Ash Shahaniyah CAMEL RACE TRACK

الشيحانية ميدان السباق للهجن

If you visit Doha in the winter (Nov - March), Ash Shahaniyah should be on your list of places to visit. Camel Racing is an important part of Qatari identity as the government promotes it extensively. They have not only created the course but offer prizes including the 'Golden Sword'. Camels themselves often have a high value. All create an entire culture and economy around the sport - that is part of the great Gulf camel focus. There are 5 tracks at Ash Shahaniyah - of varying lengths, where camels and their robot jockeys careen around an oval track. Each track has a companion car track, where the trainers race around in their 4x4 vehicles as if veritable Max Verstappens, screaming encouragement to their robot jockey & camel via walky-talky! Racing schedules are here www.hejen.qa/races or training happens on most days in the early mornings or late afternoons. There are plenty of opportunities for photography. The main events have senior ruling family members in attendance and large prizes. The start is to the right of the entrance road & after the camels complete the vast oval track, the finish and grandstand are to the left. Given the race is several kilometres, you can catch both start and finish, and there is no charge for grandstand entry. Use the toilets in the petrol station on the Dukhan Highway before the track (or McDonald's is on the south side of the highway going into Doha - just east of the elevated roundabout) - and buy water.

Typical hours - as per race

Rough GPS - 25.402, 51.205 Street - signed off Dukhan Highway - Al Rayyan / الريان Public Transport - Bus 708 & 709 from Green Line Metro Al Riffa

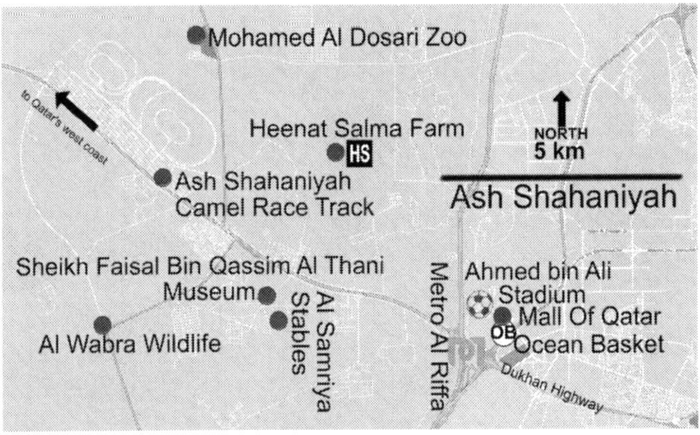

SHEIKH FAISAL BIN QASSIM AL THANI MUSEUM

متحف الشيخ فيصل بن قاسم آل ثاني

- An eclectic private museum collection created by its eponymous founder, the Chairman of City Centre in Doha, amongst other businesses.

Purpose-built in 1998, the museum is the wide-ranging accumulation of items by Sheikh Faisal Bin Qassim Al Thani.

The museum is spread over a large area with well over a dozen halls. It's over 200m in length, fortunately on a single floor. The exhibits come from a wide geographical area, including Japan & the USA and a vast time span, from geology of millions of years ago, through to the late 20th century.

Sheikh Faisal's museum

The museum's exhibits are well laid out, though without a particular focus and, unfortunately, without much information. There are highlights. A vast range of boats from The Gulf region are laid out, mostly indoors; there are so many that it's difficult to take each one in. A weaponry section is set amongst general material about Qatar, including its rulers. There are mannequins with Qatari costumes, though it would be good if the mannequins themselves were more appropriate. The collection of vehicles, motorcycles, and other transport, including palanquins, is remarkable. The cars are mainly from the USA and include some of the earliest vehicles used in Qatar, all it would appear in road-worthy condition. Part of the interior of a house from Damascus has been moved into Qatar and set up, as if in use. There are enough beautiful carpets to cover a football stadium; the collection goes on and on.

It's a remarkable collection. Outside, and next to the

museum, is the leaning mosque of Qatar. It's possible to view Oryx in the ticket price - the area is away from the museum.

Sheikh Faisal's museum

Typical hours - Mon-Thurs 09:00-17:00 Fri 14:00-19:00 Sat 10:00-18:00 Entry charge - QAR 50 (75 with tour)

Rough GPS - 25.351, 51.262 Street - Al Dukhan Highway - Ash Shahaniyah (near) / الشحانية Public Transport - Public Transport - Bus 708 & 709 from Green Line Metro Al Riffa

Contacts - visitors@fbqmuseum.org www.fbqmuseum.org

Al Samriya Stables / اسطبلات السامرية - A well-established livery stable - Al Samriya Stables also offers riding & other lessons. With four arenas and a range of horses, most people who wish to learn or ride are catered for. There are ride options outside the arenas.

Typical hours - 07:00-11:00-13:00-15:00 daily Entry charge - riding from QAR185 -

Rough GPS - 25.351, 51.262 Street - Al Dukhan Highway - Ash Shahaniyah (near) / الشحانية Public Transport - Public Transport - Bus 708 & 709 from Green Line Metro Al Riffa

- Contacts - +974 4490 2359 info@alsamriyaestate.com www.alsamriyaestate.com

Also here is Al Samriya Doha – a Marriot hotel - Contacts +97444309777 www.marriott.com

Mohamed Al Dosari Zoo / حديقة ومحمية محمد الدوسري - An example of a local private zoo, set up in the manner of a poor mid-20th-century animal display, with animals in crowded pens and cages. Extra displays and activities, including Horse & Camel rides, have an added charge.

Typical hours - 07:00-19:00 Sat-Friday Entry charge - QAR10/ -

Rough GPS - 25.440, 51.224 Street - off the Dukhan Highway taking the exit before Al Shahaniyah Camel Race Track - Ash Shahaniyah / Public Transport – no public transport. - Contacts - +974 44908785 AlDosariZoo@Hotmail.com

Al Wabra Wildlife / منطقة حيوان الوبرة - Set up in the mid-1970s as a private zoo, Al Wabra has more recently developed into a breeding zoo. The animals include Arabian Goitered Gazelle, Arabian Mountain Gazelle and Arabian Oryx. Other species include Sand Cat and Cheetah.

Typical hours - Not open to the general public.

Rough GPS - 25.346, 51.176 Street - southwest of Ash Shahaniyah Camel track - Ash Shahaniyah / الشحانية Public Transport - No public transport - Contacts - office@alwabra.com www.alwabra.com

CHAPTER 9
SERVICE PROVIDERS - TOURS, EVENTS, RESTAURANTS, HOTELS

Tour Providers

ONES TO CONSIDER INCLUDE

Air tours around the Doha area are a terrific way to see the city, though they do have restrictions regarding the air space they can fly in. If you have a choice of times - sunset is a magical time - when the lights start coming on over West Bay. **Asfary** offers several flying experiences, including Hot Air Balloon, with a small basket rather than a large one, Paragliding or Gyrocopter with a pilot, Helicopter, and small Plane. There are some weight restrictions on Paraflying and the Gyrocopter. **Qatar Flying Club** offers small fixed-wing flights. The extremely well established **Gulf Helicopters** provide helicopter flights and photo tours. In all cases, booking several days in advance is suggested. Some experiences are only private to you - others are usually made as part of a group of other passengers. Transport to the place of departure is your responsibility - it may be in the centre of Qatar at Ash Shafallahiyah 25.696 51.361 (60km from central Doha)

Typical hours and cost - as per request

- Contacts - asfary.com / www.qatarflyingclub.net / www.gulfhelicopters.com

Blue Pearl - offers a range of land and sea activities that are great for all ages. KiteSurf, Standup Paddleboarding (SUP), Kayak, Fatbiking in Doha and in the area around the city, and wilderness camping and other eco-activities.

Rough GPS - 25.369, 51.548 Street - off Lusail Expressway - The Pearl / اللولو No public transport - Contacts - +974666 02 830 hello@clubbluepearl.com www.bluepearlexperience.com

Doha Bus - Group Bus tours throughout Qatar - a 24 hop-on hop-off operation, including Souq Waqif (look for the Kiosk on Bank St, etc.). If you have two or more people in your party, it's worth comparing the cost of private tours by other companies. A different type of bus venture is offered as a 4x4 vehicle into the sand dunes south of Doha.

Typical hours and cost - as per request from QAR154 -

Rough GPS - 25.268, 51.495 Street - Doha Expressway/Al Amir St - Al Nasr / النصر Public Transport Metro Al Sudan - Contacts - +97444422444 hello@dohabus.co www.dohabus.com

Falcon Tours - City Tour, Desert Safari, Dhow and Game Fishing, Yacht

Typical hours and cost - as per request

Rough GPS - 25.289, 51.539 Street - Building No: 38

7th floor Abdullah Bin Jassim St, Doha, Qatar - Souq Waqif / سوق واقف Public Transport - Bus 76, 177 Metro Gold Line Souq Waqif - Contacts - +974 3144 0129 info@falcontoursqatar.com www.falcontoursqatar.com

Golden Adventures Qatar - City Tours, Tours to northern & western Qatar, Desert Safari

Typical hours and cost - as per request

Rough GPS - 25.267, 51.545 Street - Al Khalidiya Street - Najma / نجمة Public Transport - Bus 11, 757 Metro Umm Ghuwailina - Contacts - +974 5501 1031 info@goldenadventuresqatar.com www.goldenadventuresqatar.com

Inbound Tours Qatar - Tours throughout Qatar, including Desert Safari, with optional overnights in the desert and Dhow trips.

Typical hours and cost - as per request

Rough GPS - 25.287, 51.532 Street - South of Souq Waqif - Souq Waqif / سوق واقف Public Transport Metro Gold Line Souq

Waqif or Red Line Al Doha Al Jadeda. - Contacts - +974 7745 1196 info@inboundtoursqatar.com www.inboundtoursqatar.com

National Cruise - Cruises in a traditional dhow around the bay at Doha. Cruises can include meals; in some dhows, a table dining experience is offered. An excellent choice is an evening cruise that takes in the lights of the skyscrapers on West Bay. The Qatari government hope to install solar power and LED lighting to make its fleet of tourist Dhows more environmentally friendly. Other tour companies are available.

Typical hours - Various times including 10:00. from QAR150 for round trip excluding snacks which are + QAR50. Private cruises are also available.

Rough GPS - 25.295, 51.533 Street - Dhow Harbour off Corniche - Dhow Harbour / ميناء الداو قبالة الكورنيش Public Transport - Bus 76, 777 Metro Gold Line Souq Waqif - Contacts - +974 77999666 sales@nationalcruise.com www.nationalcruise.com/

Qatar International Tours (was Qatar International Adventures) - City tours, Desert Safari, Dhow Cruise, Game Fishing, Helicopter. In mid-summer Whale Sharks appear off the Qatari coast – ask if trips to search them out are possible,

Typical hours and cost - as per request

Rough GPS - 25.270, 51.517 Street - 1st Floor, Office # 7, 16 Al Rawabi St - Rawdat Al Khail / روضة الخيل Public Transport - Bus 602 from Msheireb Bus Station Contacts - +974 4455 3954 info@qittour.com qittour.com/

Q-Explorer - A range of programs in Qatar, essentially Q-Explorer offer most of what Qatar can provide, including a variety of City Tours, Desert Safaris, Kayaking, Scuba and Sea Excursions.

Typical hours and cost - as per request

Rough GPS - 25.318, 51.528 Street - Doha Tower, Al Corniche - West Bay / الخليج الغربي Public Transport - Metro Red Line West Bay - Contacts - +974 4472 5146 info@q-explorer.com www.q-explorer.com

Sea excursions - Several companies offer game fishing as a

private activity (not a group program). Qatar's game fishing is an excellent way to enjoy cooler temperatures at sea and, usually, not too rough seas. Equipment and bait are supplied; you need to bring your passport. You stand a chance of catching sea bass, tuna, or grouper (hamour). Much of the fishing from Doha is between Banana Island and off Al Wakrah. The start may be from the Dhow Harbour off the Corniche. Dhow cruises are available from **Arabian Adventures** (possibly Qatar's oldest tour operator) who also offers a complete range of tours - typically, you will join other people. Private yacht tours are also a possibility. For sea tours that are simply for sightseeing or leisure, an exciting time to do it is to take in dusk and enjoy the city lights of West Bay.

Typical hours and cost - as per request - seas are calmer in the morning - the West Bay lights make sunset attractive

Dhow Harbour Rough GPS - 25.295, 51.533 Street - Dhow Harbour off Corniche - Dhow Harbour / ميناء الداو قبالة الكورنيش Public Transport - Bus 76, 777 Metro Gold Line Souq Waqif - Contact - www.arabianadventuresqatar.com/

Possible Events In Qatar

Arabian Horse show - Doha

These are held annually – however, it's always best to check if they will occur.

Jan - Qatar International Book Fair - DECC - Large retail book fair - compensating for the lack of bookshops in Qatar

Jan - Marmi Festival - Katara (base) - Falcon and Saluki hunting festival. Hawking displays and more in Khor Al Udaid area. - http://algannas.website/

Feb - Katara International Arabian Horse Festival - Katara - Festival focused on Arabian Horses and their equipment. There are horse events held during the festival. kiahf.qa/

Feb - Al Adaid Desert Challenge - Khor Al Udaid - Off-road (up to 60km) cycling & running event - promoted with the Qatar tourism council - www.aladaid.qa/

Feb - Al Shaqab International Equestrian Competition - Al Shaqab - A major CHI (Concours Hippique International) Showjumping and Dressage event - www.alshaqab.com

Feb - The Amir's Sword Festival - an Equestrian event at Qatar Racing and Equestrian Club

March - Aspire International Kite Festival - Aspire - Professional kite displays and family kite flying events.

March - May - Amir of Qatar Football Cup - various rounds and venues

March - Amir Camel Racing Festival/ Purebred Arabian Camel Festival Al Shahaniya racetrack

April - QTF Tennis Open - Khalifa Complex - Tennis tournament - one of many throughout the year. - http://www.qatartennis.org/ check for more

Sept - S'hail Hunting & Falconry - Katara - A significant event about hunting and falconry. - s-hail.qa

Sept - Qatar Shopping Festival - City-wide - A retail event promoting shopping in Qatar

Oct Formula 1 - Losail International Circuit www.formula1.com

Nov - Qatar International Boat Show - The Pearl - An international boat show aimed at the local market - with some regional overspill - qatarboatshow.com.qa/

Nov - Katara Dhow Festival - Katara - Traditional Dhows, under sail and more. - www.katara.net/

Dec - Qatar Balloon Festival - Several days of multiple hot-air balloon events

Dec - Qatar National Day - Nationwide - especially the Corniche - Patriotic events celebrating Qatar as a nation

Dec - Souq Waqif and Souq Al Wakrah Spring Festival - Souq Waqif and Souq Al Wakrah - Entertainment and cultural events in Souq Waqif and Souq Al Wakrah

Hotels And Restaurants

Souq Waqif restaurants

Restaurants are grouped geographically. They are chosen to offer a reasonable meal in that location only, not to suggest any comparison with those in other locations. For example, in Al Ruwais, Iskender Pasha is included; however, other restaurants would squeeze it out if it were in Doha.

In Souq Waqif there is a wide choice, the government is the property owner, and they expect visitors to have a good meal whatever the price.

There is an excellent offering of good hotel and standalone restaurants in Doha. So, if you do prefer a more traditional international dining experience, closer to that in a western city, choose a restaurant from within the better hotels or in Souq Waqif, Katara & The Pearl.

In general, local restaurants outside hotels offer freshly cooked food, often against your order. In the lower-cost options away from tourist areas, they cater for the local population. Often they have incredibly authentic cuisine, such as Pakistani, Turkish, and southern Indian. The downside is that general hygiene may not be as high as McDonald's or 5* hotels, and service may be haphazard. After all, they do not have layers of management and head offices to lay down consistent standards. The price does reflect these lower standards.

Hotels are also listed geographically. Here the intention is simply to show some choices – not give an exhaustive critique. If you use a booking site or even a hotel's own website, you will see the very latest opinions of clients.

The area around Souq Waqif from Msheireb Metro hub – through to the National Museum offers a broad selection at many price points. The advantage in this area is that you have Metro stations Msheireb, Souq Waqif or the National Museum to use to get around. Around Msheireb and Souq Waqif - Park Hyatt, Al Najada Doha, and C-Hotel and Suites are worth looking at.

Prices for hotels vary seasonally, and you may have a loyalty card with an international chain that might decide where you stay for you. The brand name 'international' hotels offer the most consistent service. Service may be patchy in the lower price range, especially in hotels not part of an international group. In these hotels that are more than a few years old, lack of maintenance starts to change their quality. In these lower cost hotels – a change of manager also does make an immediate difference.

Major hotels and their restaurants will usually have alcohol available (the minimum age to drink alcohol in Qatar is 21 years old. An ID is often needed); Ramadhan may affect alcohol availability; elsewhere, alcohol is not available.

All hotels and restaurants rely on staff who work on a contract of a couple of years within Qatar. The result is that the hotels might struggle to keep consistent standards.

Restaurants are stared by the dollar price (charges will be in QAR) of a typical lower-cost meal for a single person in that restaurant.

US$ 5-9 **

US$ 9-13 ***
US$ 13-19 ****
US$ 19-25 *****
US$ 25 + ******

Hotels are stared by the dollar price (charges will be in QAR) of their cheapest room, out of their peak season.

US$ 0-60 *
US$ 61-90 **
US$ 91-125 ***
US$ 126-190 ****
US$ 191-250 *****
US$ 251+ ******

RESTAURANTS

CORNICHE, SOUQ WAQIF & CENTRAL DOHA

Bandar Aden - Authentic, in all respects, with Yemeni food, meat and rice-based. The service is very patchy, and cleanliness is not ideal; however, the food is freshly prepared. Extremely popular. They must be getting something right. Ask for cutlery or go Yemeni style and choose a sitting on floor meal indoors and use your right hand.

Typical cost range - ** Rough GPS - 25.290, 51.533

Street - Abdullah Bin Jassim St, Public Transport - Metro Gold Line Souq Waqif Typical hours - 06:00-23:00 (Friday 12:30-23:00) - Contacts - +974 44375503 / bandaraden@yahoo.com / http://www.bandaraden.com/

Icons Coffee - In the western area of Souq Waqif, about 50m south of the camel pens. This fresh-looking coffee shop has everything needed to give you a boost when sightseeing, coffee, delicious cakes and more.

Typical cost range - ** Rough GPS - 25.289, 51.532

Street - Inside Souq Waqif Public Transport - Metro Gold Line Souq Waqif Typical hours - 10:00-midnight - Contacts - 974 4408 7777

Shujaa Restaurant - Small, always busy, and inexpensive; share a table with others and enjoy this restaurant's golden anniversary in 2022. The food is loosely Lebanese in style. Meat-based dishes are available in the evening. This is a stone's throw away from the luxury of Parisa and just south of the more expensive Al Shurfa. Anticipate a rushed service, and apart from that, you are not likely to be disappointed.

Typical cost range - ** Rough GPS - 25.289, 51.533

Street - near Corniche in Souq Waqif Public Transport - Metro Gold Line Souq Waqif Typical hours - 14:00-midnight - Contacts - +974 5586 7895

Al Shurfa Arabic Restaurant - One of the more interesting views in Doha from this restaurant's upper floor balcony - it overlooks the Corniche and is great following sunset. The Middle Eastern food is coupled with Arabic games and water pipes (also known as hookah/hubbly bubbly/shisha) and makes a good dinner choice. One of two restaurants within the small Al Jumrok Hotel.

Typical cost range - *** Rough GPS - 25.289, 51.533

Street - off Al Corniche Public Transport - Metro Gold Line Souq Waqif Typical hours - 12:00-23:00 - Contacts - +974 4433 6666 / res.vswq@tivolihotels.com / www.tivolihotels.com/en/souq-waqif-al-jomrok-boutique-hotel?

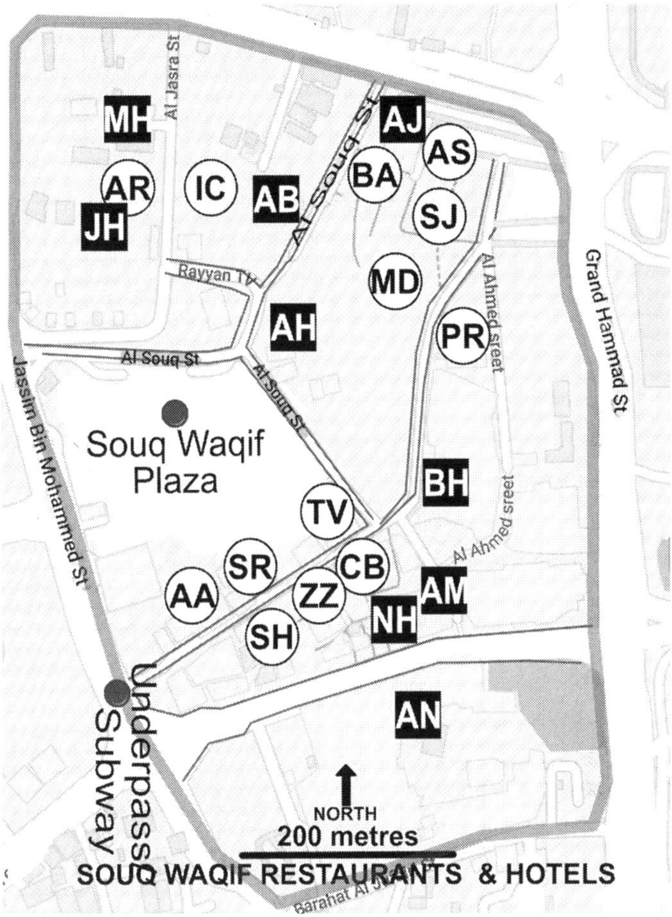

The Village - Stylish dining in one of three restaurant options here, just west of the Golden Thumb in Souq Waqif. Choose from Arabic, Iranian or Turkish cuisines. The other branch on the Salwa Rd (25.265308, 51.498197) is comparable - but not quite as beautifully decorated.

Typical cost range - ***** Rough GPS - 25.287, 51.533

Street - Al Souq St Public Transport - Metro Gold Line Souq Waqif Typical hours - 08:00-23:30 - Contacts - +974 4411 1243 / www.thevillageqatar.com

Argan - This opulent restaurant in a modern Moroccan style offers an update on Moroccan cuisine - with a few international dishes thrown in. It's inside the Al Jasra Hotel - illustrating that the Tivoli group do have a remarkably good dining choice in Souq Waqif.

Typical cost range - ****** Rough GPS - 25.289, 51.531

Street - Al Jasra St, Doha, Qatar Public Transport - Metro Gold Line Souq Waqif Typical hours - 13:00-23:00 - Contacts - +974 4433 6872 / www.tivolihotels.com/en/souq-waqif-al-jasra-boutique-hotel/restaurants

Parisa

Souq Waqif (Also at Sharq Village) - A destination in itself with décor a fusion of style from the Golestan Palace in Tehran.

The Persian food is good, with matching service and, usually, light live music in the background. This is dining as a total sensory experience.

Typical cost range - ****** Rough GPS - 25.288, 51.533

Street - Inside Souq Waqif Public Transport - Metro Gold Line Souq Waqif Typical hours - 12:00-midnight - Contacts - +974 4441 1494 / dining.sharq@ritzcarlton.com / http://www.ritzcarlton.com/en/hotels/qatar/sharq-village/dining/parisa-souq-waqif

Parisa

Saravana Bhavan is a very well-established vegetarian restaurant (a major franchise from India). The food is authentically South Indian. There are other branches in Doha.

Typical cost range - * Rough GPS - 25.283, 51.537

Street - Ras Abu Abboud St Public Transport - Metro Gold Line Souq Waqif or Red Line Al Doha Al Jadeda. Typical hours - 07:00-15:00/17:30-23:00 Friday 07:00-11:30 12:30-23:00 - Contacts - +974 4443 5557

Al Adhamiyah - This is an exceedingly popular restaurant south of Souq Waqif - serving Iraqi style food that is meat & rice-based. Have one of their great fruit juices. It's possible to dine indoors or outside. The interior is exceptionally atmospheric, especially upstairs - with extensive use of a '*mashrabiya*' style decoration. The service reflects how busy they are and its relatively low cost.

Typical cost range - ** Rough GPS - 25.286, 51.532

Street - Ali Bin Abdullah St, Doha, Qatar Public Transport - Metro Gold Line Souq Waqif Typical hours - 12:30-midnight (Midnight) - Contacts - +974 4432 4326

Lamazani Grill - Busy, excellent value Persian style kebab restaurant. The location and decoration may not have the appeal of some other options - but a 30-minute walk from Souq Waqif does have its rewards.

Typical cost range - *** Rough GPS - 25.280, 51.537

Street – Khaybar Rd off Ras Abu Abboud St Public Transport - Metro Gold Line Souq Waqif. Typical hours - 12:00-01:00 (Friday 14:30 -01:00) - Contacts - +974 55526345 (Mobile) / info@lamazani.com / www.lamazani.com

Al Nahham Restaurant at Banana Island Resort - Offering Lebanese / Gulf style Arabic food with indoor or outdoor dining overlooking the sea. The prices are justified, in general, by a premium experience.

Typical cost range - ****** Rough GPS - 25.295, 51.646

Street - Banana Island Public Transport - Metro Gold Line Souq Waqif & Ferry from Dhow Harbour 25.292135, 51.534429 Typical hours - 13:00-17:00 / 19:00 - 17:00 - Contacts - +974 4040 5116 / fbreservations.adoh@anantara.com / www.anantara.com/en/banana-island-doha/restaurants/al-nahham

Azraq At Banana Island - With various cuisines and an international buffet offering the wide selection of a typical Gulf style main dining restaurant, though slightly skewed towards seafood. Choice of indoor or outdoor dining.

Typical cost range - ***** Rough GPS - 25.295, 51.646

Street - from Corniche 25.292010, 51.534803 Public

Transport -, Metro Gold Line Souq Waqif & Ferry from Dhow Harbour 25.292135, 51.534429 Typical hours - 06.30 -23.00 - Contacts - +974 4040 5050 / fbreservations.adoh@anantara.com www.anantara.-com/en/banana-island-doha/restaurants/azraq

HOTELS & RESTAURANTS
CORNICHE AREA

Q Lounge & Restaurant at Banana Island - Overlooking a pool, beach sea and, in the distance, Qatar Airways taking off and landing at HIA, the Asian / Indian style food is also good.

Typical cost range - ****** Rough GPS - 25.295, 51.646

Street - Banana Island Public Transport - Metro Gold Line Souq Waqif & Ferry from Dhow Harbour 25.292135, 51.534429 Typical hours - 06.30-10:30 / 12.00-23.30 - Contacts - +974 4040 5116 / fbreservations.adoh@anantara.com / www.anantara.-com/en/banana-island-doha/restaurants/q-lounge-and-restaurant

Riva At Banana Island - A Mediterranean themed restaurant with a remarkably good mix of taste and service.

Typical cost range - ****** Rough GPS - 25.295, 51.646

Street - Banana Island Public Transport - Metro Gold Line Souq Waqif & Ferry from Dhow Harbour 25.292135, 51.534429 Typical hours - 13:00-22:00 (Closed Sunday) - Contacts - +974 4040 5116 / fbreservations.adoh@anantara.com / www.anantara.com/en/banana-island-doha/restaurants/riva

Afghan Brothers (one of seven branches all are comparable) - Very Good value Afghani (& Pakistani) serving meat and rice-based style food with a local Qatari style. Might only have spoons; ask for knife and fork - or use hands. Takeaways are also available, as are assorted Afghani sweets.

Typical cost range - * Rough GPS - 25.273, 51.496

Street - Al Mirqab al Jadeed St Public Transport - Metro Joaan Metro 1km over busy rd. Typical hours - 07:00-01:00 - Contacts - +974 4488 8556 / Alnasr@afghanbrothers.com / www.afghanbrothers.com

Pak Pakwan Restaurant - This is a busy, small local restaurant with good Pakistani food. Fair value grilled meats and curries are supported by rice dishes with food and, usually, quick service.

Typical cost range - ** Rough GPS - 25.286, 51.523

Street - Al Diwan St Public Transport - Metro Msheireb (Hub) Typical hours - 11:30-23:30 (Friday 12:30-23:30) - Contacts - +974 3382 2399

Turkey Central Restaurant - A large, simple restaurant where you probably will be sharing a table with other diners. This is a well-established Turkish restaurant geared to high turnover business, especially with take-aways. It offers excellent value food.

Typical cost range - ** Rough GPS - 25.274, 51.496

Street - Al Mirqab Al Jadeed St Public Transport - Metro Gold Line Joaan Typical hours - 09:30-01:30 - Contacts - +974 4443 2927

SMAT Restaurant - A contemporary version of Qatari & Gulf food, with lightly spiced meat and rice, though it offers much more than that. The restaurant's location is good on the eastern Corniche, overlooking a small park and, beyond that, the sea. Well worth a visit if you have visited the National Museum or Museum of Islamic Art.

Typical cost range - **** Rough GPS - 25.289, 51.547

Street - East Corniche Public Transport – Gold Line National Museum Typical hours - 08:00-01:00 - Contacts - +974 4410 6600

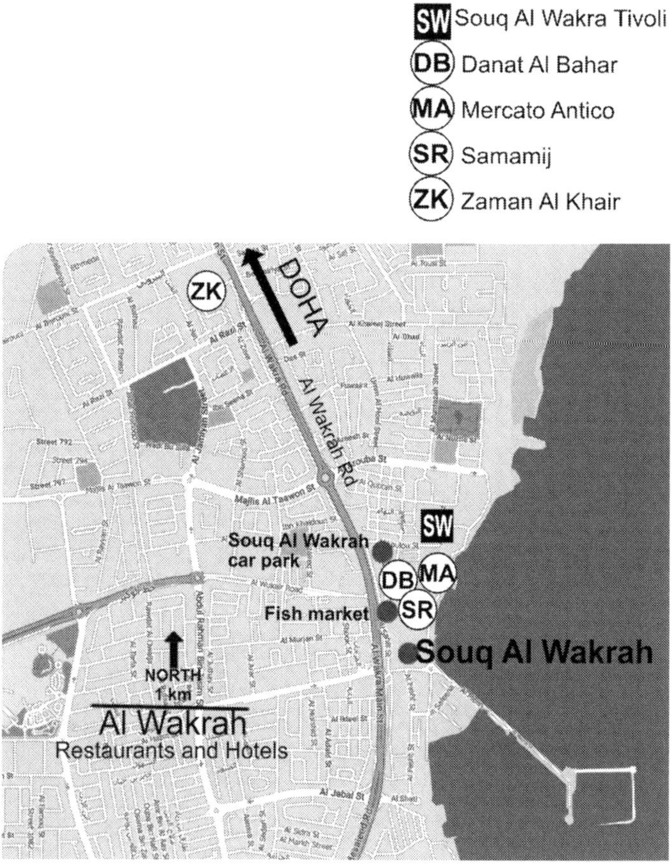

Danat Al Bahar +974 7770 7085 & **Samamij** +974 5999 9061. These two small fish restaurants are next to each-other near the car-park area of Souq Al Wakrah (a few minutes west of the sea). They so similar they may well be operated by the same management. These are popular in the evening and offer a good selection of sea food. The area they are in has a number of other options - so have a look before you decide where to eat.

Hours - 13:00-01:00 daily. Typical cost range *** Rough GPS - 25.170, 51.608

Zaman Al Khair Restaurant - A well-established Lebanese / Syrian restaurant with excellent mezze, mains and fruit juice. This is on route to Inland Sea – with a choice of dine-in or takeaway.

Typical cost range - *** Rough GPS - 25.186, 51.600

Street - Al Wakrah Main St Public Transport – MetroLink from Al Wakrah Typical hours - 08:00-midnight - Contacts - +974 4498 6111 / info@zamanalkhairrest.com / www.zamanalkhairrest.com

Mercato Antico (Also Branch in Tawar Mall) is a rustic-style restaurant with an extremely simple set-up. Overlooking the beach, a sepia-toned interior contrasts with blue sea and sky. Premium-priced Pasta and Pizza are largely worth the visit.

Typical cost range - ****** Rough GPS - 25.172, 51.611

Street - off Al Wakrah Main St Public Transport – MetroLink from Red Line Metro Al Wakrah Typical hours - 16:00-midnight (Friday & Saturday 13:00-midnight) - Contacts - +974 4441 0020 / info@mercato-antico.com / www.mercato-antico.com/en/

WEST BAY

The M Restaurant, The Pullman Hotel West Bay. This is an exceptional restaurant, offering a fine international dining experience focused on meat. The menu has a limited range - enabling the team to excel at their offering. Typical cost range ***** appx GPS 25.323,51.525 Street Al Shatti Public Transport Red Line Metro DECC Contacts +97459989982 www.themqatar.com

Royal Istanbul Restaurant (Behind West Bay Petrol Station) - The name aside is just a simple Turkish restaurant, popular due to its convenient location and takeaway service.

Typical cost range - * Rough GPS - 25.326, 51.517

Street - Al Istiqal St / Al Intisar Public Transport – Red Line

Metro DECC Typical hours - 11:00-midnight - Contacts - +974 4498 1268 / RoyalIstanbul@BakeMartDoha.com /

The W Hotel does have some excellent options

Spice Market (W Hotel) - Set in the W Hotel, this is a general Asian themed menu offered in a room with very subdued lighting. A very popular option, with co-operative staff.

Typical cost range - *** Rough GPS - 25.328, 51.530

Street - Diplomatic St Public Transport – Red Line Metro Doha Exhibition and Convention Center (DECC). Typical hours - 07:00-midnight (Friday from 08:00). - Contacts - +974 4453 5135 / bnfreservations.wdoha@whotels.com / www.spicemarketdoha.com/

La Spiga by Paper Moon (W Doha) - A small Italian Restaurant with a wine bar in the W Hotel. The décor is more anonymous than Italian, while outside the overlooking skyscrapers may not be to everyone's taste.

Typical cost range - ***** Rough GPS - 25.328, 51.530

Street - Diplomatic St Public Transport - Metro Doha Exhibition and Convention Center (DECC) Typical hours - 12:00 - 16:00 / 17:00-midnight - Contacts - +974 4453 5135 / bnfreservations.wdoha@whotels.com / www.laspigadoha.com

Market By Jean-Georges - A straightforward European design for the restaurant, with a similar approach to the quality food. With cuisine from the British Isles through Lebanon - to Japan, it's a broad offering.

Typical cost range - ****** Rough GPS - 25.328, 51.530

Street - Diplomatic St Public Transport - Metro Doha Exhibition and Convention Center (DECC) Typical hours - 06:00-11:00/12:00-16:00/17:00-23:30 (Friday 12:00-16:00/17:00-23:30) - Contacts - +97444535135 / bnfreservations.wdoha@whotels.com / www.marketdoha.com

Wahm (W Hotel) - Live music and a fashionable bar in the W Hotel in Doha.

Typical cost range - ***** Rough GPS - 25.328, 51.530

Street - Diplomatic St Public Transport - Metro Doha Exhibition and Convention Center (DECC) Typical hours - 17:00-02:00 - Contacts - +974

4453 5135 / bnfreservations.wdoha@whotels.com / www.wahmdoha.com

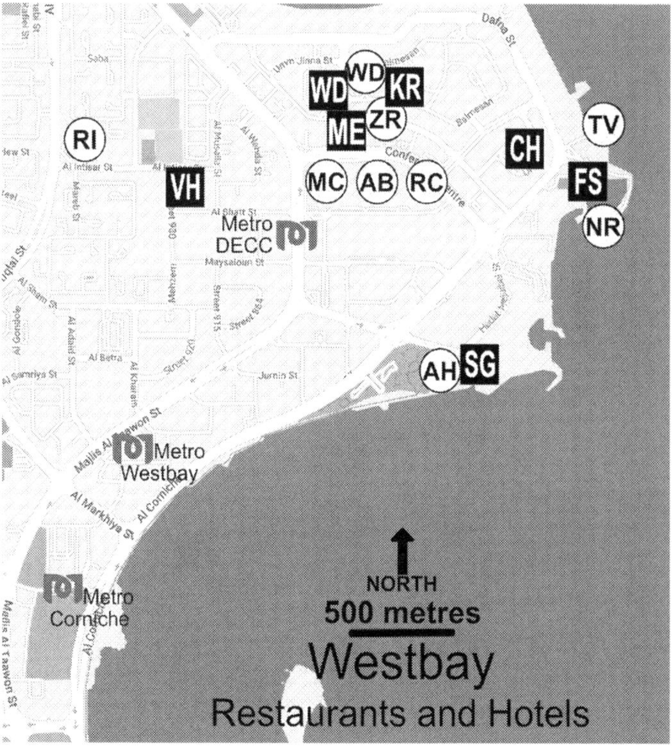

W Café (W Hotel) - Set in the W Hotel, this is an excellent alternative coffee shop to Starbucks, at not much more cost.

Typical cost range - *** Rough GPS - 25.328, 51.530

Street - Diplomatic St Public Transport - Red Line Metro Doha Exhibition and Convention Center (DECC). Typical hours - 07:00-midnight (Friday from 08:00) - Contacts - +974 4453 5135 / bnfreservations.wdoha@whotels.com / www.wcafedoha.com

Applebee's (Chain) - Part of the APPLEBEE Franchise, one of several branches in Doha. American style Ribs and fast food options. Predictable food quality and efficient service.

Typical cost range - **** Rough GPS - 25.326, 51.530

Street - Conference Centre Public Transport – Red Line Metro Doha Exhibition and Convention Center (DECC) Typical hours - 10:00-23:00 - Contacts - +974 4493 4880 / contact form / www.applebeesme.com/qatar/

Olive Oil Rotana City Centre (all-day dining breakfast/lunch/dinner) - A reasonable buffet in the Rotana that is very convenient for the Conference Centre and City Centre Mall. The food is a typical Gulf International style.

Typical cost range - **** Rough GPS - 25.324, 51.533

Street - Diplomatic St / Conference Centre St Public Transport - Metro Red Line Doha Exhibition & Conference Centre (DECC) Typical hours - 06:30-23:30 - Contacts - +974 4445 8727 / Contact Form / www.rotana.com

Sridan - A wonderfully comfortable restaurant offering an Arabian style menu in a convenient location for DECC and City Centre Mall.

Typical cost range - ***** Rough GPS - 25.325, 51.533

Street - Conference Centre/Diplomatic St Public Transport - Metro Doha Exhibition and Convention Center (DECC). Typical hours - 6.00am – 10.30am / 12.00noon – 3.00pm / 6.00pm – 10.00pm - Contacts - +974 4429 5000 / Contact Form / www.marriott.com **Trader Vic's** (Hilton) - Part of the established chain of Polynesian-themed restaurants - it's been in the region for almost 40 years. Frequent theme nights add to the appeal. They have a dress code to gain entry.

Typical cost range - ***** Rough GPS - 25.327, 51.541

Street - Diplomatic St Public Transport - Metro Doha Exhibition and Convention Center (DECC) Typical hours - midday-midnight - Contacts - +974 4423 3118 / www.tradervicsdoha.com/

Al Hubara Restaurant - Well established venue in the slightly dated public lobby of the Sheraton. The good is generally good, though an unadventurous international style.

Typical cost range - ****** Rough GPS - 25.318, 51.536

Street - Al Corniche Sheraton Public Transport - Metro Red Line Doha Exhibition & Conference Centre (DECC) Typical hours - Breakfast Buffet: 06:00 AM - 11:00 AM

Lunch Buffet: 12:00 PM - 15:30 PM / Dinner Buffet: 19:00 PM - 23:30 PM / Friday Brunch: 12:30 PM -16:00 PM - Contacts - +97444853000 / F&Breservations.doha@sheraton.com / www.alhubararestaurant.com

Nobu - Worth visiting for the views, as it's just off the beach - with fantastic views over West Bay. This is a decidedly premium Japanese style, mainly seafood offering; the service and food struggle to match the price. Although a beachfront location, there is a dress code.

Typical cost range - ****** Rough GPS - 25.323, 51.541

Street - Diplomatic St (Four Seasons Marina) Public Transport - Metro Red Line Doha Exhibition & Conference Centre (DECC) Typical hours - 18:00-01:00 (Friday 12:30-16:00) - Contacts - +974 4494 8600 / contact form / www.fourseasons.com/doha/dining/restaurants/nobu_doha/

THE PEARL AND KATARA

Layali In Lagoona Mall - A reasonable Lebanese restaurant in a building that looks like an afterthought in an expensive area. The interior is more on-point, as is the food.

Typical cost range - *** Rough GPS - 25.377, 51.526

Street - off Pearl Boulevard Public Transport - No public transport Typical hours - 09:00-23:30 - Contacts - +974 44310005 / layali@adaragroup.co / www.layalirestaurantqatar.com/

L'wzaar Seafood - Seafront seafood restaurant in Katara, what's not to like? From Sushi to Fish & Chips, a complete range of seafood overlooking the sea in Katara. In cooler weather, choose outdoor, especially in the afternoon when the sun drops behind the building; otherwise, ask for window seats.

Typical cost range - **** Rough GPS - 25.358, 51.526

Street - off Al Moasses St/Lusail Highway Public Transport - Metro Red Line Katara Typical hours - 12:00 16:00 - 19:00-23:30 (Friday 13:00 16:00 - 19:00-23:30) - Contacts - +974 4408 0710 / info@lwzaar.com / www.lwzaar.com/

WEST BAY HOTELS & RESTAURANTS

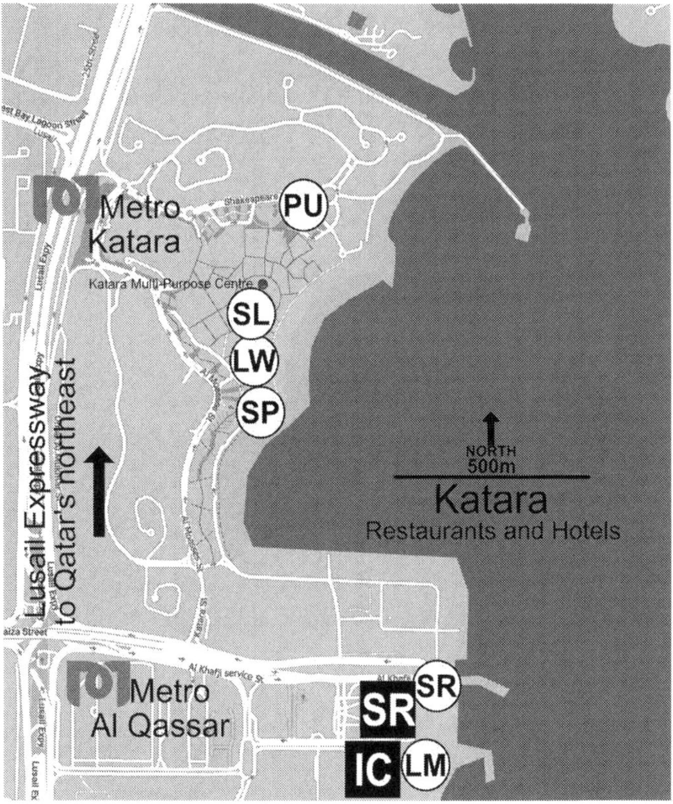

Sukar Pasha - Turkish restaurant set directly on an extension on the Katara beach. Indoor dining or in less humid weather, choose outdoor. The location is difficult to beat; however, the service and quality of food is patchy, which is unexpected at its premium price.

Typical cost range - **** Rough GPS - 25.357, 51.527

Street - off Lusail Expressway Public Transport - Metro Red Line Katara Typical hours - Fri 08:00-11:00/12:30-01:00 - Contacts - +974 4408 2000 / info@sukarpasha.qa. / http://sukarpasha.qa

Al Sufra - Uniformly excellent Lebanese food and wine. The service and attractive, subdued Arabic inspired ambience does make for a relaxing meal.

Typical cost range - ***** Rough GPS - 25.376, 51.549

Street - Marsa Malaz Kempinski, Pearl Boulevard Public Transport - No public transport Typical hours - 12:30-midnight - Contacts - +974 4035 5011 / restaurants.-marsamalaz@kempinski.com / www.kempinski.-com/en/doha/marsa-malaz-kempinski-the-pearl-doha/dining/restaurants/al-sufra/

Saffron Lounge - Elegant surroundings and good north Indian food. With the 3 monkeys outside, it's an easy place to find.

Typical cost range - ***** Rough GPS - 25.359, 51.526

Street - off Lusail Express (next to Katara Hall) Public Transport - Metro Red Line Katara Typical hours - 12:00-22:00 (Friday 13:00-23:00) - Contacts - +974 4408 0808

Yasmine Palace - An opulent complex in The Pearl with four dining locations (one is a café style). The overall concept is Arabian Nights - with Levant style food. The location isn't the easiest to get to - but the food, ambience and service make it a worthwhile journey.

Typical cost range - ***** Rough GPS - 25.365, 51.543

Street - Porto Arabia Drive The Pearl Public Transport - No public transport Typical hours - 07:00-midnight - Contacts - +974 7711 1504 yasminepalace.com/

Hakkasan (St. Regis Doha) – One of the more the most expensive dining options in Doha, it's reasonable to expect it to be the best, and it may well be. The stylish decor and ambience set the theme for excellent Chinese cuisine, with a style that reflects the restaurant's interior. Being well established does mean that the restaurant has had more than enough time to find what works and what doesn't. The restaurant does run a restrictive door policy, including for children below 11 - booking for tables advised.

Typical cost range - ****** Rough GPS - 25.350, 51.529

Street - east of Lusail Highway Public Transport – Red Line Metro Al Qassar Typical hours - 19:00-23:30 (also weekends 13:00-16:00) wine bar (18:00-01:00) - Contacts - +974 4446

0170 / reservation.hakkasan@stregis.com / www.hakkasan.-com/locations/hakkasan-doha/

Morimoto (Mondrian Doha) - Stylish Japanese restaurant in the Mondrian hotel (part of Accor) The Pearl with food and service equal with cost.

Typical cost range - ****** Rough GPS - 25.377, 51.523

Street - Pearl Boulevard/ Lusail Expressway Public Transport – Red Line Metro Legtaifiya & MetroLink Typical hours - 18:00-23:30 (Closed Sunday) - Contacts - +974 4045 5999 / Wineanddine-mondriandoha@sbe.com / www.morganshotel-group.com/mondrian/mondrian-doha/

Nozomi (Marsa Malaz Kempinski) - With a view over the man-made lagoon around Marsa Malaz Kempinski, Nozomi is an excellent Japanese restaurant in a premium hotel. The food and service meet expectations, but the interior and exterior don't live up to them.

Typical cost range - ****** Rough GPS - 25.377, 51.549

Street - Pearl Boulevard/ Lusail Expressway No public transport Typical hours - 19:00-23:00 (Thurs & Friday also 12:00-15:30) - Contacts - +974 4035 5089 / info@nozomidoha.com / http://www.nozomi-doha.com/

Toro Toro (Marsa Malaz Kempinski) - Overlooking the lagoon of Marsa Malaz Kempinski, this is a taste of Latin America in Doha, complete with occasional Havana cigar smoke.

Typical cost range - ****** Rough GPS - 25.377, 51.549

Street - The Pearl Boulevard No public transport Typical hours - 19:00-01:00 (Friday 19:00-02:00) - Contacts - +974 4035 5101 / contact form / www.torotorodoha.com

Vine (St Regis) - An elegant restaurant with a spacious interior and options to dine outside. This is one of the better all-day dining options in Doha. Vine serves an international range of foods, though they have theme evenings throughout the week.

Typical cost range - ****** Rough GPS - 25.350, 51.529

Street - off Lusail Highway Public Transport - No public transport Typical hours - 06:00-11:00/18:00-23:00 and Friday (12:30-16:00) - Contacts - +974 4446 0105 / dining.reservations@stregis.com / www.vinedoha.com/

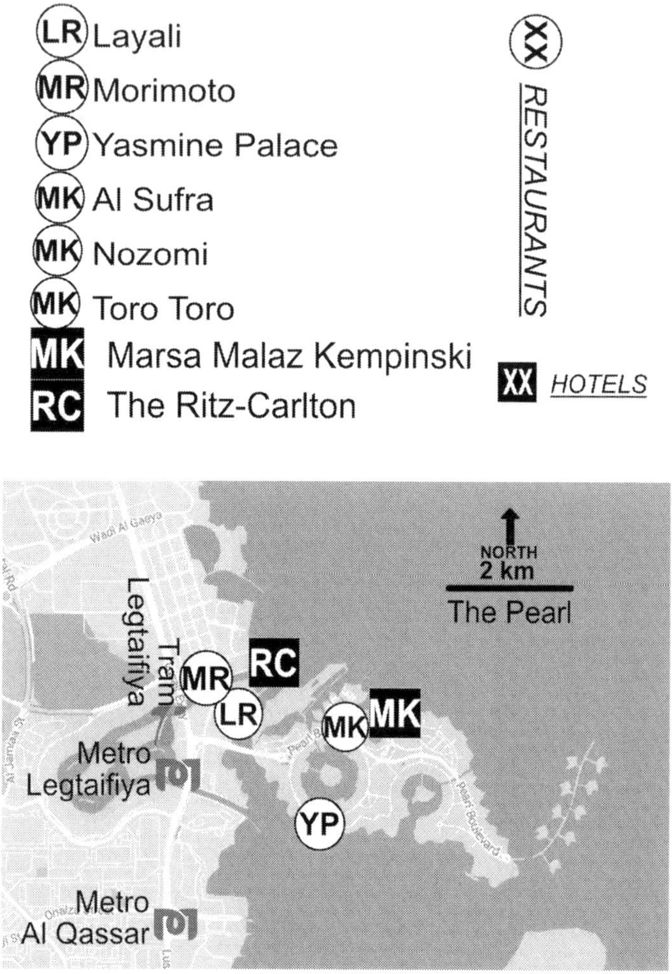

DOHA SOUTH & EAST

The Cellar - This is now a Hyatt managed property. With a good range of drinks, this Spanish themed restaurant is a welcome change from the plethora of Middle Eastern and Indian -sub-continent cuisines throughout Doha.

Typical cost range - *** Rough GPS - 25.268, 51.554

Street - Al Nahda School St / C Ring Rd. Public Transport - Metro Red Line Umm Ghuwailina Typical hours - 12:00-02:00 -

Contacts - +974 4402 3454 / Contact Form / www.hyattrestaurants.com/en/dining/qatar/doha/spanish-restaurant-in-hamad-International-airport-the-cellar

Al Nafourah Garden - A change from a Rotana to Hyatt management, but still a nice courtyard dining experience. Not the widest choice of food in this Lebanese restaurant, but what there is offers a delightful selection. The water pipes add to the experience.

Typical cost range - **** Rough GPS - 25.268, 51.554

Street - Al Matar St Public Transport Red Line Metro Umm Ghuwailina Typical hours - 12:00-02:00 - Contacts - +974 4402 3333 / www.hyattrestaurants.com/en/dining/qatar/doha/lebanese-restaurant-in-doha-s-business-district-al-nafourah-garden

Paper Moon (1st Floor Jaidah Square Complex) - A comfortable modern style restaurant with the possibility of indoor or outdoor tables. This may be the nicest overall experience in an Italian restaurant in Doha.

Typical cost range - ***** Rough GPS - 25.273, 51.545

Street - Umm Ghuwailina St / Al Matar St Public Transport - Metro Red Line Umm Ghuwailina Typical hours - 11:30 - 22:45 - Contacts - +974 4016 6000 / info@papermoondoha.com / www.papermoondoha.com/

Jazz Club (Oryx Rotana) - An excellent choice for a night out. There is usually live music, occasionally televised sports - supported by a good selection of drinks, sliders, & burgers.

Typical cost range - ****** Rough GPS - 25.268, 51.554

Street - off Al Matar St/ C Ring Rd Public Transport - Metro Red Line Umm Ghuwailina Typical hours - 17:00-02:00 (Closed Saturday) - Contacts - +974 4402 3444 / www.hyattrestaurants.-com/en/dining/qatar/doha/International-restaurant-in-al-matar-street-jazz-club

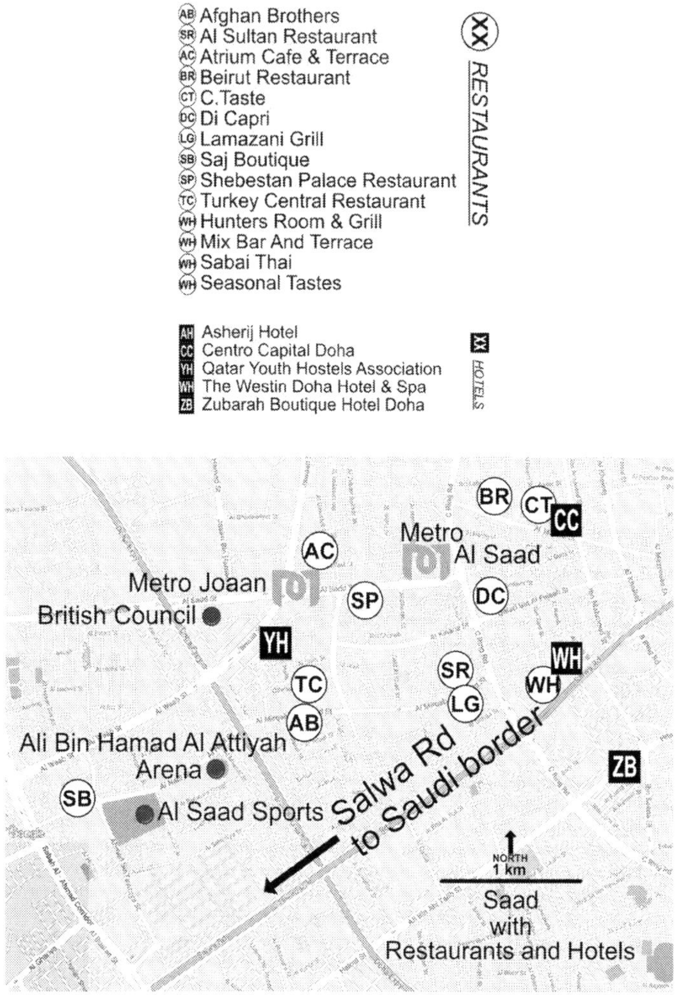

EDUCATION CITY AND DOHA WEST

Saj Boutique - Fast-food Arabic style with the staple Shawarma (flat pitta type bread with meat or falafel filling) type takeaway nicely cooked and presented. Though famous as a takeaway - the restaurant is well laid out - one of 2 branches.

Typical cost range - * Rough GPS - 25.270, 51.477

Street - Al Wab St / Al Bustan St No Public Transport -

Metro Gold Line Gold Line Al Sudan Typical hours - 07:00-01:00 - Contacts - +974 6607 8444

Al Sultan Restaurant - Al Saad - Good value, though with a tired decor, Lebanese restaurant (one of two in a chain) with a selection of Fruit Juices.

Typical cost range - ** Rough GPS - 25.274, 51.505

Street - Al Mirqab Al Jadeed Public Transport - Metro Gold Line Al Saad Typical hours - 08:00-23:00 - Contacts - +974 4441 1865 / info@al-sultanrestaurant.com / www.al-sultanrestaurant.com/

Beirut Restaurant (With Branches) - Simple well established, low-cost, popular Lebanese restaurant.

Typical cost range - ** Rough GPS - 25.285, 51.509

Street - Al Jazeera St Public Transport - Metro Gold Line Al Saad Typical hours – 02:30-23:00 Contacts - +974 4435 5258 / info@beirutrest.com / www.beirutrest.com/

Summer Land (Qatar Petroleum Service Station) - Turkish & Syrian style restaurant offering low priced food. This is one of the larger, of many, restaurants in this petrol station forecourt. It offers dine-in and takeaway. There must be a dozen other choices in the same petrol station forecourt that are ideal for a late-night takeaway or a picnic when driving north.

Typical cost range - ** Rough GPS - 25.350, 51.457

Street - Doha Expressway (Al Shamal Road) /Al Khafji St No Public Transport Typical hours - 08:00-02:00 - Contacts - +974 4444 2056

Atrium Café & Terrace - With live piano music and light international food in a spacious atrium - this is a good choice for a quick meal if in the area.

Typical cost range - **** Rough GPS - 25.284, 51.496

Street - Al Manara St, Jawaan St, Public Transport - Metro Gold Line Joaan Typical hours - 07:00-23:30 - Contacts - +974 4 424 7777 / info.mdoh@millenniumhotels.com / www.millenniumhotels.com/en/doha/millennium-hotel-doha/atrium/

C.Taste (Centro Capital Hotel) In Al Jazeera St - A limited but well produced international menu from this modern well run all-day restaurant in the Centro Hotel.

Typical cost range - **** Rough GPS - 25.284, 51.512

Street - Al Jazeera St Public Transport - Metro Gold Line Al Sadd - 1km away Typical hours - 06:00-22:30 - Contacts - T: +974 4455 5000 / centro.capitaldoha@rotana.com / www.rotana.com/centrohotels/qatar/doha/centrocapitaldoha/dining

Di Capri Ristorante (La Cigale Hotel) - Vivid ambience with a hint of the late 1950s modern Italy. The food lives up to the promise.

Typical cost range - **** Rough GPS - 25.280, 51.508

Street -, C Ring Rd /Suhaim Bin Hamad Street Public Transport - Metro Gold Line Al Sadd Typical hours - 11:30-15:00 / 07:00 - 23:00 - Contacts - +97144288840 / info@lacigalehotel.com / http://www.lacigalehotel.com/sub_-category.php?intCategoryId=4

Ocean Basket (Mall of Qatar) - Seafood as fast-food. A reasonable choice if visiting Mall of Qatar or Villaggio Mall

Typical cost range - **** Rough GPS - 25.324, 51.350

Street - Dukhan Highway / National Day Ceremonial Road (a complicated junction) No Public Transport - Typical hours - 11:00-23:00 (Friday 01:00-23:00) - Contacts - +974 4490 2944 / www.qatar.oceanbasket.com/

Shebestan Palace Restaurant is an extremely well-established Persian restaurant with a subdued, classic, and spacious interior. The food and service are less polished than in other Persian restaurants in Doha, though at an appreciably lower price.

Typical cost range - **** Rough GPS - 25.281, 51.504

Street - Al Saad St Public Transport - Metro Gold Line Al Saad Typical hours - 12:00-midnight - Contacts - +974 4432 1555

Seasonal Tastes (Westin Hotel) - An International restaurant with nightly themed food nights

Typical cost range - ****** Rough GPS - 25.275, 51.514

Street - Salwa Rd Public Transport - Metro Gold Line Bin Mahmoud Typical hours - 18:30-23:00 - Contacts - +974 4492 1555 / dining.doha@westin.com / www.seasonaltastesdoha.com/

Three Sixty (360) Torch Doha - Mediterranean & Seafood restaurant (no alcohol) set on the 47th floor of The Torch. The food is good, but what makes this an outstanding restaurant is the revolving view. This is best enjoyed from just before sunset (arrive early to catch the skyscraper lights coming on in West Bay). The other restaurants in The Torch are also good, but the revolving restaurant does make it especially worth the journey. Very Smart Casual, or suit & dress (national dress).

Typical cost range - ****** Rough GPS - 25.262, 51.445

Street - off Al Waab Street, Al Buwairda St Public Transport - Metro Gold Line Sport City Typical hours - 12:00-15:00 / 19:00-23:00 - Contacts - +974 4446 5600 / reservation@thetorchdoha.com / www.thetorchdoha.com.qa

NORTHEAST QATAR

Maha Al Khaleeg (it was Miknas Cafeteria) - A low-cost restaurant opposite the harbour in Al Khor, with Indian food - especially with a south Indian flavour. Outside seating is available.

Typical cost range - * Rough GPS - 25.686, 51.514

Street - Al Khor Coastal Rd / Al Khor Town Rd No Public Transport - Typical hours - 05:00-midnight - Contacts - +974 500 60179

Pearl Of Beirut Restaurant - Straightforward restaurant – moved from its seaside original location. As the name says, it's a Lebanese style restaurant - the food is good value, and the new restaurant is cleaner than the original.

Typical cost range - * Rough GPS - 25.675, 51.500

Street - Corniche Al Khor (opposite fish harbour) No Public Transport Typical hours - 06:30-23:00 - Contacts - +974 4472 0123

Turkiye Kebab - The main restaurant upstairs offers Turkish meals in the north of Qatar. Takeaways are available.

Typical cost range - * Rough GPS - 25.679, 51.497

Street - Al Khor Coastal Rd / Al Khor Town Rd No Public Transport Typical hours - 10:00-23:00 - Contacts - +974 4411 4150

DUKHAN & WEST COAST, CENTRAL QATAR, AL RUWAIS & NORTH COAST

Iskender Pasha - About as far north as you can get in Qatar.

This inexpensive restaurant is basically furnished with simple Turkish and Mediterranean food. Several other restaurants (including Tea Time) are on the same street; compare these if you wish.

Typical cost range - * Rough GPS - 26.126, 51.204

Street - Madinat Al Shamal Rd / Al Ghayra Rd Public Transport - Typical hours - 09:00-23:00 - Contacts - +974 3357 4304

VARIOUS LOCATIONS

Tea Time - A Qatari Gulf-wide franchise. Spiced tea, with a wide range of options, is the theme. The snack food isn't quite as good as the tea, but this is an excellent alternative to a burger.

Typical cost range - * - various locations (13+) in Qatar including Souq Waqif 25.287, 51.533

Typical hours - 24 Hours - Contacts - teatime.qa/

Wrap It - In food court of several shopping malls (Gulf Mall, Landmark Etc) - The Gulf's most popular snack, the Shawarma, is branded here as Wrap-it. A shawarma in The Gulf is a pitta/Lebanese style bread - split open and stuffed. Here you can individually select the filling, a Subway style of getting precisely what you want.

Typical cost range - * - various locations

Typical hours - 09:00-23:30 (or as in specific food court opening hours)

Of course you will find the usual franchises McDonalds, Starbucks and many many more – all over Doha.

HOTELS

Hotels are stared by the dollar price (charges will be in QAR) of their cheapest room, out of their main peak season (Christmas and major events). In those periods booking well in advance is suggested.

US$ 0-60 *

US$ 61-90 **

US$ 91-125 ***

US$ 126-190 ****

US$ 191-250 *****
US$ 251+ ******

CORNICHE, SOUQ WAQIF & CENTRAL DOHA

This area has an excellent range of hotels. It's also a very popular area for leisure visitors. Advance booking is suggested to get your preferred hotel during any potentially busy period. As a location for straightforward short stay (a few nights) tourism, hotels within walking distance of Msheireb's Metro are ideal. The reason is the Metro station serves 3 metro lines – one of which, the Red Line, serves the airport. Next to the station is the Karwa bus station – with a good range of bus routes & the MetroLink on the road to the south. It's also worth looking east from Msheireb, as that includes the Souq Waqif Metro and National Museum Metro

Century Hotel - Spacious rooms and good facilities in a convenient location. The hotel is new - unfortunately, the staff may also be as their service is inexperienced. A choice of 3 dining options Well located for National and Islamic Art museums & with good access to National Museum Metro (Gold Line). Number of rooms - 215

Typical cost range - * Rough GPS - 25.286, 51.547

Street - Sheraouh St Public Transport - National Museum Metro Location in Qatar - Al Hitmi الهتمي - Contacts - +974 4445 5111 / info@centuryhoteldoha.com / www.centuryhoteldoha.com

Grand Qatar Palace Hotel - Simple style, locally operated and slightly dated, especially the bathrooms with their simple shower & bath. However, the standard is acceptable, and the hotel offers fair value. Established hotel, with a choice of restaurants, small pool and a gym. About 1 kilometre to Souq Waqif and Msheireb Museums. There are several comparable hotels adjacent to this. Number of rooms - 92

Typical cost range - * Rough GPS - 25.281, 51.530

Street - Al Areeq St. Public Transport - Metro Msheireb (Hub) Location in Qatar - Msheireb مشيرب - Contacts - +974 4441 4140 / info@grandqatarpalacehotel.com / www.grandqatarpalacehotel.com

Kingsgate Hotel - Modern functional, and colourful - part of the Millennium Hotels chain. A small pool and gym with reasonable facilities for the price. The key bonus is the proximity to Souq Waqif (600metres), Gold Souq, and a kilometre away from the Islamic Museum or National Museum Number of rooms – 140. It's also directly opposite the Gold Line Souq Waqif Metro.

Typical cost range - * Rough GPS - 25.286, 51.538

Street - Ali bin Abdullah (Al Mirqab Roundabout) Public Transport - Metro Gold Line Souq Waqif Location in Qatar - Old Al Ghanim الغانم - Contacts - +974 4408 5555 / reservations.kgdoh@millenniumhotels.com / www.millenniumhotels.com/en/doha/kingsgate-hotel-doha/

Ramada Encore by Wyndham - Simple, bright decor giving a sense of space in relatively compact rooms. Small pool, gym restaurant About 1 kilometre to Souq Waqif and Msheireb Museums. There are several equivalent hotels adjacent. Number of rooms - 111

Typical cost range - * Rough GPS - 25.280, 51.530

Street - Al Areeq St Public Transport - Metro Msheireb (Hub) Location in Qatar - Msheireb مشيرب - Contacts - +974 4444 3444 / info@ramadaencoredoha.com / www.ramadaencoredoha.com

The Town Hotel Doha is a new hotel with generally attractive and simple muted colour decor. Single restaurant, small pool on the roof (often closed). About 1km to Souq Waqif and Msheireb Museums. There are several similar hotels adjacent. Number of rooms - 120

Typical cost range - * Rough GPS - 25.280, 51.530

Street - Al Areeq Public Transport Metro Msheireb (Hub). Location in Qatar - Msheireb مشيرب - Contacts - +974 4410 7100 / reservations@thetownhotelqatar.com / www.thetownhotelqatar.com

Tourist Hotel - A budget hotel with inexpensive middle-east style decor. Small gym and simple restaurant. Highly convenient to National Museum and close to Museum of Islamic Art and less than 2km from Souq Waqif, I Number of rooms - 120

Typical cost range - * Rough GPS - 25.287, 51.547

Street - Al Aaliya St Public Transport Metro GoldLine National Museum Location in Qatar - Al Hitmi الهتمي - Contacts - +974 4432 1321 / contact form / www.touristhoteldoha.site

Jouri Hotel - With a warm, welcoming theme and good service, this hotel is part of Katara Hospitality, the Qatari government group. Other hotels within the group include The Avenue. The facilities are suitable for a short stay with 3 restaurants and a small gym and spa. Well located for the National and Islamic Art museums & with reasonable access to National Museum Metro (Gold Line). Number of rooms - 136

Typical cost range - ** Rough GPS - 25.287, 51.545

Street - Muthaf St Public Transport - National Museum Metro Location in Qatar - Al Hitmi الهتمي - Contacts - +974 4004 1000 / info@jouridoha.com / www.jourihotel.com/

Saray Musherieb Deluxe Hotel Residence just outside the main Msheireb Area it is close to the Metro- Comfortable, though using domestic fittings for kitchens. Rooms in muted earth tones encourage sleep. Small pool, gym, sauna, Number of rooms - 216

Typical cost range - ** Rough GPS - 25.283, 51.522

Street - Al Meyyah

Street/Al Adhwaa St Public Transport - Bus, Salwa Rd (100m) Location in Qatar - Msheireb مشيرب - Contacts - +974 4015 0555 / contact form / www.saraymsherebhotel.online/

Fraser Suites Doha – Nice rooms of various sizes; many have sea views (ask for these). Choice of dining, gym, spa and rooftop pool with great views. Museum of Islamic Art, National Museum, Corniche are close and just over a kilometre away is Souq Al Waqif. Number of rooms - 138 apartments (there are several hotels close to this).

Typical cost range - *** Rough GPS - 25.290, 51.544

Street - Al Meena St near Corniche Public Transport - Metro GoldLine National Museum Location in Qatar - Al Mirqab المرقاب - Contacts - +974 442 43443 / sales.doha@frasershospitality.com / www.doha.frasershospitality.com

Al Najada Doha Hotel by Tivoli - A fresh spacious property focusing on service and ambience. Well-appointed hotel with a range of facilities (some shared with adjacent Al Najada Hotel by Tivoli) short walk from Souq Waqif, museums and Corniche. Straightforward access to transport. Number of rooms - 151

Typical cost range - **** Rough GPS - 25.285, 51.534

Street - Barahat Al Jufairi

Street, Grand Hamed St Public Transport - Metro Gold Line Souq Waqif Location in Qatar - Msheireb مشيرب - Contacts - (+974) 4470 4444 / alnajada@tivolihotels.com / www.tivolihotels.com/en/al-najada-tivoli

Alwadi Hotel – With clean lines it excels in the excellent location for leisure and business and the service and attention to detail. 3 restaurants and lots more in nearby areas. South-west of Souq Waqif Number of rooms - 213

Typical cost range - **** Rough GPS - 25.286, 51.531

Street - Wadi Msheireb St. Public Transport - Souq Waqif Metro Msheireb Tram Location in Qatar - Msheireb مشيرب - Contacts - +974 4009 9999 / Reservations.alwadihotel@accor.com / all.accor.com/hotel/8395/index.en.shtml

Sharq Village & Spa, Ritz-Carlton - Established hotel. Opulent Arabesque style with a series of low rise buildings set like pleasure pavilions in a manicured environment. Choice of restaurants, including incredibly scenic outdoor options, pools, gym, 250m beach. Near National Museum & Museum of Islamic Art, Dhow yard and along the Corniche to Souq Waqif and more of Doha's sights. Number of rooms - 174

Typical cost range - ***** Rough GPS - 25.284, 51.557

Street - Corniche Public Transport - Metro GoldLine National Museum Location in Qatar - Al Corniche الكورنيش - Contacts - +974 4425 6666 / sharq.leads@ritzcarlton.com / www.ritzcarlton.com/en/hotels/qatar/sharq-village

Souq Waqif Boutique Hotels - Tivoli a collection of 9 individual properties in central Doha. The style is restrained but opulent. Most of these hotels are small and might share some facilities, after a short walk, say from one hotel to another for breakfast. Surrounded by Souq Waqif and close to Qatar's leading museums.

Typical cost range - ***** Rough GPS - 25.289, 51.532

Street - Al Souq St Public Transport - Metro Gold Line Souq Waqif Location in Qatar - Souq Waqif سوق واقف - Contacts - +974 4433 6666 / / www.tivolihotels.com/en/qatar/souq-waqif-doha

The Westin Doha Hotel & Spa - Modern exterior is matched with the interior. Spa, gym, and fitness, along with sheltered gardens. Several good restaurants - southwest of town centre Number of rooms - 364

Typical cost range - **** Rough GPS - 25.275, 51.514

Street - Salwa Rd Public Transport - Bus 31, 32, 33.34, 137, 136, 301 Location in Qatar - Fereej Bin Mahmoud فريج بن محمود - Contacts - +974 4492 1555 / No email / www.marriott.com/hotels/travel/dohwi-the-westin-doha-hotel-and-spa/

Banana Island Resort Doha by Anantara - A stylish resort with access, by boat, to Doha's attractions giving a sense of getting away. This is a small, 25 hectares, island about 1/2 hour boat ride from Doha's Dhow Harbour. A private 600m beach with 9 dining options (some included under suggested restaurants). A Surf Pool, main Pool, and Bowling Alley supply a range of activities. Open views to Doha and across to the Airport, with a surprising lack of noise. Number of rooms - 141 Rooms

Typical cost range - ****** Rough GPS - 25.295, 51.646

Street - In Doha Bay Public Transport - Metro Gold Line Souq Waqif & Ferry from Dhow Harbour 25.292135, 51.534429 Location in Qatar - Banana Island Doha Bay جزيرة بنانا - Contacts - +974 4040 5050 / doha@anantara.com / www.anantara.com/en/banana-island-doha

W Doha

WEST BAY

Marriott Executive Apartments - A 24 story tower with comfortable furnishings and decor. Offers good value for money. Pool, gym and well-appointed rooms and suites. Modern, easy to use kitchens and bathrooms. Just off the Corniche in West Bay, close to DECC and City Centre Mall Number of rooms - 254

Typical cost range - *** Rough GPS - 25.328, 51.530

Street - 'Diplomatic Area Doha, Qatar Diplomatic St' Public Transport - Bus 74, 777 Metro Doha Exhibition and Convention Center (DECC). Location in Qatar - West Bay الخليج الغربي - Contacts - +974 4497 1111 / contact form / www.marriott.-com/hotels/fact-sheet/travel/dohec-marriott-executive-apartments-city-center-doha/

The Curve Hotel - Excellent value for the location, though the large number of rooms would benefit from more restaurants and facilities. Roof Top pool, gym, a few dining options. The DECC and City Centre Mall, along with the modern sights in West Bay, add to the location's appeal. Number of rooms - 600

Typical cost range - *** Rough GPS - 25.326, 51.538

Street - Diplomatic St Public Transport - Metro Doha Exhibition and Convention Center (DECC) Location in Qatar - West Bay الخليج الغربي - Contacts - +974 400 78888 / reservation@ezdancurve.qa / www.ezdancurve.qa/

Fraser Suites West Bay Doha - As you would expect from the chain, the rooms offer clean, relaxed surroundings and excellent options for a business traveller. A rooftop pool, gym, 3 restaurants. A modern hotel with a good range of facilities. The Fraser Suites near the National Museum offer a better pick for tourists. Close to the DECC and City Centre Mall. Number of rooms - 396 rooms (one of Doha's largest hotels) on 46 floors.

Typical cost range - **** Rough GPS - 25.325, 51.522

Street - Al Intisar St Public Transport - Metro Doha Exhibition and Convention Center (DECC). Location in Qatar - West Bay الخليج الغربي - Contacts - +974 4495 5000 / sales.westbay-doha@frasershospitality.com / www.westbay-doha.frasershospitality.com/en

Intercontinental (Beach & Spa) Doha Hotel - This is an

attractive relatively low rise hotel with a beach protected by Al Safliya Island. A mix of hotel and adjacent apartments on a 400m beachfront. With 10 dining outlets, several pools and a very stylish interior. Relatively close to Katara - a 3km walk is possible along the coast with a slight detour around Magical Festival Village Number of rooms - 375

Typical cost range - **** Rough GPS - 25.348, 51.528

Street - East of the Lusail Expressway, on Onaiza St Public Transport – Red Line Metro Al Qassar Location in Qatar - West Bay الخليج الغربي - Contacts - +974 4484 4444 www.ihg.com/intercontinental/hotels/us/en/doha

W Doha - Modern, fresh with almost an Oriental touch. Choice of dining options, pools and gym. So many greeters that it can be overwhelming. Ask from rooms in the middle of the tower – they are quieter. The DECC and City Centre Mall, along with the modern sights in West Bay, are nearby. Number of rooms - 442

Typical cost range - **** Rough GPS - 25.328, 51.530

Street - Diplomatic St Public Transport - Bus 57, 74, 76, 777 Metro Doha Exhibition and Convention Center (DECC). Location in Qatar - West Bay الخليج الغربي - Contacts - +974 4453 5000 / wdoha.reservations@whotels.com / www.marriott.com/hotels/travel/dohwh-w-doha/

Four Seasons Hotel Doha - Restrained and opulent - the style is welcoming and hints at the Arab world. A restricted beach and views are facilities to this hotel. The height of the hotel gives sea views from many rooms. A small marina and Nobu restaurant complete the marine theme - there are 8 other dining venues. The DECC and City Centre Mall, along with the modern sights in West Bay are nearby. Number of rooms - 232

Typical cost range - ***** Rough GPS - 25.325, 51.539

Street - Diplomatic St Public Transport - Metro Doha Exhibition and Convention Center (DECC). Location in Qatar - West Bay الخليج الغربي - Contacts - +974 4494 8888 / contact form / www.fourseasons.com/doha/

Kempinski Residences & Suites - The tallest hotel in Doha (till the next one) offers a luxurious stay with most suites having sea views. The style is modern and simple. All you could expect from an upmarket hotel, plus unexpected facilities such as a boardroom - for the company on the move! Just off the Corniche in West Bay, close to DECC and City Centre Mall Number of rooms - 368 on 60 floors

Typical cost range - ***** Rough GPS - 25.328, 51.531

Street - Diplomatic Area Public Transport - Metro Doha Exhibition and Convention Center (DECC). West Bay الخليج الغربي - Contacts - '

+974 4405 3333' / reservations.doha@kempinski.com / www.kempinski.com/en/doha/residences/

Sheraton Grand Doha Resort & Convention - This is a very well established, exceptionally well-located hotel (it's possibly overall the best-located property in Doha). It's probably focused on the business traveller, but it is still an excellent leisure choice. Beach, pools, gym, racquet courts and more - with probably the best pub in town. Check out the 'whale shark fountain' in the park to the west. The DECC and City Centre Mall are close. Number of rooms - 371

Typical cost range - ***** Rough GPS - 25.318, 51.536

Street - Al Corniche Public Transport Metro Red Line Doha Exhibition & Conference Centre (DECC) Location in Qatar - West Bay Al Corniche الخليج الغربي / الكورنيش - Contacts - +974 4485 4444 / sheraton.doha@Sheraton.com / www.marriott.-com/hotels/travel/dohsi-sheraton-grand-doha-resort-and-convention-hotel/

The St. Regis Doha - Clean, fresh, slightly Arabic in feel. The grounds, though, are smaller than the number of rooms would suggest. Over 10 dining choices, a small beach, pool, gym and all the little touches you would hope for at the cost. a modern mix of buildings and close to Katara - less than 3km walk is possible along the coast with a slight detour around Magical Festival Village Number of rooms - 336

Typical cost range - ****** Rough GPS - 25.350, 51.529

Street - East of the Lusail Expressway, on Onaiza St Public Transport - No public transport Location in Qatar - West

Bay/The Pearl الخليج الغربي - Contacts - +974 4446 0000 / The hotel avoids showing emails. / www.marriott.com/hotels/travel/dohxr-the-st-regis-doha

THE PEARL & KATARA

Marsa Malaz Kempinski - One of the better hotels in Doha, set on a man-made island in a man-made lagoon. The hotel aims to supply a genuine 5* service to its guests; it includes a Butler service. The hotel encourages guests to linger with 11 dining options, a small private beach, and tennis courts. A short drive from Katara and the other modern developments of The Pearl and West Bay. Number of rooms - 281

Typical cost range - ***** Rough GPS - 25.376, 51.547

Street - Pearl Boulevard Public Transport - No public transport Location in Qatar - The Pearl اللولو - Contacts - +974 4035 5555 / reservations.marsamalaz@kempinski.com / www.kempinski.com/en/doha/marsa-malaz-kempinski-the-pearl-doha/

The Ritz-Carlton - This is a well-established hotel with amazingly comfortable luxury rooms. It lacks the opulent style of Ritz-Carlton's Sharq Village Hotel. Overlooking the sea with grounds, pools and access to a man-made beach and marina. Convenient for Katara's cultural mix and the business area of West Bay. Number of rooms - 374

Typical cost range - ***** Rough GPS - 25.380, 51.532

Street - off Lusail Expressway Public Transport - No public transport Location in Qatar - The Pearl اللولو - Contacts - +974 4484 8000 / doha.reservations@ritzcarlton.com / www.ritzcarlton.com/en/hotels/qatar/doha

DOHA SOUTH & EAST

Al Liwan Suites - An older style accommodation with spacious, slightly dated rooms. As an established hotel (10 years old), it offers a non-pretentious place to stay that gives excellent value. Options of 3 locations for meals; the best is the rooftop with Frangipani and a take on an old Qatari house. Small pool, gym, airport transfer, this is an older area in Doha (relatively speaking) that offers interest and reasonably easy access to tourist areas and Airport. Number of rooms - 84 rooms/suites

Typical cost range - * Rough GPS - 25.275, 51.547

Street - Umm Ghuwailina St Public Transport - Metro Red Line Al Jadeda Location in Qatar - Umm Ghuwailina ام غويلينا - Contacts - +974 44242888 / mohsen.khattab@alliwan-suites.com.qa / www.alliwansuites.com.qa/

Chairman Hotel - With comfortable furnishings and spacious rooms - the hotel offers excellent value. A single dining choice. In one of the older areas of Doha. Number of rooms - 68

Typical cost range - * Rough GPS - 25.269, 51.538

Street - Najma St Public Transport - Al Mansoura Metro, Location in Qatar - Najma نجمة - Contacts - +974 4426 0444 / reservations@chairmenhotel.com / www.chairmenhotel.com/

Holiday Inn Doha - The Business Park - Modern, with a range of facilities expected in a Holiday Inn with Pool and gym.

There are three dining options Convenient to the Airport and transport to other areas. Request quiet rooms.

Number of rooms - 307 Typical cost range - * Rough GPS - 25.273, 51.543 Street - Al Matar St Public Transport - Metro Al Doha Al Jadeda Location in Qatar - Najma نجمة - Contacts - +974 4031 3333 - holidayinndoha@ihg.com / www.ihg.com/holidayinn/

DOHA CENTRAL SOUTHEAST HOTELS & RESTAURANTS

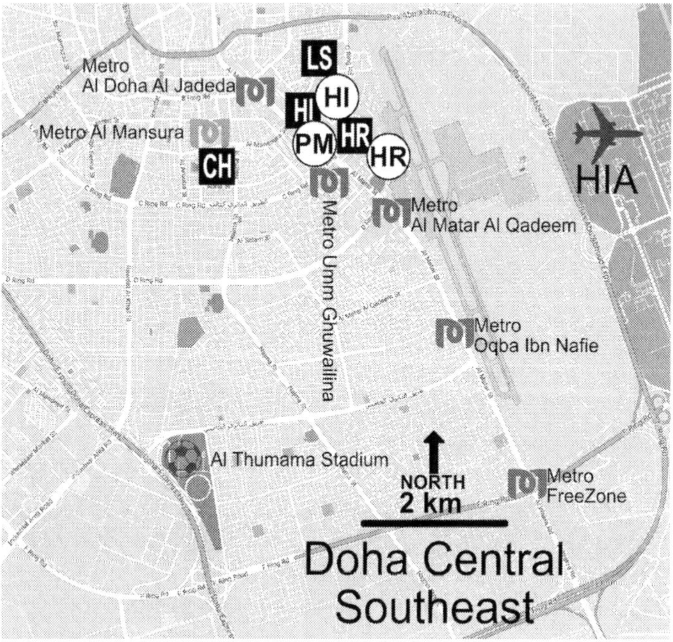

La Villa Suites - Very old-fashioned rooms that offer reasonably good value with a small kitchenette. Rooms are furnished differently – look at yours before checking in. A single dining choice. Close to the Najma souq area - with a wide variety of low-cost goods. Number of rooms -

Typical cost range - * Rough GPS - 25.271, 51.539

Street - Ibn Firnas St Public Transport - Al Mansoura Metro and MetroLink buses Location in Qatar - Najma نجمة - Contacts - / info@lavillahospitality.com / lavillahospitality.com/

Strato Hotel by Warwick - Comfortably furnished, though with patchy service. Consider this hotel if you have early morning or late night flights or a short stay. Rooftop pool, gym, Sauna and a couple of dining options. Convenient for Airport, National Museum and Museum of Islamic Art. Number of rooms - 97

Typical cost range - * Rough GPS - 25.269, 51.552

Street - C Ring Rd / Al Matar St Public Transport - Metro RedLine Umm Ghuwailina Location in Qatar - Umm

Ghuwailina ام غويلينا - Contacts - +974 4041 4444 / info.stratohotel@warwickhotels.com / warwickhotels.com/strato-hotel/

Al Madina Suites - This has a slightly older look offset by spacious rooms and comfortable facilities. Buffet style restaurant and gym. The hotel is located in an older area (around 30 years old) of Doha - less than 2km from Souq Al Waqif and Corniche. Number of rooms - 40 small suites with a small kitchenette

Typical cost range - ** Rough GPS - 25.276, 51.534

Street - Al Nada Street Public Transport - Red Line Metro Al Jadeda Station Location in Qatar - Al Mansoura المنصوره - Contacts - +974 4431 8800 / info@almadinasuites.com / www.almadinasuites.com/

Holiday Villa Hotel & Residence - A very distinctive hotel architecture, with a large open courtyard overlooked by 10 stories. Though an Asian chain, the service standards are generally lower than many other international chains. This is offset by the excellent value for money otherwise. Five restaurants, a pool and a gym. There is a wide range of room options, each with different decor; ask to see before checking-in. Close to local car rentals, though far from Corniche and other tourist areas. A large public park is opposite the entrance. Number of rooms - 356 rooms in a large complex

Typical cost range - ** Rough GPS - 25.265, 51.525

Street - Rawdat Al Khail St / C Ring Road No Public Transport Location in Qatar - Al Mansoura المنصوره - Contacts - +974 4408 4888 / info@holidayvilladoha.com / www.holidayvilladoha.com

Hyatt Regency Oryx - A former Rotana Hotel – it is still a modern functional hotel gym, Pool Spa & several restaurants, straightforward access to Airport and Transport Number of rooms - 400

Typical cost range - *** Rough GPS - 25.268, 51.554

Street - off Al Matar St Public Transport - Metro Red Line Umm Ghuwailina Location in Qatar - Umm Ghuwailina ام غويلينا - Contacts - +974 4402 3333 / contact form / www.hyatt.com/en-US/hotel/qatar/hyatt-regency-oryx-doha/dohrd?

AL WAKRAH, MESAIEED & SOUTH QATAR

Souq Wakra Tivoli - South of Doha on a public beach in a leisure area. A charming hotel, in a modern reimagined village setting. The hotel is one or two floors set around a series of courtyards. In general, the hotel lives up to its high government classification. The low density and courtyard style means that you are unlikely to feel you are in anything other than a private home. A choice of 5 restaurants, including Mahaadeg, with views of The Gulf. Number of rooms - 101

Typical cost range - **** Rough GPS - 25.174, 51.610

Street - Al Loulou St Public Transport - Al Wakrah Metro & MetroLink bus Location in Qatar - Al Wakrah الوكرة - Contacts - +974 4428 7888 / souqalwakra@tivolihotels.com / www.tivolihotels.com/en/souq-al-wakra-tivoli

Sealine Beach, A Murwab Resort - Low rise property, with only 35 rooms in the main building- this is a chalet & villa property. Owned by a Qatar government organisation, though not run by a brand name chain, unlike several others in Doha. This is one of the more established hotels in Qatar. Pool, gym, Spa and 1.3km beach. Not far from the sand dunes and inland sea. Number of rooms - 95 Units

Typical cost range - ***** Rough GPS - 24.862, 51.514

Street - Sealine Beach Rd Public Transport - No public transport Location in Qatar - Khawr Al Udaid / Mesaieed مسيعيد / خور العديد - Contacts - +974 4021 4000 / info@sealinebeachqatar.com / www.sealinebeachqatar.com/

Education City & Doha West

Asherij Hotel - Newly built hotel with decorations in an Arabic style. Limited services, a small gym and a coffee shop. Larger suites have a small kitchenette. Rooms have different decorations - ask to see what's available. A mix of residential and business, this is just inside the C Ring Rd and about a 2.5km walk (if you want) to the Corniche. Number of rooms - 100

Typical cost range - * Rough GPS - 25.282, 51.508

Street - Al Quds St /Majda St Public Transport - Goldline Metro Al Saad Location in Qatar - Fereej Bin Mahmoud فريج بن

محمود - Contacts - +974 440 828 28 / info@asherijhotel.com / www.asherijhotel.com/

Premier Inn Doha Education City. The hotel offers outstanding value with comfortable simply furnished rooms. This modern accommodation could be a good choice for a business person. A pool, gym and restaurant add to the appeal. The hotel does offer a complimentary shuttle into town. This area is principally the educational focus of Doha, about 10km west of the Corniche. In the general area are the new Qatar National Convention Centre, National Library, Mataf Arab Museum of Modern Art and Shaqab Equestrian Stables Number of rooms - 219

Typical cost range - * Rough GPS - 25.322, 51.430

Street - east of Garafat Al Rayyan Rd Public Transport - Metro GreenLine Education City - 800m walk or Grey Tram Line Location in Qatar - Education City المدينة التعليمية - Contacts - +974 4007 8333 / reservations.dec@mena.premierinn.com / global.premierinn.com/en/hotel/doha-education-city

Qatar Youth Hostels Association - A relatively simple accommodation offering, though far from basic. Its focus is on students, or similar. A basic coffee shop and do-it-yourself laundry. Number of rooms - 40

Typical cost range - * Rough GPS - 25.317, 51.464

Street - Jawaan St Public Transport - +974 4421 7157 Public Transport Joaan. As with so many lower-cost hotels, there is only the possibility to book through online agencies.

Centro Capital Doha - Simple, clean rooms create a modern look. All-day dining, with a bar, A small rooftop pool & gym, and 2 good restaurants. A newer area of Doha - about 2km walk from Corniche Number of rooms - 229

Typical cost range - ** Rough GPS - 25.284, 51.512

Street - Al Jazeera St Public Transport Metro Goldline Al Sadd - 1km away Location in Qatar - Fereej Bin Mahmoud فريج بن محمود - Contacts - +97444555000 / Contact Form / www.rotana.com/centrohotels/qatar/doha/centrocapitaldoha

Zubarah Boutique Hotel Doha - A small, well-run hotel with warm, comfortable facilities. Limited facilities include a small Spa and three small dining options. Mainly in a mix of a residential and small business area. Number of rooms - 45

Typical cost range - ** Rough GPS - 25.270, 51.518

Street - Al Rawabi St No Public Transport - Location in Qatar - Rawdat Al Khail روضة الخيل - Contacts - +974 4447 0000 / info@zubarah.com / www.zubarahhotels.com/

The Torch Doha - The most distinctive hotel in Doha, opened for Asian Games. Rooms are simple in appearance alongside modern, opulent design. The restaurants are unique and all worth a visit, esp 360.

The Torch

There are no grounds. Eight dining options, gym and a remarkable small swimming pool. Near are sports stadiums and Villaggio Mall. It's well out of the city centre. Number of rooms - 163 rooms on 51 floors.

Typical cost range - **** Rough GPS - 25.262, 51.445

Street - off Al Waab

Street, Al Buwairda St Public Transport - Metro GoldLine Sport City Location in Qatar - Baaya / Aspire اسباير / بعيا - Contacts - +974 4446 5600 / reservation@thetorchdoha.com / www.thetorchdoha.com.qa

The Westin Doha Hotel & Spa - Modern exterior is matched with the interior. Spa, gym and fitness, along with sheltered gardens. Several good restaurants - southwest of town centre Number of rooms - 364

Typical cost range - **** Rough GPS - 25.275, 51.514

Street - Salwa Rd Public Transport - Bus 31, 32, 33.34, 137, 136, 301 Location in Qatar - Fereej Bin Mahmoud فريج بن محمود - Contacts - +974 4492 1555 / No email / www.marriott.com/hotels/travel/dohwi-the-westin-doha-hotel-and-spa/

• • •

NORTHEAST QATAR

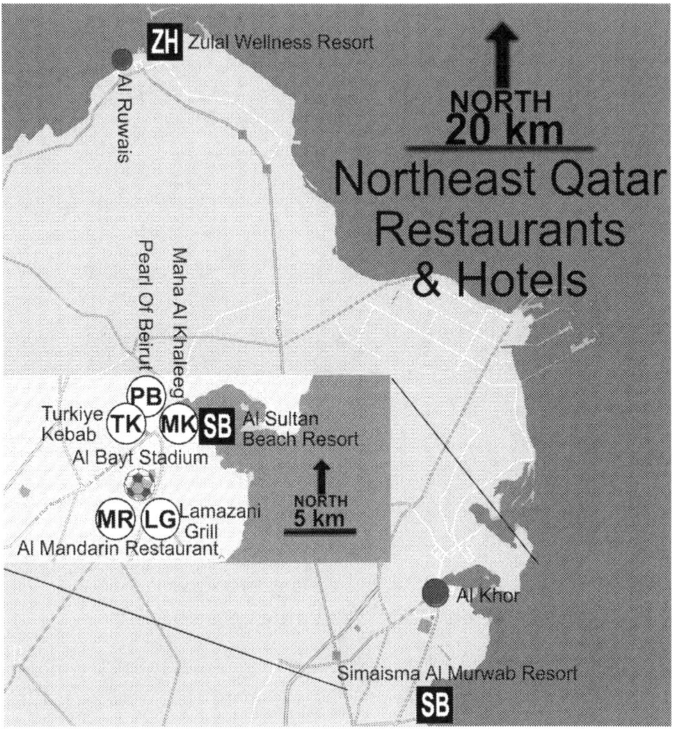

Al Sultan Beach Resort - Quirky hotel with a pool near a beach. A premium price compared to 5* hotels in Doha for this hotel's more modest offering. Along with the beach (and a mangrove swamp), a Pool and a simple restaurant are the key assets. The staff are helpful. Number of rooms - 187

Typical cost range - **** Rough GPS - 25.685, 51.522

Street - Corniche Al Khor Public Transport Bus 702 & 722 from Lusail Location in Qatar - Al Khor الخور - Contacts - +974 4472 2555' / / www.alsultanbeachresort.com

Simaisma Al Murwab Resort - A property of villas set overlooking the sea. Owned by a company of the Qatari government. Pool, gym, Tennis and beach Opportunities for scuba diving Number of rooms - 52 all villa

Typical cost range - ****** Rough GPS - 25.584, 51.488

Street - off Al Khor Coastal Rd Public Transport - No public transport Location in Qatar - Sumaysimah سميسمة - Contacts - +974 4479 9555 / info@simaisma.com / www.simaisma.com/

DUKHAN & WEST COAST, CENTRAL QATAR, ALRUWAIS & NORTH COAST

Zulal Wellness Resort - A newish upmarket hotel on Qatar's northern tip. Opposite the hotel are two islands, and a few kilometres away is Al Ruwais town. Number of rooms - 120

Typical cost range - ***** Rough GPS - 26.155, 51.242

Street - Public Transport Non - Location in Qatar - Al Ruwais الرويس - Contacts - +974 4008 4999 / info@msheireb.com / www.msheireb.com/zulal-wellness-resort/

Hilton Salwa – One of Qatar's newest hotels. Set on an expansive beach of 3+km in a location where it can only appeal as a resort property. With over 20 dining options to support 360 accommodation units (villa, suites etc) there has to be an option for everyone. A key attraction is a water adventure park.

Number of rooms 361, Typical cost range - **** Rough GPS 24.848 ,50.857 Public Transport non - Location in Qatar – Salwa Road, southwest coast - Contacts +974 4423 6666 www.hilton.com

CHAPTER 10

GENERAL BACKGROUND

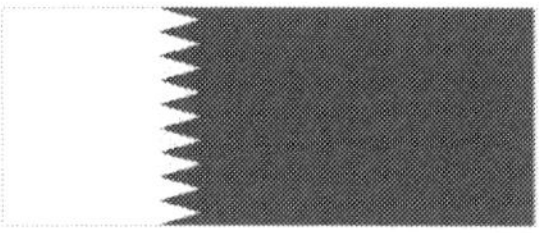

Geography: The State of Qatar occupies a Peninsula halfway down the east coast of the Arabian Peninsula (the western coast of The Gulf), bordered to the south by Saudi Arabia. The coastline is about 550km long and bounds the country to the west, north and east. Low hillsides in the northwest and dunes in the southeast are the most noticeable topography. There are several minor islands, including Halul, Shirawah and Al Ashat. The total land area of Qatar is approximately 11,627 square kilometres (sq. km).

Capital: Doha, on Qatar's east coast, is the capital, economic and population centre of Qatar.

Economy: Qatar is one of the world's wealthiest nations in GDP per capita. Oil and Natural Gas are the basis of this wealth; and this is predicted to continue for the next century.

Population: The Qatar Government assessed the mid-year population in March 2023 (psa.gov.qa) at 3,005,069 appx. This gives a population density rate of 258 persons per sq. km; most are on Qatar's east coast.

Climate: Qatar has a hot, humid desert climate with long summers and, from November to February, short warm winters.

Language: Arabic is the official language; however, English, Hindi/Urdu & Bengali are widely spoken.

Government: Qatar is a hereditary monarchy. The ruler appoints the Government.

Religion: Islam is the official religion of the country.

Qatar National Day: Qatar's National Day is the 18th of December & is an official holiday.

Flag: The flag is white and 'Qatar maroon', with a vertical border of nine white serrations between the two colours. The maroon suggests the imperial purple of ancient civilisations, which used dye obtained from shellfish exploited in Qatar. The nine serrations are for the nine Gulf sheikhdoms under a British treaty in 1916. Qatar considered forming a union with these in the late 1960s.

Work Hours: Government: From 07:00-14:00. Friday and Saturday are the weekend breaks. Companies: Office hours typically from 08:00-midday / 16:00-20:00 (or 08:00—17:00). Friday & Saturday is the weekend. Retail and services have longer hours. In major shopping malls, the working hours may be 10:00-22:00, with supermarkets working an hour either side of this. In malls they are typically open 7 days a week. Friday opening hours are after mid-day prayers – till late night.

Local Time: Three hours + Greenwich Mean Time

Currency: The official currency is the Qatari Riyal (QAR—sometimes QR), which is divided into 100 Dirhams. The exchange rate is fixed at US$ = 3.65 QARs.

Geography

On the eastern coast of the Arabian Peninsula, Qatar, a Peninsula itself, is one of the world's smallest states at 11,627 square (sq.) kilometres (km), stretching about 190km south-north and a maximum of 90km east-west. This country includes offshore islands, such as Halul, some 97km to the northeast of Doha, Al Ashat 60km south of Doha and Fasht Ad Dibal northwest of Al Ruwais in northern Qatar.

Qatar is part of the Arabian Shelf, the eastern sedimentary areas of the Arabian Plate that are moving north and being subducted under the Iranian/Eurasian plates. The geology of

Qatar includes surface areas of gravels and sandstone of the Hofuf Formation formed by rivers over the last 1.5million years. The Hofuf Formation lies over the Dam Formation of the Miocene Period (23-2.6million years ago approximately). This formation is clay and limestone, found mainly in the southwest of Qatar. Below the Dam Formation is the Dammam Formation, much of which is a chalky limestone and dolomite. The Dammam Formation extends over most of Qatar and was created during the Middle Eocene (48-38million years ago). The Dammam Formation is a karst limestone environment that has sinkholes and caves. Typical sinkhole examples can be found off the Salwa Road to the northwest and southeast of the Rawdat Rashid Interchange (GPS 25.172, 51.327). The sinkholes and caves are thought to have developed from about 560,000 years ago. They often collect water run-off and locally are called *dahl*. Below the Dammam Formation is the Rus Formation, chalky limestone and marl/clay also formed during the Middle Eocene (48-38 million years ago).

The key structural elements within the Qatar rock formations are anticlines; these are rock strata that have been forced into a convex (curving up and then down) arch. Here, Qatar's wealth, its oil and gas, is trapped in the upper part of the arch where suitable 'capping' rock is found. The primary anticlines are the Qatar Arch that spreads from the south of the country into Iran; in this arch's northeast is the vast North Gas Field. Others include the Dukhan Anticline that flows from the south to the northwest a few kilometres inland from the coast up to the area of Dukhan. This uplift has exposed the fossiliferous Dam Formation and has trapped the Dukhan oilfield to its west.

Almost devoid of notable contours, Qatar's highest point is in the southwest at Qurayn Abu al Bawl (GPS 24.717, 51.047), also listed as Al Galail. This is next to a security installation, so do take care about photography and activities here and at all government buildings. The location overlooks the Saudi Arabian border 19km away, taking advantage of the 103 metres elevation; access is west from route 59 at GPS 24.713, 51.069. The land gradually drops in general elevation from there towards the north. However, there are low hills in the north, and the general flatness makes any rock outcrop noteworthy. Shallow dry valleys that, in Arabic, are called *wadi* are found throughout the country.

The Khor Al Udaid area has dune and *sabkha* (mud, sand, gypsum salt flats). The sands are aeolian (wind-blown) in origin, while the *sabkha* that often looks like a solid surface might be a quicksand-like trap waiting for unwary drivers.

To Doha's west and northwest are karst limestone areas with depressions symptomatic of erosion and sinkholes. North of Doha, the coast is sand, created following changes in the level of The Gulf which, when lower over 10,000 years ago, allowed sand from the extensive exposed seabed to be blown inland.

Qatar shares a single land border, of 87km, with Saudi Arabia. This was ratified in 2001. It has sea borders with Bahrain to the west, the United Arab Emirates (UAE) to the east and Iran to the north, and the sea borders with Saudi Arabia to the southwest and southeast. Khor Al Udaid, an inlet of The Gulf in the southeast of Qatar, is with Qatar, and Saudi Arabia is immediately to its south..

The sea border with Bahrain was also agreed in 2001. The ratification with Bahrain resulted in the Hawar Islands, a few hundred metres off Qatar's west coast, being certified as Bahraini territory. Areas disputed with Bahrain and awarded to Qatar at the same time were Al Zubarah [PAGE 122] in Qatar's northwest mainland, the isolated islets of Fasht Ad Dibal northwest of Al Zubarah and Jinan Island northwest of Dukhan on the west coast.

Be cautious near an international border in Qatar as Bahrain, Saudi Arabia and the UAE arrest people who are in their territory illegally.

Climate

Qatar's is a desert climate with scorching, humid summers and warm winters. During July, Qatar's hottest month, the temperature peaks at over 48Celsius (C) in Doha and drops to a night-time minimum of 29C, with humidity up to 90%. In the coolest month, January, the highest temperature might be 31C and a minimum of 12C. Humidity may reach 100% if a night fog forms, but typically during the day it's around 40%. Rain is unlikely at any time of year, with the highest probability during December-March. Winds are usually light, coming from the south in the summer and from the north in winter, when weather systems drop south from Asia. Springtime can have dust-storms, which may originate over Iran, and these can last up to a few days.

Note that the average (Celsius) is what it says and does not stand for the absolute maximum.

Note that the average (Celsius) is what it says and does not stand for the absolute maximum.

Month	Jan	Feb	Mar	Apr	May	Jun	Jul	Aug	Sep	Oct	Nov	Dec
Avg Max (C)	23	25	30	35	41	43	44	43	40	37	31	26

Nature

With Qatar's extreme desert climate, plants and animals have constant stress to survive. Add in an increasingly developed human environment, and for many these pressures increase; though some have taken advantage of new man-made environments.

Flora

Qatar's fauna ultimately depends on its 300+ species of flora. The dominant trees include *ghaf Prosopis cineraria.* This large tree, with its feathery leaves, grows in sandy soils (though not usually in dunes) and in Qatar from the central region through to the north. The *ghaf's* leaves can trap moisture from fog, and the resultant water dripping to the ground becomes the tree's own irrigation system. The Christ's thorn tree, *Ziziphus spina-christi,* grows in rocky *wadi* environments. The flowers are a source of prized honey. Its small fruit is eaten by animals and, in the recent past and occasionally today, by humans. Its densely branched habit and 20 metres height make it an ideal shade tree when planted in villages. A similar tree, *Ziziphus mauritiana,* has been introduced, probably from Malaysia. Three species of Acacia are found, *'Salam' Acacia ehrenbergiana* is found in loose sandy soils. Its appearance varies but is usually a very ragged bushy shape of less than three metres in height. *'Garat'*, *Acacia nilotica,* resembles Salam, though slightly smaller and less bushy. *'Simr'*, *Acacia tortilis / Vachellia tortilis,* is spread throughout Qatar and, as with other Acacias, prefers well-drained sandy soil. This tree is the classic umbrella Acacia also found in Africa and, unlike the other Acacia of Qatar, its flower is creamy coloured rather than yellow. All Acacia have roots that can penetrate deep into the soil and fractured rock, up to 30m depth, in search of water. The trees respond to drought by dropping their leaves, which will regrow rapidly after rains.

On the north coasts and at Al Wakrah, south of Doha, the Mangrove *Avicennia marina* grows on muddy areas in the intertidal zone. Mangrove's aerial roots absorb oxygen, water and nutrients in a muddy, stagnant lagoon type environment, while the leaves excrete salts from seawater. In Qatar, around Al Thakira, they grow up to around five metres high.

Animals

Qatar's land mammals in historical times may have included the Asiatic lion and Asiatic cheetah along with their prey that would have included antelope and gazelle. Today the number of land mammals and their variety has reduced. Smaller mammals are the most common.

Dwarf gerbil, *Gerbillus nanus;* Wagner's gerbil, *Gerbillus dasyurus;* Cheesman's gerbil, *Gerbillus cheesmani;* are widely dispersed small rodents. Cheesman's gerbil is probably the most readily seen towards dusk in sandy areas. Look for a light russet colour rodent about 11 centimetres (cm) in body length with a slightly longer tail and rear legs that are somewhat longer than the forelegs. These are opportunistic feeders, preferring seeds & grain though eating insects if other food is scarce. They probably breed throughout the year, and each litter may have up to eight young and are vital food for owls and foxes. Jirds are related to gerbils, though they are larger at up to 16cm, with a more rat-like appearance. The Libyan jird, *Meriones libycu's* and Sundevall's jird, *Meriones crassus,* are omnivorous and occupy sandy or rocky desert in Qatar. With its long kangaroo type rear legs, the Egyptian jerboa, *Jaculus jaculus,* occupy a similar niche to the gerbil. The more familiar house mouse, *Mus musculus,* and house rat, *Rattus rattus,* join these small rodents in Qatar.

The desert hedgehog, *Paraechinus aethiopicus,* is relatively small at up to 25 cm. As with most other hedgehogs, this is a nocturnal animal that eats insects and small animals. This hedgehog breeds once a year with a litter of perhaps six young. Cape hare *Lepus capensis* is comparable to the European brown hare in appearance and is up to 68cm in length. As with most other desert animals, it is active from dusk to dawn, sheltering under vegetation during the day. This animal breeds throughout the year with perhaps up to six litters annually and four leverets in each. The hare's adult size and the lack of larger predators in Qatar mean it is most vulnerable only when young – except if hunted by humans.

The largest predators in Qatar include three canids and possibly the honey badger, *Mellivora capensis,* which might live in the south of the country. The honey badger is omnivorous, about 75cm long, excluding the tail and may have a couple of cubs annually.

An adaptive predator, the golden jackal, *Canis aureus,* has a body length up to 85cm long and a tail of about 25cm with a weight of 14kilograms (kg). This jackal possibly breeds with feral dogs in Qatar. Pure animals have a coat of a rusty brown colour, with black back. Like most jackals, this is omnivorous, feeding on small rodents, lizards and carrion, which it supplements with fruit and vegetation for a well-rounded diet. They breed once a year and give birth to up to six pups. Found throughout Qatar the red fox, *Vulpes vulpes arabica,* is a subspecies of the red fox, though with a less intense red colour. Ruppell's fox *Vulpes rueppelli sabaea* is a pale coloured desert-living fox, up to 74cm long, including its tail, weighing in at less than 1.9kg. They breed once a year with up to six pups. Like the jackal, these foxes are omnivorous, eating small animals, large insects and plant products.

Bats include desert long-eared bat, *Otonycteris hemprichii*, and Geoffrey's trident leaf-nosed bat, *Asellia tridens,* which are both insectivorous.

Reintroduced species include the **Arabian oryx**, *Oryx leucoryx,* which has become the logo of Qatar Airways. The oryx can be up to 175cm long, 100cm at shoulder height and weigh up to 70kg, with both sexes having twin horns of up to 65cm. Their natural habitat is a desert environment, both stony and sandy, where they might roam in family groups of about ten animals. The white colour of the coat helps reflect the heat, while in colder weather, the hair raises to expose the darker skin, allowing it to absorb heat.

Arabian Oryx

The Arabian Oryx can breed throughout the year with a single calf born eight months after mating. Calves are well camouflaged in desert conditions, having a mid-brown coat. Extinct in the wild by 1972, due to hunting, a breeding population had been set up in several zoos worldwide, most notably at Phoenix and San Diego Zoos, and animals were reintroduced into their original countries from the mid-1970s. In Qatar, this reintroduction was focused initially on Al Wabra Wildlife Preservation, a private zoo; later other locations bred the animal. The Arabian oryx can obtain its water in winter by eating fresh vegetation, including grasses and leaves.

The other major mammal reintroduced to Qatar is the Arabian sand gazelle, *Gazella subgutturosa marica,* locally called *reem*. Due to hunting, the animal was extinct in Qatar by the end of the 1950s.

Sand Gazelle

It was reintroduced in the mid-1990s, notably in Al Reem Reserve. The males can grow to a length of 110cm and weigh 30kg. Both sexes have horns, though the male's are substantially larger. In a safe environment, population growth can be rapid, as this gazelle can breed after it is about 18months, and in about 30% of live births twins are born after a gestation period of just over five months.

Camels

Qatar would hardly seem an Arab country without the Camel, *Camelus dromedaries*, the dromedary.

The word Camel comes from the Arabic جمل (Jamal, a male Camel). The word dromedary, the single-humped camel variety, from the Greek *dromus,* meaning race/racecourse or running, very apt in the world of Camel racing today. All living dromedaries are domesticated animals, the wild type having disappeared perhaps 2,500 years ago. This domestication started, at least, by 1,000BC, probably in southeast Arabia when the wild

Camel population was declining in numbers, probably due to predation by humans.

Male Camels can be two meters in height at the shoulder and weigh 600kg; females are perhaps 10% shorter in height and 30% less in weight. The single hump is a fat bearing organ and as fat can release water, if used due to lack of food, it allows better survival in drought. The Camel is a herbivore and grazes on the ground and browses bushes and trees, though nowadays, a substantial proportion is supplied as hay or other animal feed. As with a cow, the Camel is a ruminant, so spends much of its day either eating or ruminating! To cope with the desert climate, the body temperature can fluctuate by more than 10C and can deal with a 30% water loss; either of these changes would kill most mammals. Camels, fortunately, can replenish water at around 20 litres a minute, helpful if finding water in a desert climate.

From around four years, the Camel can breed, with typically a single baby born after a gestation period of some 15 months, which may then live for some 50 years. In captivity, the dromedary has bred with the llama. In the wild in areas such as Iran, where their ranges overlap, dromedaries can breed with the two-humped Bactrian Camel. In Turkey, the breeding of Bactrian and dromedary is specifically done at Izmir province, where the result is large single-humped animals, whose males compete in Camel 'wrestling' events.

Camels have been used historically for transport, milk, meat, clothing and more; it, therefore, is probably more helpful than cattle. Today in Qatar, they are bred for the prestige they bring, especially for racing. Camels are used for short races from about aged 18 months – 24months, the prime age is around six years, and these older Camels can race at around 40kmph. Though children were used as jockeys for their light-weight, from 2007 the 'rider' has been a simple robot, with a rotating whip to encourage the animal's speed. Prizes can be hundreds of thousands of Qatari Riyals and luxury cars. Though the sales value of the winner, which can reach US$ 1,500,000, must be an added benefit. These high prices are obtained for animals that, like thoroughbred racehorses, have a known and admired lineage.

Other Camels might take part in Camel beauty contests or milking contests. Again, the value of a successful animal might run to more than US$1,000,000, with the most expensive Camel ever being sold for US$ 2,720,000 in the UAE (though rumours say one has been sold for US$9,500,000). Camels have been banned from these beauty contests for having Botox injections to enhance the flop of the lip. As they say, beauty is in the eye of the beholder.

Cemels

Birds

There have been 325 bird species recorded in Qatar, excluding introductions such as the red-necked Ostrich, which is a zoo-based bird in Qatar. Of these birds, about 119 species are relatively common, 83 are scarce but expected to be seen at some stage in the year, 38 are seen regularly but are uncommon, some 39 have only been seen one or two times, and there are around 46 vagrant species. The overall number of species seen in Qatar is gradually increasing, principally due to new environments being created by man. These include vegetated areas such as farms, parks and golf clubs and, less attractively, rubbish dumps where birds such as Eagles, especially Steppe Eagles, feed.

Three invasive species are probably amongst the most easily birds seen around Doha. The Indian mynah, *Acridotheres tristis,* is an aggressive resident, breeding throughout Doha and its surroundings. It out-competes and can kill the young of similar-sized birds and lives very freely alongside people.

Indian Mynah

The Indian house crow, *Corvus splendens,* nests in trees and is found towards the coast in areas of human habitation. The house crow scavenges refuse and, like the mynah, can live alongside people. From Africa or India, the rose-ringed parakeet, *Psittacula krameri,* is a common resident breeder and, like the mynah, probably results from escaped cage birds. This is the parakeet seen in London and other cities worldwide that were not part of its original range. Another parakeet, the larger Alexandrine, *Psittacula eupatria,* is also found in Doha. These birds feed on nuts, fruit and seeds and therefore can damage cultivation in Qatar.

Flamingo

Off the coast of Doha at Al Aaliya Island (a restricted location north of The Pearl), some 500 pairs of Socotra cormorant *Phalacrocorax nigrogularis* nest. This endangered species breeds in winter in various months, but always as a synchronised event in any given colony. The great cormorant, *Phalacrocorax carbo,* occurs in lower numbers.

Birds readily seen coast include greater Flamingo *Phoenicopterus roseus* from around November to April. They might also be found inland at Irkhaya Farm (25.013, 51.163) along with the black-crowned night Heron, *Nycticorax*, grey heron, *Ardea cinerea*, purple heron, Ardea *purpurea*. Smaller shorebirds are mostly winter visitors and include Grey Plover, *Pluvialis Squatarola*, Common Ringed Plover, *Charadrius Hiaticula*; Little Ringed Plover, *Charadrius Dubius*; Kentish Plover, *Charadrius Alexandrines*; Lesser Sand Plover, *Charadrius Atrifrons*; Greater Sand Plover, *Charadrius Leschenaultia*; Common Snipe, *Gallinago*; European Black-Tailed Godwit, *Limosa*; Bar-Tailed Godwit, *Limosa Lapponica*; Eurasian Whimbrel, *Numenius Phaeopus*; Eurasian Curlew, *Numenius Arquata*; Common Redshank, *Tringa Tetanus*; Marsh Sandpiper, *Tringa Stagnatilis*; Common Greenshank, *Tringa*

Nebularia; Green Sandpiper, *Tringa Ochropus*; Wood Sandpiper, *Tringa Glareola*; Terek Sandpiper, *Xenus Cinereus*; Common Sandpiper, *Actitis Hypoleucos*; Ruddy Turnstone, *Arenaria Interpres*; Sanderling, *Calidris Alba*; Little Stint, *Calidris Minuta*; Dunlin, *Calidris Alpine*.

Gulls and terns, which are mostly migratory species, include Slender-Billed Gull, *Chroicocephalus Genei*; Common Black-Headed Gull, *Chroicocephalus Ridibundus*; Great Black-Headed Gull, *Larus Ichthyaetus*; Steppe Gull, *Larus Barabensis*; Gull-Billed Tern, *Gelochelidon Nilotica*; Caspian Tern, *Hydroprogne Caspia*; Lesser Crested Tern, *Thalasseus Bengalensis*; White-Winged Tern, *Chlidonias Leucopterus*; Saunders's Tern, *Sternula saundersi* (seen throughout the year); whiskered tern, *Chlidonias hybrid* (seen throughout the year);

European Roller

Inland from Doha, some attractive migrants that should be seen include the flashing blue of the European roller, *Coracias garrulous*; the deeper blue of the Indian roller, *Coracias benghalensis*, both these rollers are similar in size to a jackdaw or feral pigeon, blue-cheeked bee-eater *Merops persicus*; European bee-eater *Merops apiaster*, Eurasian hoopoe, *Upupa epops*, which though most migrate through Qatar some stay rather than moving on.

Expect to see common kestrel, *Falco tinnunculus,* and Western osprey, *Pandion haliaetus,* which is resident along much of the coast and breeds in Qatar. Arriving in winter are Western Marsh Harrier, *Circus aeruginosus,* and Pallid Harrier, *Circus macrourus*, Steppe Eagle *Aquila nipalensis.*

Steppe Eagle & Indian House Crows

Smaller migratory species include the much sought after hypocolius, *Hypocolius ampelinus,* found in scrub, Rufous-Tailed Scrub Robin, *Erythropygia Galactotes*; Spotted Flycatcher, *Muscicapa Striata*; Ed-Spotted Bluethroat, *Luscinia Svecica*; Black Redstart, *Phoenicurus Ochruros*; Common Redstart, *Phoenicurus*; Rufous-Tailed Rock Thrush, *Monticola Saxatilis*; Whinchat, *Saxicola Rubetra*; European Stonechat, *Saxicola Rubicola*; Northern Wheatear *Oenanthe*; Isabelline Wheatear, *Oenanthe Isabellina*; Desert Wheatear, *Oenanthe Deserti*; Pied Wheatear, *Oenanthe Pleschanka*.

Less common birds include crab-plover, *Dromas ardeola,* a distinctive wader with black & white plumage and a heavy bill, at Simaisma, though the resort may change their numbers. North African red-necked Ostrich, *Struthio Camelus,* has been introduced to the Al Reem reserve.

Lizards

Geckos are the most numerous lizard in species and overall numbers; Arabian desert gecko, *Bunopus tuberculatus*, rough-tailed gecko, *Cyrtopodion scabrum*; Heyden's gecko, *Hemidactylus robustus*, are all found.

The yellow-belly house gecko, *Hemidactylus flaviviridis*, as its name suggests is the species commonly seen inside buildings where they feed on insects. This may well be the most commonly seen lizard in Qatar.

Other lizards include Persian Leaf-Toed Gecko, *Hemidactylus Persicus*; Arabian Short-Fingered Gecko *Stenodactylus Arabicus*; Slevin's Short-Fingered Gecko, *Stenodactylus Slevini*; Gulf Short-Fingered Gecko, *Pseudoceramodactylus Khobarensis*; Persian Rock Gecko, *Pristurus Rupestris*; Arabian Desert Lizard, *Acanthodactylus Opheodurus*; Blanford's Short-Nosed Desert Lizard, *Mesalina Brevirostris*; Hadhramaut Sand Lizard, *Mesalina Adramitana*; Yellow-Spotted Agama, *Trapelus Flavimaculatus*; Arabian Toad-Headed Agama, *Phrynocephalus Arabicus*; Eastern Skink, *Scincus Mitranus*.

Arabian Toad-Headed Agama

The strangest lizard of Qatar is Zarudny's worm lizard, *Diplometopon zarudnyi*, a limbless subterranean lizard. The largest lizards are Desert Monitor *Varanus griseus* which can reach over 90cm from the nose to the tip of the tail. They are active hunters and eat other reptiles including the Egyptian spiny-tailed lizard *Uromastyx aegyptia* which is slightly smaller at up to 80cm.

There is a toad species, the African common toad *Sclerophrys regularis* that may have been introduced from Egypt. Though Qatar is a hyper-arid country, these toads are expanding their distribution making use of artificial irrigation systems.

Snakes include Sindh Saw-Scaled Viper, *Echis Carinatus Sochureki,* a venomous ambush hunter of perhaps up to 50cm in length; possibly the Desert Black Snake, *Walterinnesia Aegyptia,* this can exceed a meter in length and is a venomous hunter of small animals; Hooded Malpolon / False Cobra, *Malpolon Moilensis,* a venomous rodent eater that grows to over 1.5m; Flowerpot Snake, *Rhamphotyphlops Braminus,* a worm-like snake of only a few cm in length, found in soil; Crowned Dwarf Snake, *Eirenis Coronella*, a small non-venomous snake of only about 30cm length; Crowned Leaf-Nosed Snake, *Lytorhynchus Diadema*, again this is non-venomous but slightly larger at up to 50cm; Clifford's Diadem Snake, *Spalerosophis Diadema Cliffordi,* a six foot long hunter of rodents that is very mildly venomous.

Insects

Moths and butterflies of Qatar are thought to number less than 35 species including the Blue Pansy *Junonia Orithya*; Clouded Yellow *Colias Croceus*; Painted Lady *Vanessa Cardui*, whose family is also familiar in Europe.

Sea Mammals

Despite being almost landlocked and shallow, The Gulf (this phrase is used in this book in preference to the Arabian Gulf that is used in the Arab World or Persian Gulf that is used elsewhere) has many sea mammals.

Bottle nosed Dolphin

These include Orca / Killer Whale *Orcinus Orca*, Bryde's Whale *Balaenoptera Edeni*, Indo-Pacific Bottlenose Dolphin *Tursiops Aduncus*, Indo-Pacific Humpbacked Dolphin *Sousa Chinensis*, Spinner Dolphin *Stenella Longirostris*, often seen leaping out of the sea and rotating its body and Dugong, *Dugong*. The Dugong can grow to around three metres and weigh some 500kg. They feed in shallow waters on seagrass, which means The Gulf is an ideal habitat. A single calf is born after a year's pregnancy and is dependent for almost two years, after which it might live for a further 65 years.

Sea Turtles

The Gulf is home to several sea reptiles, including the Hawksbill turtle *Eretmochelys imbricate* and Green Turtle *Chelonia mydas*, both of which are found in Qatar's seas.

Green Turtles are the most common in Qatar's waters, where they feed on seagrass but do not appear to nest in Qatar, while Hawksbill do nest, but the adults move elsewhere to feed in coral reefs. The Hawksbill has a hawk beak-like shaped mouth, while the Green Turtle's is more rounded.

The most detailed knowledge of any turtle is for the Green Turtle; however, it is likely that the Hawksbill has a similar lifestyle in most respects.

Only female turtles return to the land and then just to lay eggs; males never return to land after hatching. The female Hawksbill may reach maturity around 20 years and Green Turtle from 25 onwards. A mature adult Green Turtle may measure 120cm shell length and weigh 170kg, while a Hawksbill may measure 85cm and weigh 65kg. The eggs are laid in a sandy beach with a relatively shallow slope. In Qatar, Fuwayrit beach is a prime location. This beach is closed, as a result, at peak nesting season 1st April to 31st July.

Mating for turtles takes place at sea near the beach, following which the female will lay eggs perhaps up to 140, with the Green Turtle repeating this four times over a few weeks. They then leave, migrating to feeding grounds that may be hundreds of kilometres away. Each turtle returns to breed after 2-3 years, undoubtedly returning to their hatching beach to breed when they mature. As with many other reptiles, the temperature of the environment surrounding the egg decides the sex of the hatchling. More females develop with a temperature over 30C and more males under 30C. The impact that global heating will have on the sex ratio is clear and presumably will have an effect on total numbers over the long term unless they relocate to different, cooler areas to nest. The nesting process is designed to camouflage the location of the eggs, but even so, foxes may find and dig up a nest and eat the eggs. Around 60 days after the eggs are laid, they hatch, and the hatchlings will co-ordinate their eruption from the nest, so they appear en-mass and scramble together towards the sea. On their way to the sea, Ghost Crabs predate the hatchlings, *Ocypode rotundata*, Gulls, Foxes and in the sea by Fish. The result of this predation and other death causes is that perhaps 990 out of every 1,000 eggs laid may never give rise to an adult. The young turtle may spend the next five years in open waters feeding on krill and other small marine life before moving to shallow waters.

Green Turtle

The Green Turtle feeds on seagrass and algae while Hawksbill is omnivorous, though preferring sea sponges, which though toxic to many sea animals, do not affect the Hawksbill turtle.

Other sea reptiles include various sea snakes, which are found generally in shallow waters and are best given a wide berth. They include the Annulated Sea Snake *Hydrophis cyanocinctus*, the Gulf Sea Snake *Hydrophis lapemoides*, Reef Sea Snake *Hydrophis ornatus* in shallow water including sandy bottomed areas, Yellow Sea Snake *Hydrophis spiralis*, Yellow Bellied Sea Snake *Pelamis platurus* which may reach over two metres and does inhabit shallow water. All are venomous.

Nature Reserves

There are 12 land reserves in Qatar, two of which also include marine areas. The reserves, in most cases, seem little different in development from places outside the reserve's boundary. Most are freely accessible.

Ash Shahaniyah covers 12sq km in central Qatar. It was a sanctuary for the endangered Arabian Oryx from Muaither farm. Today there is also a pen for ostriches.

The 54sq km Al Masshabiya reserve is in southwest Qatar, near the Abu Samara border. Here there are sandy plains with some hills and valleys, and seasonal grass, herbs and wild trees grow on sand dunes in the reserve. Arabian Oryx, gazelle and other endangered animals were settled here.

The Al Eraiq reserve is next to Al Masshabiya and is intended to protect its vegetation from overgrazing.

In north-east Qatar, 64km from Doha, Al Thakhira was chosen as a natural land and sea reserve and included the small island of Um Far opposite the housing at Al Thakhira and natural mangroves. The reserve has rich marine biodiversity and *Avicenna marina* mangrove.

The Al Reem reserve lies on the western coast and covers around 16 percent of Qatar's total land area and has distinctive calcareous formations alongside the western coast. The reserve is recognised under UNESCO's Man and the Biosphere Program.

The Al Wasil nature reserve measures around 36sq km. It was chosen in line with the biodiversity strategy aims and to limit the rapid urbanisation on Qatar's eastern coast.

Khor Al Udaid, also known as the 'Inland Sea', was made a land and sea nature reserve in 2007 and stretches over around 1833sq km. It has large, white sand dunes and presents a unique mix of geological terrains and environmental factors, creating potential natural habitats for various flora and fauna species.

Despite it being a reserve, 4x4 vehicles use it as a recreation area, and tourist camps line the shore.

The 53sq km Al Rafa reserve is found near Al Rayyan and Al Wajba areas, west of Doha.

Smaller reserves are the Sunai reserve, northwest of Doha; Um Al Amad Reserve 25km northeast from Doha; Um Qarn 30km north from Doha.

Finally, Irkaya Farm is off the Abu Samra Road about 50km west of Doha in the south-central plain of Qatar. Though also a nature reserve, the area is a man-made environment of sewage settling ponds and agricultural pivot fields and it is these that attract wildlife, most especially birds.

Agriculture

Perhaps the key reason man has been able to survive on the Qatar peninsula is access to the sea and a symbiotic relationship with the Camel. Searing heat, intense sun and lack of rain mean that agriculture in Qatar depends on man-made help, which includes permanent irrigation. Farming, as a result, has in the past been subsistence, with limited scope for crops and a vast range area needed for animal grazing.

There are no permanent rivers in Qatar, so most water, until recently, was a direct result of local rains with the run-off fed into localised water catchment features. Qatar's soils are relatively shallow, with high salt levels and low nutrients due to the high evaporation and high temperatures. These issues do make any form of crop cultivation difficult.

Today, most water for agriculture in Qatar is pumped up from two aquifers: the Aruma aquifer in southwest Qatar (recharged from the west and Saudi Arabia) and the more critical Rus aquifer northwest of Doha.

Agriculture is probably possible over less than 300sq km of Qatar, while the actual use is around 85sq km.

Date Palm

The quintessential tree of Arabia, the **Date Palm** *Phoenix dactylifera,* is grown over about 24sq km in Qatar. Date Palms have been cultivated in The Gulf region since the Bronze Age. The lack of large quantities of water needed for successful growth must have made date cultivation a peripheral activity in Qatar.

The date tree, in modern agriculture, is almost entirely dependent on man for fruit production. The tree is single-sex, and therefore female flowering trees need a separate male tree for pollination. Male date trees do not produce fruit and thus 'waste' space. Therefore, an artificial ratio of around one male tree to 100 female trees is created. This results in each female tree requiring artificial pollination.

Artificial irrigation is needed for date palms in Qatar today. This is typically by drip-feed irrigation. After about 8 years, the tree can produce fruit. Date Palms can grow to a height of around 20 metres, living approximately 90 years, depending on the variety. All aspects of the tree and date fruit cultivation are labour intensive; however, the fruit which ripens in mid-summer has a high value, so there is a reward. Ripe dates have a high sugar content, so the fruit, after either drying or being compressed into a mass, is not easily damaged by bacteria or fungus. The date fruit can therefore be stored and used after perhaps two years. Qatar now has around 600,000 date palms, producing about 21,000 tons of fruit.

Other agriculture

Root vegetables include beet, carrots, onions and potatoes, while greenhouse crops include cucumbers, peppers, strawberries and tomatoes. Other fruit and vegetables are almost all imported along with wheat imports of over 250,000tons.

Livestock

Qatar's livestock animals include more than 128,000 head of sheep, 78,000 goats, and over 22,000 cattle that are principally used as dairy cows. These animals are mainly imported or the descendants of recently imported animals. Most cows are at the Baladna Farm (the name means 'our country' farm), north of Doha at Al Khor. Poultry and egg production can supply over 600,000kg of meat a year and 250,000,000 eggs.

Following the economic blockade of Qatar, the country hopes to further improve its food security.

There are well over 1,000 horses, seen in equestrian centres and also used by officials in Souq Waqif. There are also around 24,000 Camels, a mix of local origin and imported animals.

All these animals rely on feed being provided, so the grass fodder is grown on large pivot fields in the south and north of the country.

Pivot field under irrigation

Baladna Farm has invested in farmland in Romania to grow fodder, which will then be imported to the Qatar farm. This fodder may be fed fresh, if grown on the Qatar cattle farm, or hay. The company is also setting up dairy operations in Malaysia and the Philippines.

Historic sea resource use

Excavations at Bin Ghannam Island (also called Al Khor Island after the nearby island or Purple Island) have revealed ample evidence of fish and mollusc exploitation. Tools found include fishhooks dating to 5610BC. This inclusion of purple in the island's name comes from the island being a base in the exploitation of purple dye from a shellfish *Thais savigny*, a murex sea snail. Vast quantities of the shellfish produce a dye that is a variety of 'Tyrian purple', the imperial purple of Rome and elsewhere. Shell middens show a lengthy timeline of occupation at this site. The structures appear to have had a cycle of use, abandonment and then reuse, over hundreds of years, perhaps as a base for seasonal activities such as Pearling. At Ras Abrouq, on the coast of west Qatar, occupation from as early as around 5,000BC with potsherds and the remains of fish found. Clearly, the coast and sea were exploited by early occupants of Qatar.

Exploitation of marine molluscs (*Pinctada sp)* the pearl oyster, has been suggested from excavations at more than a dozen sites on the coast of Eastern Arabia dating from between the 6th-4th millennium BC. This activity included Pearl diving, and was a seasonal practice, which in historical times was concentrated between April-September with the Pearls exported, probably to Mesopotamia.

Population & Gdp

During the 21st century, Qatar's population (figures given by the United Nations and Qatar's government) has increased almost as rapidly as its economy (figures from World Bank).

As of March 2023 the Qatar Government assessed the population (psa.gov.qa) at 3,005,069 appx. 72% male & 28% female. This overwhelming skew towards males is because of the large numbers of single male migrant workers employed for their labour and skills. It is thought that (as a rough approximation)

Indian nationals make up 25% of the total, Bangladeshi 12 %, Nepalese 13% and Pilipino around 10%. Citizens of Qatar probably account for less than 13% of the total population and British nationals around 1%, with those from the USA lower than 0.5%.

Much of this rise in population has been due to the economic impetus provided by Natural Gas and, to a lesser extent, oil. Rising government income & expenditure has led to massive urban development and large-scale investment projects. These include the Port, Airport, Metro system and vast new towns such as The Pearl and Lusail. High profile events, along with their infrastructure, include the 2006 Asian Games, 2011 Arab Games, F1 (Formula 1 Grand Prix) Qatar Grand Prix 2021, FIFA Arab Cup, football 2022 World Cup and upcoming Asian Cup (12 January – 10 February 2024).

Year	Population	GDP Billions of Dollars
1950	25,000	
1960	47,000	
1970	108,000	
1980	222,000	17.63
1990	474,000	6.27
2000	591,000	18.09
2010	1,699,435	119.17
2011	1,732,717	167.78
2012	1,832,903	186.83
2013	2,101,288	198.73
2014	2,172,065	206.23
2015	2,235,355	161.74
2016	2,291,368	151.73
2017	2,338,085	161.10
2018	2,674,320	183.34
2019	2,687,871	175.84
2020	2,684,329	144.41
2021	2,677,001	179.68
2022	2,909,134	

The contract to hold an annual race of the F1– the first being 8 October 2023 has cemented Qatar’s position as a major host for sports events. The workers for all these has fuelled the tremendous increase in Qatar's population. Population growth is expected to continue until 2070, when it may reach 3,400,000 and gradually drift slightly lower after that.

Towns And Major Divisions

In 2015, the regional break up of population (according to Qatar's Planning and Statistical Authority, QPSA) by administrative region shows Doha, Al Wakrah to its south, and

Al Dayyan to Doha's north on the central east coast have a combined population of 50% of the total population in Qatar. Given that much of Qatar is within 60 minutes' drive of the Corniche in Doha, most of the country's towns and villages are within the potential commuter belt of Doha.

Municipalities in Qatar (appx figures)	
Doha	956,457
Al Rayyan* (south-west Qatar)	605,712
Al Wakrah* (southeast Qatar)	299,037
Umm Salal (central Qatar)	90,835
Al Khor (north-east Qatar)	202,031
Al Shamal (north Qatar)	8,794
Al Dayyan (east central Qatar)	54,339
Al Shahaniyah (central west Qatar)	187,571

*Effectively suburbs of Doha.

Al Khor الخور: GPS - 25.680, 51.496; [PAGE 112] location – Al Khor is about a 50km drive, north, from central Doha. Public transport -: the Bus station feeding into Al Khor is Lusail – next to the Metro station a 50-minute journey. Focused around a sea lagoon with patches of mangrove, including Bin Ghannam Island , this town has a variety of natural habitats. The fishing harbour, with dozens of dhows and a small retail fish market. Though there are a few historical sites, these are not a 'must see'. Probably the one of most interest today is the house of the grandfather of Sheikh Tamim bin Hamad Al Thani, his mother's father, Abdullah Bin Nasser Al Misnad. The old house is south of the small harbour, just west of a children's play area on the junction of Al Khor Road and Al Arab St. Within Al Khor are restaurants and accommodation. To the north of the main town, Al Khor Community is purpose-built housing for employees at

Qatar Gas and other employers at Ras Laffan 20km to the north. Outlying areas include Al Thakhira and Ash Shafallahiyah.

Al Ruwais الرويس: GPS - 26.131, 51.200; [PAGE 118] location - one of the longest drives in Qatar is the 90 minutes, 110km drive between Al Ruwais, on the coast in northwest Qatar and Doha. Public transport -: Bus stations feeding into Al Ruwais are Al Gharafa Bus Station & Al Khor. Al Ruwais is a port town whose new port was built in 2011 to replace the now-abandoned old port in the town's south. The port principally receives regional cargo, including fruit, vegetables and livestock. These shipments have substantially increased since the Qatar boycott. The port also serves as a fishing port. To the north of the town are sandbar type islands. Southwest of Al Ruwais are several ruined settlements including Al Jamal, Al Khuwair and, 24km southwest, Al Zubarah. The older town of Al Ruwais is just to the modern port's east, with mangroves to the town's east. Offshore are usually dozens of small fishing boats. There are limited accommodation and dining options.

Al Wakrah الوكرة: GPS - 25.177, 51.604; [PAGE 77] location - it's just over 20km drive between Doha and, to its south, Al Wakrah. Public transport -: feeder bus stations are HIA, Industrial Area Bus Station, Al Sudan Bus Station - and into the souq. There is a Metro station, Al Wakrah, on the Red-Line, use the MetroLink bus. Al Wakrah is one of the older, still occupied, settlements in Qatar, dating to at least 1845; today, it is rapidly being subsumed by Doha.

Doha الدوحة: GPS - 25.291, 51.533. [PAGE 45 onwards] By far the largest city in Qatar, probably all the other towns serve as suburbs, dormitory or service towns for Doha. Most of Qatar's key attractions are in Doha, including Souq Waqif, Museum of Islamic Art, Msheireb Museums, National Museum and Katara. Doha's places of interest are listed separately under their names.

Dukhan دخان : GPS - 25.420, 50.794; [PAGE 130] location - Dukhan is about 80km drive west of central Doha Public transport -: Feeders bus station is Industrial Area Bus Station: for the 90-minute journey. Dukhan is a mid-20th century town created to service the nearby Oil Fields. As a 'company town', access is against permit. The area to its north includes Zekreet and the area around 'Film City'.

Lusail لوسيل GPS - 25.417, 51.503; [PAGE 108] about 20km north of central Doha. Public transport is Lusail Metro (Red Line) which has a MetroLink feeder bus service and Lusail Tram. Lusail was empty, sabkha and desert less than 20 years ago. Coastal landfilling and excavation have resulted in a new town and coastline. The development is still at a relatively early stage; however, it does have the 2022 World Cup main stadium, the Lusail Multi-purpose Arena and Lusail Circuit. Place Vendome - another massive shopping mall. The marina area will service sea-based leisure craft and up-market housing. Qetaifan Island will have a range of hotels, including floating hotels. Perhaps the most iconic building is Katara Towers, a crescent-moon shaped building primarily used as a hotel.

Katara Towers - Lusail

Mesaieed (Also Umm Said) **مسيعيد**: GPS - 24.990, 51.549; location - south of Doha by some 40km. Public transport -: Bus feeder stations HIA a 90-minute journey. Mesaieed is a significant town founded after the 2nd World War. Receiving piped crude oil from Dukhan and gas from Ras Laffan and islands near Idd Al Shargi, this is a key industrial area. This flow of gas supports fertilizer, steel and aluminium plants. A major artificial industrial port services other exports. The town has substantial housing projects within it, enabling much of the workforce to have a short commute. Recreational facilities include cricket & football, and there are restaurants. However, the closest hotels are in Sealine, about 20km south of Mesaieed and Al Wakrah, about 20km north of Mesaieed.

Ras Laffan رأس لفان: GPS - 25.892, 51.560; location - Ras Laffan is some 80km north of Doha. Public transport-: Lusail has links to Al Khor south of the industrial area of Ras Laffan. Ras Laffan is an extensive industrial development and is the major employer in northern Qatar, forming part of Qatar's massive energy industry. To its northwest is Al Jassasiya's Rock Carvings [97].

The Pearl اللؤلؤة GPS 25.368, 51.551 [PAGE 107] is an extensive man-made development to the north of Doha. Public transport includes the Legtaifiya Metro station on the Red Line – with free MetroLink buses (05:50-22:00 daily) running into the development. It is primarily man-made islands, principally with apartment housing, though hotels, retail and restaurants abound. The style is a modern take on a European Mediterranean town, intended to be reminiscent of the atmosphere of Venice, with waterways and high rise buildings!. Many of the properties are available to buy or long lease. Other areas in Qatar also have similar purchase options, including Al Khor Resort, Msheireb, Old Ghanim and more. The most visited sections of The Pearl are Porto Arabia, Viva Bahriya and the Qanat Quarter, each of which are enclosed lagoons with a Pearl-like Island in their centre.

Government, Politics And International Relations

Qatar is a Monarchy whose head of state bears the title of Amir (sometimes spelt Emir) and honorific title Sheikh. The ruler is the head of state, head of government, overseer of the judiciary and commander-in-chief of Qatar's military and security forces.

Unlike, to an extent, the United Kingdom and the United States of America, the head of state in Qatar is treated, written and talked about with considerable respect by the very deferential Qatari society. *Lese-majesty* (offense against the sovereign) is a crime in Qatar.

A Prime Minister chairs the Council of Ministers; their Ministries deal with their respective functions. Semi-government bodies also administer and execute the policies of the Government.

A Shura Council (Consultative Assembly) was set up in 1972, with 45 members who act as individuals rather than members of a political party (which are not permitted). The people who can vote are Qatari nationals, defined (broadly) by law as men and women who were long term residents of Qatar in 1930 or their descendants. The voting age is aged 18 or older. The candidates themselves must be Qatari and over 30. From 2021 there have been 30 members who are elected and 15 appointed by the Amir. Currently all elected members are Male, and the Amir appointed one Female member.

Though Qatar is not a democracy, the Government seeks a consensus from Qatar's nationals for its policies and their implementation.

Qatar is a member of the Gulf Cooperation Council, a six-member body whose other members are Bahrain, Kuwait, Oman, Saudi Arabia and the UAE.

Qatar's international relations have often been at odds with Saudi Arabia and other states, including Bahrain, the UAE, and Egypt's current Government. Notable was the 2017 Qatar diplomatic crisis with those four states. Areas of dispute have included claimed Qatari support for Islamic groups and the development of the Al Jazeera media group, with its dynamic and investigational style of reporting.

Al Jazeera studio Doha

Oman and, to a lesser extent, Iran have historically good ties with Qatar, these have improved since 2017. Since the dispute with Saudi Arabia, Qatar has pivoted towards Turkey, with its industrial and military capability. Military ties have also been enhanced with Britain and the USA.

Food security has also been a focus since 2017. Farm investments have been made in Australia, Malaysia, Oman, Philippines, Romania, Sudan and more.

Using the wealth available to its Government, Qatar has made considerable investments within the economies of key allies, including Britain, France and the USA.

Economy & Money: Banks, ATM and Money in General

Credit and debit cards are widely accepted in Qatar. Transport options and most major services such as petrol stations, restaurants, hotels and so on accept cards. Contactless (tap & go) is the norm, except when using an ATM (cash machine). If your Bank permits you to advise them the countries you will travel to – use that reporting ability. ATMs are easy to find in major shopping areas, some hotels and petrol stations. Normally you will have a charge of a few dollars per cash withdrawal and the exchange rate between your card's currency and QAR. Apple Pay and Google Pay can be used in many places. Be sure you have some Qatari Rials, though US$ are often accepted in tourist places. If you want to use US$s, bring notes issued after 2007 as earlier notes are not taken. If Qatari Riyals are not available in your own country, HIA does have exchange counters in arrivals. Money Exchanges are spread through towns and in many malls. If exchanging major currencies, the rates are comparable in any Qatari money changer. There are also exchange counters in departures, or you could drop your Qatari money into local charity boxes.

Cash

Qatar issues currency in notes (Riyals) and coins (Dirhams). The coins are of little value, with 100 dirhams in 1 Qatari Riyal, and their use is declining. Coins are now only minted in 25 dirhams & 50 dirhams, each having their value on the reverse and on the obverse the date on top with the emblem of Qatar below. There are several hundred QAR dirhams in 1 US$ (unlike the dirham - AED - of the UAE).

Notes are available in values of 1, 5, 10, 50, 100, 200 and 500 Riyals. Each denomination has a distinct colour palette and images. All have Arabic on one side and English on the other.

Economy

Qatar's oil and natural gas resources are the country's main economic engine and government revenue source. They make up around 60% of GDP, 85% of exports, 70% of total government revenue (depending on the fluctuations of oil and gas prices). Key export destinations are Japan, India, South Korea and China. Qatar has agreed to supply LNG (Liquid Natural Gas) to Germany. It supplies around 16% of its LNG to the EU countries as an alternative to Russian gas imports into Europe.

Imports of non-food items are overwhelmingly from the USA and China.

As the government receives much of its income from oil income rather than taxation, its spending drives Qatar's high economic growth and per capita income levels. Robust state spending on public entitlements and booming construction spending, looks set to keep overall economic growth high for many years.

The income from oil and gas that flows into the government is in effect a profit sharing with the production companies. The spending of this income by the Government is the critical engine of the economy.

Using a common source of GDP figures – this is how Qatar compares with some other countries.

Country	IMF est. GDP 2023 US Dollars Billion	IMF est. GDP Per Person 2023 US Dollars
Qatar	219.57	124,834
Luxembourg	86.97	142,490 (2021)
Switzerland	869.60	87,963
United States	26,854.59	80,035
United Kingdom	3,158.93	56,470
United Arab Emirates	498.97	88,221
Saudi Arabia	1,061.902	64,836

GDP (per capita) per wage-earning Qatari is substantially higher than the above raw figures suggest. This gives them an exceptionally high standard of living. The opposite is also true, the low paid manual labourers may earn around US$s 300/400 a month.

Budget	2020 Billion Dollars	2021 Billion Dollars
Total revenue	57.81	43.86 (planned)
Oil Revenue	46.03	
Non-oil revenue	11.78	
Total expenditure	57.67	53.34
Surplus/Deficit	0.14	-9.48

Some figures are omitted Expenditure all figures rounded .

Qatar's reliance on oil and natural gas is likely to remain for the foreseeable future. Proved natural gas reserves exceed 25 trillion cubic meters - 13% of the world's total and the third-largest in the world. Proved oil reserves exceed 25 billion barrels, allowing production to continue at current levels for about 56 years. Despite the dominance of oil and natural gas, Qatar has made significant gains in diversification into non-oil sectors. These include manufacturing, construction, and financial services. The leisure industry and tourism are also an increasing factor. In recent years these non-oil & gas sectors have approached half the total GDP.

Expenditure all figures rounded	2018 Billion Dollars	2019 Billion Dollars	2020 Billion Dollars	2021 Billion Dollars
Government employees' Salaries and Wages	14.36	15.68	16.16	15.86
Current Expenditure	14.72	15.41	15.89	16.63
Small projects	1.236	1.07	0.96	1.10
Major Projects	25.52	24.61	24.66	19.75
Total Expenditure	55.82	56.78	57.67	53.34

Major expenditure headings	US$ total
Defence & Security	11.57
Public Finance	10.93
Municipality and Environment	6.93
Education	4.75
Health	4.53
Culture & Sports (this includes the 2022 World Cup stadiums)	3.57
Transportation and Communication (this includes HIA, the Metro, Lusail Tram and various IT projects)	3.15

However, much of the diversification away from oil and gas also relies on 'added value' products making use of that oil and gas. These include Petro-chemicals (ethylene and methanol extracted from gas by super steam heating) which are fundamental to the plastic industry. Fertilizers (ammonia also created from gas, combined later with nitrogen and urea that uses ammonia and CO2) and finally using gas as a power source for iron and steel smelting.

The major industrial area is **Mesaieed Industrial Area** south of Al Wakrah. The primary industries produce lubricants, fertiliser (as a joint venture with Norsk Hydro using gas as a raw material), fuel additives, vinyl, and chemicals. Using gas as an energy source are aluminium and steel smelters (another joint venture with Norsk Hydro). A major electricity production unit uses natural gas as a power supply. Construction aggregate is both locally sourced and imported, for example, gabbro, an igneous rock similar to basalt, is imported from Oman. North of Mesaieed is the **Hamad Port**, a man-made commercial container port and coastguard and adjacent military port constructed from 2010 in a former area of *sabka*. It handles general containers, machinery, vehicles, imported grain and livestock. Associated with Hamed Port is a port and commercial district, **Um Alhoul.** This is a Free Zone for smaller scale manufacturing, warehousing & logistics, business services and commercial – retail, services, offices. Um Alhoul also is home to a major electricity and water desalination plant that will produce 2.52GW electricity and 514 million litres of water, per day.

North of Doha is **Ras Laffan** which is Qatar's original petrochemical complex, with several LNG plants. Ras Laffan is Qatar's export facility for LNG from Qatar's North Field.

International Transport.

This has a focus on **Hamad International Airport**, which supports the development of Qatar as an international communications hub. Qatar Airways with over 200 passenger jets and more than 25 cargo only jets, uses the airport as its hub and spoke centre serving over 83 countries and 146 destinations. Tourism is a significant focus of diversification. The number of visitors was planned to increase from 2.9million in 2016 to 5.6million in 2023, grow expenditure from US$ Billion 4.75 in 2016 to US$ Billion 10.99 in 2023, an increase in direct contribution to GDP from 3.5% to 4%. Supporting this has been a major redevelopment of **Doha Port** next to the Museum of Islamic Art. This is a leisure port, a destination for cruise ships and leisure marine operations in general. It has 3 or 4 weekly visits by cruise ships and is capable of handling cruise ships of more than 183,000 tonnes and 300m long.

To the south of HIA is **Ras Bufontas**, a free trade zone

which is focused on light industry, emerging technologies and service businesses.

Oil & Gas

Qatar's history of exploration for oil is inextricably linked with oil exploration generally in the Middle East. This is because Qatar is within the historical commercial contract called the 'Red Line Agreement'. This 'Red Line Agreement' grew from an arrangement by Calouste Gulbenkian, who was Armenian born in Ottoman Turkey in 1869, but in 1902 became a British citizen. He was well connected with the Ottoman Sultan Abdul Hamid II, who had just ascended to the throne.

Gulbenkian had promoted the prospects for oil in Mesopotamia (Iraq), which at the time was in the Ottoman Empire. Such was the clear prospects that the Ottoman sultan had large areas of land in Mesopotamia transferred from government ownership directly to his personal control, as the '*Liste Civile*', which also nullified earlier exploration agreements. Over time, German interests obtained small concessions from him in modern Iraq. During this period most of the territory in Persia was signed for exploration under a 1901 agreement with a Briton, William K. D'Arcy. He later unsuccessfully also sought exploration rights within Ottoman domains.

The Young Turk revolution in 1908 altered the economic situation in favour of British interests in the Ottoman Empire. In 1910, the National Bank of Turkey was set up to support British interests in the Ottoman Empire with Calouste Gulbenkian as a director.

Calouste Gulbenkian

He negotiated an agreement between various interested parties, and in 1912 Turkish Petroleum Co was founded. Shares were distributed - 25% Deutsche Bank (which was also involved in the Berlin-Constantinople-Baghdad Railway project), 25% to a subsidiary of Shell (Anglo-Saxon Petroleum) and 50% for National Bank of Turkey, of which Gulbenkian controlled 15%, excluded was D'Arcy. The outcome of the agreement was a non-compete clause that the partners would only work in cooperation with each other within the territory agreed, in effect a form of cartel.

Despite all this manoeuvring, no company was granted an exploration agreement. Finally in 1912, it was agreed that Anglo-Persian Oil Company (a successor to D'Arcy) would obtain 47.5% of Turkish Petroleum Co, Deutsche Bank 25%, Anglo-Saxon Petroleum Co would obtain 22.5%, and Calouste Gulbenkian would receive 5%, after which he became known as 'Mr 5%'. Shortly after this, the Ministry of Finance in Turkey granted a concession lease. 1st World War paused final negotiations, resulting in German shares being transferred to the French Government's Compagnie Francaise des Petroles.

After the 1st World War, the United States of America wanted to have oil exploration rights in the region. Several USA companies co-operated as the 'Near East Development Corporation' NEDC. During several years of negotiations, an eventual agreement was reached that the USA could join the cartel. The share was Anglo-Persian Oil Company, Royal Dutch/Shell, the Compagnie Francaise des Petroles and NEDC at 23.75 % each and Gulbenkian still at 5%.

He was either essential to the success of the operation or a superb negotiator. Gulbenkian's interest in oil was transferred to his foundation as Partex. Partex was sold to a Thai organisation in 2019. The agreement was signed in July 1928 and the company named Petroleum Concessions Ltd. The territorial boundaries of the agreement were formed when a map was produced with a red-line drawn through it, marking the boundaries of the concession area. The red-line ran from Turkey to the south, covering the Levant, Iraq and the Arabian Peninsula (except Kuwait). This agreement collapsed after 2nd World War and the establishment of Saudi Arabia.

Qatar was included in this general situation through a new subsidiary, Qatar Petroleum Co.

In Qatar, the first talks for exploration took place in 1922. The Anglo-Persian Oil Company (of that cartel) surveyed in 1926, but no oil was found. After a workable oil discovery in

Bahrain in 1932, a further concession for Qatar was signed on 17 May 1935 with Anglo-Persian representatives for 75 years. In return 400,000 rupees was given on signature and 150,000 rupees to be paid annually, and additionally with royalties. Britain agreed to supply enhanced security. In October 1938, the first oil well was sunk in **Dukhan,** and oil was found in 1939. However due to 2nd World War, exports did not begin until 1949.

During the early 1950s labour for Qatar's oil industry was initially foreign. Later Qatari nationals were increasingly employed. This increase in the number of Qatari nationals employed led to improved labour rights and higher wages for the workforce.

Offshore-oil was explored by the International Marine Oil Company, and Shell Qatar got these fields in 1952. Following this, oil was discovered in 1960 at Idd Al Shaqi, (the concession was later acquired by Occidental Petroleum of Qatar). These offshore fields use Halul Island, just under 100km north-east of Doha for oil storage and export.

Qatar joined OPEC in 1961, a year after the organisation was formed. In 1973, the Qatari government obtained 25% of Qatar Petroleum Co shares. In February 1977, the company became wholly owned by Qatar's government.

In 1971, Qatar discovered the **North Dome Gas Field** (**South Pars)** in The Gulf. This field straddled the maritime border between Iran and Qatar. Production started in 1981 which, eventually, turned out to be the largest gas field in the world. In 2015, Qatar supplied to the UAE about 7.548Billion Cubic Meters of gas and Oman 2.067Billion Cubic Meters of gas via the Dolphin Gas Project, which was established in 1999.

The Qatar Government withdrew from OPEC on 1st January 2019 (during the Qatar boycott period), explaining that it wished to increase gas production by 43%. Oil production in Qatar is some 1,530,000 barrels per day (2020) and 171 Billion cubic meters of gas a year.

Culture

Culturally Qatar is full of contrasts, jaw-droppingly modern, yet deeply conservative; remarkably insular yet potentially open.

Although most people living in Qatar are not Qatari nationals, this section gives an overview of Qatari nationals unless noted otherwise.

There are two fundamental, almost inextricably linked, areas in Qatar that impact its culture; the role of the family, both nuclear and extended and of Islam.

The Qatari nuclear family, Grandparents, Parents and Children form the key social unit in Qatar. The extended family, which includes first cousins and other cousins, creates other units. Finally, the larger social unit, a Tribe, offers a social framework for its members and an identity familiar to other Qataris.

Marriage

Marriages are generally made with the parents' agreement. In many cases, the family has arranged or organised these. Marriages from within the extended family account for around 42% of the total (Qatari Government Ministry of Development Planning and Statistics - MDPS - 2016 statistics report – now the Qatar Planning and Statistics Authority QPSA). Within all marriages, 24% are first cousins. Typically, according to the MDPS report, male Qataris are 26 when they first marry, and females are 24. Polygynous marriage is allowed in Qatar, and the MDPS figures show they are around 8 % of marriages. Fertility rates (the number of children a woman has during her life) has declined from 4 in 2007 to 2.6 in 2019 for Qatari females according to MDPS & the later QPSA figures.

Marriages are often regarded as an agreement between the bride's and groom's families. A contract, *Melcha* (*Milka*), is drawn up and witnessed by suitable people, ideally including the Imam (religious leader) of the major local mosque. Typically, a dowry is paid by the male's family to the female's, after agreement on what it should be.

The *Shabka*, a celebratory event, might be held by the

families to present gifts. This celebration is followed by agreeing on the date for the marriage, which might be weeks or months away. Before the actual night of the wedding, a '*henna* party' may be held for the females of the families. This might be in a commercial hall specially built for weddings or a hotel's ballroom. An event on the night of the marriage is held; the bride and females will have a separate venue from the groom and men. Only female guests usually attend the bride's party, perhaps with a strict no camera rule; however, the memory will be enhanced as guests receive a gift. At all celebratory events, the chief participants are at one end of the room and guests always formally greet them.

The men's event is complete with sword dancing and traditional music until, perhaps in a chain of hooting cars, the men's party leads the groom to his new bride.

Traditionally, socialising occurs from within the extended nuclear family, with male members and female members forming separate groups during the week. Social activity, during the week, centres on coffee shops and modern malls, along with informal groups in parks and beachside locations.

At weekends, relaxing with the nuclear family is the focus, though as can be imagined, first cousins of both a husband and wife may be included as they are also the brother or sister of a spouse.

A significant source of an individual's identity in Qatar is their Tribe. A Tribe is a group of people who share a common identity that, in many instances, is the belief they are descended from a single man and, by implication, his wives. It may be that a Tribe is a historical accretion of smaller units that today share a collective identity.

Names & titles

Historically the head of a Tribe and also major sections within a more prominent Tribe would have the honorific/title Sheikh (a daughter or wife will be a Sheikha). As Sheikha can also be a female's name, check what is the family name to see which of the two possibilities you have. If it's Al Thani, you will have the honorific. In Qatar, a Sheikh title is now reserved exclusively for members of the ruling Al Thani family. The word Amir, which means, in this example, prince, is reserved for the ruler. These uses and exclusions do vary in other countries. A Tribe's members will have the tribal name as their family name/surname, for instance, Al Kubaisi (Al means 'the', one of the members of the Tribe). A member of this Tribe might be called Mohammed bin Ali bin Abdullah. His first name, Mohammed, is followed by '*bin*', which means son (of), Ali (his father), the son of Abdullah, who therefore is Mohammed's Grandfather. A female has a similar name line-up, for example, Fatima bint Ali bin Abdullah Al Kubaisi; here, the first name is Fatima. The word '*bint*' means daughter, in this case of Ali. On marriage, both the man and woman keep their birth names; however, children have their first name, followed by their father's name and so on.

Town and Country

Qatar has two intermingling cultures; a *Bedouin* one, the traditional nomadic society. Historically, a Tribe may have had a territory, which was acknowledged as their collective land that other people could enter with permission. Traits such as bravery alongside generosity, epitomised through hospitality, are core to bedouins' culture. Alongside this culture is the *hadhr,* a culture of settled people. In Qatar, this is mainly on the coast. The fixed location for these families allowed for educational establishments to develop. However, although the family was settled, male members might be away for weeks, months or occasionally years at a time as they worked in Pearling or commerce overseas. This obliged women to be involved in many areas in society that men might have otherwise occupied.

Social Greetings

Greetings between members of the same sex is a matter of tradition, perhaps a 'cheek kiss', once on each cheek if you know each other, maybe twice on the same cheek if you are more than acquaintances, a multiplicity if you are friends and haven't seen each other for a long time. A nose kiss may be given if they are perhaps from the same family. Occasionally a person may kiss the forehead of another person; this is a sign of deference to that other person. Usually, during these greetings, the right hand is held, or the right hand is placed on the left shoulder of the other person.

Verbal greetings in Qatar are often formulaic and lengthy. Qataris inquire about the other person's health and family, and the other person reciprocates these. If between men, these enquiries are never about a man's wife, as this is considered disrespectful.

Between a Qatari and non-Qatari, a normal handshake will be used, often the hand is held for a long time by people who are friends.

Often, even if you have invited a Qatari person or group of Qatari people for coffee or a meal in a restaurant, there will be a good-natured disagreement after the meal amongst everyone as to who will have the 'honour' of paying for the meal. Each person will happily pay, especially if you are the only foreigner. However, if you have invited people - insist; and accept the reciprocal invitation.

Although achieving consensus is preferred, within Qatar decisions are top-down without real delegation of responsibility or authority. This is the form of decision making in many businesses, where the culture is Arab and, to an extent, other Asian cultures. Even in the choice of restaurant, the senior person is deferred to.

In businesses and areas such as meetings for work, a person is addressed using the type of their university degree or job title, followed by first name, Engineer Ahmed or His Excellency Khalid. To an extent, this explains some of the importance of achieving certification. It may be that a man is called *Abu* Mohammed or *Abu* Miriam; *Abu* means father, and here he is being acknowledged as a father. It is also a sign that he is known well by the person who addresses him, as they also know his child's name. A similar range of address terms are used for women though the term *umm*, which means mother, is used.

Qatari Clothing

Clothing for both sexes is expected to be modest – in respect of concealing the body. Qatari men wear the white *thobe* (it may be a dark colour in winter), either with a small stand-up collar

(Mandarin style or western formal shirt collar). Both styles have cuffed sleeves often worn with cufflinks. The *thobe* is usually tailor-made for the wearer incorporating a choice of material quality, shade of material, overall design and fit. Under the *thobe*, lightweight long *sirwal* pants are worn, and also a vest (undershirt). The *ghutra* headdress is usually a heavily starched white cloth (it may be red & white or other design), formed from a square of material and folded once across two corners to form a triangle, the longest edge forms the front with the apex of the two shorter edges down the back. It is worn in several styles according to the wearer's preference; very distinctive to Qatar is what is known as a 'cobra' style, which you will know when you see it. Under the *ghutra* is a small *ghafiya* cap that gives some grip for the *ghutra* and stops any oil from the hair from touching it. The black circle of rope, *agil,* on the *ghutra* (often with a long tasselled cord at the back that is a very Qatari style) was in the past used to hobble the front legs of a Camel; some religious men do not wear this on the *ghutra*. The men wear formal sandals, or possibly shoes, and in addition to the cufflinks wear a stylish watch and frequently a pen in the *thobe's* chest pocket. Worn for prestige on special occasions such as weddings is a *bisht* - a traditional long, white, brown or black lightweight Arabic cloak trimmed in gold thread.

The man's ensemble explicitly states the wearer's identity; he is a Qatari.

Qatari women typically wear a black (or another colour) cloak *abaya* worn over the shoulders and reaches just above the ground. Over her head and covering the hair and neck is a scarf *shayla,* also known as a *hijab*. Under this *abaya* and *shayla* may well be the latest fashion from New York, London, Paris or Milan, elaborate Lebanese style fashion or only jeans and T-shirt, along with western style underwear.

DO'S AND DONT'S

The below is intended to be helpful and create awareness, obviously circumstances will have an impact in any outcome. A short-term visitor is likely to come and go in Qatar without having to even consider any of these.

Criticism

Things that would cause embarrassment and loss of face to a Qatari should absolutely be avoided. Criticism might be given indirectly, circumspectly, and never in front of others to prevent that loss of face. Advice on what to do where any criticism is possible is worth looking for through a person known to you both, who is more senior to the person you want to address.

Pointing with a single finger, making a fist or banging a desk to make a point are not acceptable behaviours. Wearing footwear in a home, showing the soles of the feet (even if covered by socks/tights) or footwear's sole should be avoided. However, this is not a critical issue as inevitably, somebody's feet will be in the general direction of another person in a large group. In traditional meals, food might be eaten with the hand. Here, avoid using the left hand to handle food, as this hand is used for personal cleansing; this use of hand restriction still applies even if you are left-handed. A drinking glass should also be held in the right hand.

Discussing Politics and Religion

Although conversations between groups of friends and family members include politics and religion, these topics are unlikely to be discussed in front of people they are less familiar with. Indeed, if you are a foreign national in Qatar, conversation about politics and religion should be avoided; discussion about the ruling family should also be cautious. In all cases, a positive, admiring viewpoint is usually the best attitude.

Do not discuss your own religion unless you are a Muslim. Proselytising is prohibited by law, and a positive viewpoint of your own religion might be misconstrued as proselytising.

Interactions with a different gender

Interaction between non-family males and females occurs within an environment considered acceptable within Islam. Naturally, there is some variance; however, in this area caution is ideal. Culturally it is inappropriate for a female to be alone with an unrelated male. This includes being in a vehicle (clearly, taxis are an elastic area where sitting in the rear is best if you are a female passenger), elevator, room and so on. These situations should be avoided as misinterpretation can easily be made by the other person or others who are aware of it.

Greeting members of the opposite sex is also an area where traditions play a role. Physically touching a member of a different sex is usually considered inappropriate; for example, a male and female would not typically shake each other's hands. In very conservative Islamic society, touching the flesh (such as a hand) of the opposite sex is considered an intimate act. In these situations, the female would take the lead in either offering or withdrawing her hand from being shaken. She should try to assess how conservative the male is. Generally, if you are the female, consider the circumstances. If it is a business meeting, a handshake might be more appropriate than in casual social interaction.

General Language

According to the Qatar Penal Code Article (290) "Anyone who makes gestures, dares to say or sing immoral things or perform an infamous deed in a public place or an open space is convicted to no more than six months in prison and to a fine of no more than three thousand riyals, or to one of these two penalties." This is reinforced by article (294) "Anyone who instigates debauchery, dissipation or adultery in public by words, gestures or any other means is convicted to no less than six months and no more than three years in prison." This applies to instances of flipping the bird, for example when in the 'privacy' of your own car.

Physical Intimacy

Avoid public display of affection with members of the opposite sex in public. Avoiding this will also avoid the possibility of a member of the public complaining to security personal that you have offended public decency. There have been regular well publicised instances of arrests for kissing in Dubai (the poster city for Gulf tourism) regarding this type of action.

LGBT+

Homosexuality is absolutely prohibited in Qatar; penalties can include several years imprisonment, physical lashing and potentially death. LGBT+ symbols and their display are an area where caution is suggested. During the World Cup in Qatar there were several instances of people wearing clothing with rainbow colours being refused entry to games. Same-sex marriage is not recognised. Consider that public homosexual sexual activity will bring a more severe punishment than similar heterosexual activity. Additionally, 'cross-dressing' in the case of men, is likely to result in arrest. Do review your own government's advice (see below).

Churches

Several churches have premises in Doha, especially to the south of the F-Ring Road, at the junction with the Doha Expressway. Their congregations include Coptic Egyptians, various denominations from India and the Philippines – including Catholic and Protestant. The principal day for services is Friday (the day off for most workers); services are also held on Sunday.

Do read your own country's foreign ministry's advice about Qatari culture www.gov.uk/foreign-travel-advice/qatar/local-laws-and-customs travel.state.gov/content/travel/en/international-travel/International-Travel-Country-Information-Pages/Qatar.html

Language Phrases

Below is a simplified range of words and phrases. They do not have the various gender specific suffixes and prefixes.

English	transliteration	Arabic
hello	marhaba	مرحبا
how are you	kayf halik	كيف حالك
I am fine	ana bikher	أنا بخير
what's your name?	ma ismik	ما اسمك
my name is	ana ismi	انا إسمي
welcome.	ahlan wa sahlan.	اهلاً وسهلاً
good morning.	sabah alkhair	صباح الخير
good evening.	masa alkhair	مساء الخير
yes	naam	نعم
no	laa	لا
welcome, help yourself	tfadhal	تفضل
thanks.	shukran -	شكراً
goodbye	maa assalama	مع السلامة
sorry	asif	آسف
please	minfadhlak	من فضلك
about / almost	yaani	يعني
where is the	ayn al	اين ال
company	ash-sharika	الشركة
hospital	mustashfaa	مستشفى
hotel	alfunduq	الفندق
restaurant	mataam	مطعم
supermarket	subermarket	سوبر ماركت

museum	mathaf	متحف
this is expensive.	haadha ghaali	هذا غالي
no it's cheap.	la inaha rakhisa	لا إنها رخيصة.
thobe	thoob	ثوب
ghutra	ghutra	غترة
aqal	agaal	عقال
black cloak (for women)	abaya	عباءة
headscarf (for women)	shayla	شيلة
veil covering face	niqaab	نقاب
face mask	birqa	برقع
furniture	athaath	أثاث
chair	kursi	كرسي
table	attawlah	الطاولة
bed	assirir	السرير
carpet	sajada	سجادة
jewels	mujawharat	مجوهرات
gold	dhahab	ذهب
silver	fudha	فضة
are these made of real gold	hal hadhih masnuwiat min aldhahab alhaqiqi	هل هذه مصنوعة من الذهب الحقيقي
vegetables	khudrawaat	خضروات
onion	basila	بصلة

cabbage	alkarnab	الكرنب
tomatoes	tamatim	طماطم
cucumbers	khiar	خيار
radishes	fjul	فجل
beans	faswlaya	فاصوليا
potatoes	bitata	بطاطا
fruits	fawakah	فواكه
watermelon	albatikh	البطيخ
lemon	liamun	ليمون
orange	alburtaqali	البرتقالي
dates	tawarikh	تواريخ
banana	mawz	موز
peaches	khukh	خوخ
grapes	aanb	عنب
walnuts	eayn aljamal	عين الجمل
I want to drink	ared an ashrab	اريد أن أشرب.
juice	aasir	عصير
orange juice	aeasir alburtuqal	عصير البرتقال
apple juice.	aasir altafahu.	عصير التفاح
coffee	qahwa	قهوة
tea	shai	شاي
bread	khabaz	خبز
rice	aaruz	أرز
cheese	jbin	جبن
one egg	bidha	البيض

how much is a dozen eggs?	kam hu dazinat min albida?	كم هو دزينة من البيض؟
meat (beef)	lahm	لحم
lamb	lahm kharuuf	لحم خروف
chicken	dijaaj	دجاج
fish	samak	سمك
shoes	jooti	جوتي
clothes	malaabis	ملابس
shirt	qamis	قميص
traditional pants	sirwaal	سروال
trousers	bantaloon	بنطلون
suit	badhla	بذلة
a dress	fistan	فستان

Islamic Religion In Qatar

In AD628, Prophet Mohammed sent an envoy Abu Al-Alaa Al-Hadrami to Munzir ibn Sawa Al Tamimi, the Sassanid governor of Qatar and the surrounding area. Similar requests were sent to all rulers of lands with - Contacts to the Hijaz, where Mecca and Medina, the two core towns under Prophet Mohammed's rule, are found. The letter asked for Munzir's allegiance to the Islamic faith, which he and some of his subjects agreed to. After more correspondence, Mohammed advised that those who did not become Muslims should pay *Jizya* a tax levied on non-Muslims. After the death of the Prophet Mohammed in 632, a widespread revolt occurred throughout the Islamic world. The new Caliph sent Abu Al-Alaa Al-Hadrami to defeat the rebels, which he did. From this date, Qatar increasingly became an Islamic country, primarily Sunni.

Though Christianity was well set up in Qatar, Islam gradually became the dominant religion. By the 10th century, probably the entire area was Islamic.

From 1787 and the Al Saud incursions, Qatar has increasingly followed the Wahhabi version of Islam based on the Hanbali school of Islam that is dominant in Saudi Arabia.

As with Christianity, there are different schools of thought within Islam. These often develop a distinct identity. The Hanbali school follows the law and culture as given in the Quran, the Prophet Mohammed's sayings, customs and records by the companions of the Prophet Mohammed. This approach is much the same way as the Bible, the sayings and traditions of Jesus and accounts made by his disciples inform the behaviour of Christians. Unlike some other Islamic schools, the Hanbali school does not accept legal or cultural interpretations from different Islamic schools of thought.

Hanbali comes from an Iraqi academic, Ahmed bin Hanbal who died in AD 855. This school of thought was followed by Imam Muhammad ibn Abd al-Wahhab (the main mosque in Doha has his name), who lived from 1703-1792. He was a student of several Hanbali theologians, who espoused ideas at the extreme of Sunni Islamic thought. Imam Muhammad ibn Abd al-Wahhab gained the support of local rulers to the north of what is now Riyadh in modern Saudi Arabia. These eventually included the ruler of a town, Diriyah, also near Riyadh, Sheikh Muhammed bin Saud. These two men collaborated to expand their political and religious territory. By 1818 this covered large areas of Arabia, including the Qatar peninsula. That state, now called the First Saudi State, fell in 1818. A Second Saudi State developed from 1824, which further increased the influence of Wahhabism in Qatar.

The basis of Islam is what has been called the Five Pillars of Islam that are incumbent on each Muslim.

Shahadah - testimony of faith each Muslim must say, in the form: 'There is no God but Allah, and Muhammad is His Prophet'.

Zakat – annual charitable giving, based on a proportion of one's wealth

Sawm - fasting during the month of Ramadhan. Not eating/drinking/smoking etc in public is also prohibited for non-Muslims.

Making the *Haj* pilgrimage to Mecca at least once during one's lifetime, if possible.

Salat prayers five times a day.

The mosque is the first and quintessential Islamic building. In Arabic, the name is *masjid* which means 'place of prostration'. The Prophet Muhammad's house, a typical 7th-century Arabic-style house with an internal courtyard giving access to its rooms, acted as the first mosque. The ceilings of the rooms were supported by columns, creating what is now called a hypostyle (meaning under columns) mosque. More prominent mosques in Arabia followed this style.

The critical function of a mosque is a place of prayer to Allah (God). However, it is acceptable to worship elsewhere. Prayers are held five times daily based on solar time (the sun's position in the sky). Therefore, the time of worship varies throughout the year and will also depend on the location on the earth. The first prayer is about 10 minutes before sunrise; second at solar noon; third late afternoon (initially based on a calculation of the time that a person's shadow became a specific proportion of their height); fourth when the entire solar disk has sunk below the horizon; fifth when, according to some Islamic schools of thought, the sun would be between 12 & 18 degrees below the true horizon, this is around 90minutes after the 4th prayer. Today, technology has, fortunately, immeasurably simplified knowing when prayer is due.

In Islam, it is preferred that for the midday Friday prayers, men gather as a community in a *masjid al jumaa* (congregational mosque) with an Imam to lead prayers. Most mosques do not have a particular Imam (prayer leader); however, in urban areas, there is a significant mosque to serve a district, the *masjid al jumaa*, which does. Many of these *masjid al jumaa* are named in memory of an individual, such as Imam Muhammad ibn Abd al-Wahhab Mosque, the State Grand Mosque of Qatar.

On entering almost all mosques, a visitor faces the *mihrab* (prayer niche), which faces Mecca, towards Qatar's southwest. This direct relationship between a mosque's main entrance and the *mihrab* is preferred. Though a mosque's purpose is to accommodate prayers, it is possible to pray in any clean, respectable place. For that, a small prayer rug can be used to ensure a clean surface on which to pray. Some major mosques in Qatar have prayer space for women and a mezzanine floor so they can hear the prayer service if they attend without being themselves overlooked by men.

Ramadhan

Ramadhan is the holy month when Muslims abstain from eating, drinking and smoking between sunrise and sunset during the entire month. Non-Muslims are affected because it is prohibited to be seen eating, drinking (of any liquid) or smoking in public places during daylight hours in Ramadhan. As a result, most restaurants are closed (though large hotel's main restaurants usually function for non-Muslims). All bars are closed, and hotels are not allowed to serve alcohol publicly. Working hours are shorter, with later starts and earlier finishes. Qataris look forward to and enjoy Ramadhan as it is a time for self-restraint and spiritual reflection. After evening prayers, friends and family are visited, and social activity continues late at night. During Ramadhan, government offices are open from 09:00-14:00, Sunday to Thursday; commercial offices that deal directly with the public will have shorter hours than normal but longer than 09:00-14:00. Banks may work from 10:00-14:00 / 21:00-23:00 (check specific timings). Other businesses and smaller shops will also have altered hours with short timings during the day and later closing at night. Major supermarkets may have unaltered timings. As Ramadhan follows the lunar calendar, it moves forwards each year (falls earlier) by about ten days.

Islam And Culture

Islam is a crucial part of Qatar's culture. It decides activity during the day due to the importance of prayer times. As has been said, it also is critical in the social interactions between males and females. Clothing and modesty are also affected by the religion, even details of how far above a person's ankles a garment should be. The foods that cannot be eaten, such as pork, how an animal should be killed and the views on alcohol, are all covered by the Quran or sayings of the Prophet Mohammed.

Education

Before 1949, Qatar had simple schools that focused on teaching the Quran. A school for boys, giving a broader education was set up in Doha in that year following the increasing income from oil exploration. Other schools were set up in 1954, and the first girl's school started in 1956. By 1976 there were 130 schools in Qatar with an equal split between boys and girls schools. In 2019 the number of schools reached 290, says QPSA.

Today Education for Qatari nationals and foreign employees of the education ministry is free within the government system. There are three streams of Education in Qatar; elementary school for children aged 6 to 12, a preparatory school for children aged 12 to 15 and secondary school for children aged 15 to 18. Up to age 15, Education is compulsory. Qatari government schools are single-sex, with English taught as a foreign language.

From 1964, there has been a variety of fee-paying international schools in the country, catering primarily for children of non-Qatari nationals. However, Qatari's can and do attend. There is a wide variety of national curricula followed at various grades, including USA (32 schools), UK (131) and Canadian (3). In private schools, the history of Qatar is taught in addition to their national curriculum. If the student is Muslim, Arabic and Islam are also taught. International schools may be coeducational or single-sex. The Qatari government supports Qatari nationals attending these, with up to QAR 28,000 as a grant.

The major Qatari university 'Qatar University' was founded in 1973; there are now seven + Qatari university-level educational institutions. Within Qatari government universities, there are scholarships available to non-Qatari nationals. Additionally, there are 19 foreign university-level establishments in Qatar. These are mainly from the USA. The first international university was Virginia Commonwealth University, and campuses are predominantly at Education City. Most of the international academic level establishments offer a limited range of courses based on their parent body supplying material and tutors. There is some segregation of the sexes at the classroom level at several universities. According to the QPSA, about 70% of students (in both government and private universities) are female. They make up around 67% of all graduates. These percentages, where female numbers in Qatar have been increasing annually, are comparable throughout The Gulf. The figures for the UK (2018) are 57% female students and in the USA (2019) 56%.

The education system is under the authority of several bodies. The Supreme Education Council oversees the education system at all levels, from pre-school through university. The Ministry of Education is gradually being subsumed by the Supreme Education Council. Finally, and in effect an autonomous body, the Qatar Foundation (for Education, Science and Community Development) aims to place Qatar at the cutting edge of Education, with an especial emphasis on the inclusion of foreign Universities.

MEDIA

Qatar, as an Arab country, is open to Arab language printed media from around the world, in much the same way as English language media from the USA is available in London, and British media is available in New York. Some of this media is based within an Arab country. Others that have a 'pan-Arab' approach, especially if they have a critical approach to Arab governments, may be found in a non-Arab location, for example, in London.

Historically in Qatar, the relatively small population of Arab speakers meant that local media received a subsidy (whether direct or by advertising & other support) through the government. Otherwise, a publication would not be financially workable. This subsidy resulted in censorship, whether from the government or self-censorship, to align with known government preferences. This also was the situation with English language newspapers. Support and overt government censorship were largely, formally, removed in 1995. However, laws within the country mean that many press houses continue to self-censor. Currently, there are two Arabic papers Al Sharq and Al Watan.

English language papers include the Gulf Times www.gulf-times.com, The Peninsula www.thepeninsulaqatar.com and

Qatar Tribune www.qatar-tribune.com. Several television stations, including Taalam and Baraaem, are aimed at children. Al Jazeera news and current affairs www.aljazeera.com/live/ also in Arabic and the Arabic only Qatar Television (a government operation). Al Jazeera's news programs are claimed to be free of government political censorship. Indeed, it has replaced other channels in Qatar and other Arab countries as many peoples preferred choice for news. It naturally has a less western-centric news focus. Despite claims to be free of government political censorship, it is hardly critical of the Qatar government and ruler.

A few magazines, include Expat Woman Qatar www.qatarexpatwomen.com, Time Out www.timeoutdoha.com.

Radio stations include Al Jazeera (Arabic and English) www.aljazeera.com/live/, Sout Al Khaleej (Arab and English) www.soutalkhaleej.fm.

CHAPTER 11
UNESCO LISTING

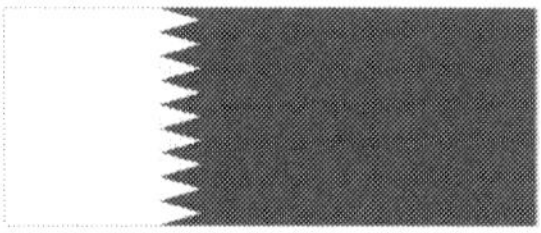

QATAR HAS A SINGLE UNESCO WORLD HERITAGE SITE, Al Zubarah, [PAGE 249], a coastal town listed in 2013 as an 'outstanding testimony to an urban trading and Pearl-diving tradition which sustained the region's major coastal towns'.

On the northwest coast of Qatar, Al Zubarah was a Pearling and trading centre that flourished from around AD1760-1811.

The town is on a ridge of slightly higher ground, with the sea to its west and sabkha to the east. The landscape was created during the mid-Holocene period (about 6,000years ago) when the seawater levels in The Gulf were up to three metres above its current level. During this period, the sea was over a kilometre inland at Al Zubarah. It has since retreated, stabilising around its current position about 1,500 years ago, with *sabkha* replacing the sea.

The entire plain on which Al Zubarah is found is currently without tree cover. This shows the impact of heat, wind, lack of rain and the high salinity of the soil, coupled with the impact of roaming livestock. Windblown sand and debris cover much of the entire town area. Periodically archaeological excavations are made, and therefore new finds are made.

Al Zubarah's establishment may have been following Portuguese attacks on other coastal area in its region. Later disruption in Iraq ruled, under the Ottoman sultans, by Mamluks who originally came to Constantinople from the region of modern Georgia may have increased the population. However the arrival from 1732 by people from the Al bin Ali family and the Al Khalifa family (currently rulers of Bahrain) of the large Utub tribal confederation provided leadership.

Basra was hit by the plague in the early 1770s, affecting its trade and allowing other centres, such as Al Zubarah, to develop. Further migration into Al Zubarah from the Basra area occurred during the Ottoman–Persian War of 1775–1776. During the period that Al Zubarah was inhabited, there were several smaller settlements in northwest Qatar. Most seem to have been impacted by the rise and decline of Al Zubarah, either negatively or positively. Al Zubarah follows the legacy of similar towns that developed around The Gulf, many of which traded with Mesopotamia in ancient times and then the Abbasid and later rulers based in Baghdad. These small towns often served a small hinterland as well as trans-ocean trade.

Following an unsuccessful attack on Al Zubarah by the Persian governor of Bahrain island in 1783, Al Zubarah's ruler, Sheikh Ahmed bin Muhammad bin Khalifa, invaded Bahrain from Al Zubarah. He captured Bahrain, which his descendants have ruled since.

The rise of the Al Saud family in Al-Diriyah, near modern Riyadh, affected the finances and appeal of Al Zubarah. The town paid tribute to the Al Saud from 1787. However, the effect of the Al Saud occupation of the Al Ahsa oasis, 140km southwest of Al Zubarah, in eastern Arabia, also increased the appeal of Al Zubarah to many families. In 1809 Al Zubarah was occupied by the Al Saud forces. However, the Ottoman sultan instructed the governor of Egypt, Mohammed Ali, to attack Al-Diriyah in 1811. Taking advantage of the general military situation, the Sultan of Oman attacked Al Zubarah in 1811. The result was it was largely destroyed. This destruction and the Al Saud confrontation at Al-Diriyah created an opportunity for the Al Khalifa of Bahrain to reoccupy the town. Though the occupants then lived in a much smaller area.

The increased assertion of British power in the Gulf complicated disputes between the Al Khalifa and the Al Thani family based in Doha. During a period of confrontations from 1868, the Al Khalifa family were gradually excluded from the Qatar peninsula. However, the rise of the Al Thani family was helped by the decline of Ottoman influence in the region, despite the Ottomans having several forts in Qatar and a governor at Al Zubarah. In 1878 Sheikh Jassim bin Mohammed Al Thani captured the town, though his hold was tenuous. Despite the town's decline, its proximity to Bahrain resulted in the building in 1938 of Al Zubarah Fort. Following this, Britain decided in 1939 that Al Zubarah was indeed part of sovereign Qatari territory – a 1937 memo gave the opinion of the Political Resident at Bushehr that it 'definitely' belonged to Qatar.

The ongoing territorial disputes between Qatar and Bahrain were settled by the International Court of Justice in The Hague in 2001. It was decided that Al Zubarah was Qatari territory, while the Hawar Islands (off the west coast) were Bahraini territory.

Despite all the legal attention, Al Zubarah had been covered by windblown sand. The sand concealed cemeteries, courtyard houses, walls, fishermen's huts, mosques, palaces, and narrow streets.

The brief period of Al Zubarah's occupation means that an authentic insight into the organisation of 18th & 19th-century towns in the region can be gained.

The town walls of Al Zubarah are the original outer wall and a smaller inner wall, built after the town's 1811 destruction. The outer wall is around 2500m long, with 22 bastions at regular intervals. The wall extended into the sea to the north and formed part of a harbour. This wall, along with the town's overall grid-like layout, suggests a planned town layout. The smaller inner wall was built later, over earlier structures and uses older building materials.

Up to 600 separate buildings are enclosed by the outer wall, suggesting a population of over 6,000 people. Neighbourhoods appear to have been planned out. Most parts of the town have courtyard-style housing, which was common throughout The Gulf until an oil economy grew. Some houses seem to have had the iconic wind towers that are found throughout the region. Many buildings have gypsum decoration suggesting a degree of wealth enabling these decorative touches.

In the southern area of the town is a large fortified palatial compound. Square in shape, its well over one hectare with nine interior courtyards and a tower on each corner. Functions found for some of the rooms include bathing areas. Date processing rooms, *madbasa,* have long troughs to collect date syrup. This is pressed out from dates that are stored in sacks stacked on top of the channels.

A smaller compound to the northeast of the fortified square palatial compound has been partially excavated. This compound is just over half the size of the larger compound, with towers on each corner. Both these compounds may have had an upper floor. A mosque is close to these two residential buildings. Early 20th century photos show it had large columns and arches supporting what is believed to be a multi-dome roof, all covered in plaster. Public squares are also found in this area of the town.

Al Zubarah Souq

In the middle area of the town, 80 metres east from the beach, was a souq that not only engaged in import & export but also appears to have been involved in a range of activities, including glass manufacture and the processing of dates for syrup. On the beach, a small fort marked an area of deeper water to its south.

Huts that are believed to be associated with fishing and Pearl diving have also been found by their post-holes found by the beach. Though these are contemporary with Al Zubarah, this type of hut structure and its function remain prevalent throughout the region.

A couple of wall barriers perpendicular to the original wall extend for a kilometre towards the more recent Al Zubarah Fort. These are thought to have directed traffic toward the town and also to act a defensive shield for the water carriers moving between the town and Qalat Murair to the town's east. Also, a water canal leads towards Qalat Murair, stopping about 500metres to its southwest. Though originally functional as a small boat canal, it appears to have been abandoned and partially infilled, probably due to its operational or economic failure during Al Zubarah's existence. In places, the barrier walls run over the canal.

Al Zubarah Fort was built by the ruler of Qatar, Sheikh Abdullah bin Jassim Al Thani in 1938 as a police outpost. It was used as a military fort until the early 1970s. The construction followed a period of confrontation with Bahrain over this area and the Hawar Islands when a Bahraini police fort was built on those islands in 1937. The single-story Al Zubarah Fort is of a type common throughout the Arabian Peninsula, with a large open courtyard, within which is a water well and rooms opening off the square.

There is a photographic exhibition about the old town within the fort.

Qalat Murair (Murair Fort – Qalat is the Arabic for fort) (GPS 25.974, 51.043) was built in 1768 by Sheikh Mohammed bin Khalifa along with water wells and a surrounding area of housing. Agriculture and livestock pens were to the fort's south and southwest. Its purpose appears to have been to defend the water canal that served Al Zubarah. Today most of its remains are below the surface. Since it was unoccupied from the early 20th century, the stones may have been re-used for building the adjacent Al Zubarah Fort.

About 1,600m north-east of Qalat Murair is a small fort Qalat Shuwail (GPS 25.979, 51.056), which was noted in 1850 by Francis Warden, Chief Secretary to the Government of India at Bombay. It is thought this fort is also contemporary with Al Zubarah town.

Both Al Zubarah and Qalat Murair are on ground that is above the current *sabkha* and earlier sea levels, shown by wave-cut platforms (levelled areas of rock or coral) offshore. The area around Qalat Murair was the location of the freshwater supply for Al Zubarah; this water supply 'floats' over seawater that intrudes inland.

There are scattered mangrove *Avicennia marina* areas along the shoreline and on the mudflats. Close to Al Zubarah and the general inland areas are salt-tolerant plants. Occasional sightings of Dugong and common Bottlenose Dolphin *Tursiops truncates* are made offshore. Socotra Cormorant *Phalacrocorax nigrogularis* roost on Um Jatila Island, just off Al Zubarah. Greater Flamingo *Phoenicopterus roseus* can be seen in winter, close to the shore during high tide. Both Green Turtle *Chelonia mydas* and Hawksbill turtle *Eretmochelys imbricata* have been seen in the water.

Some agriculture associated with Al Zubarah was developed 5km southeast of the town and at Al Jumail 18km north on the coast.

Qatar also has three UNESCO inscriptions on the Representative List of the Intangible Cultural Heritage of Humanity.

Falconry [PAGE 59/80/100] as a sport is included as a UNESCO Intangible Culture. Falconry in Arabia is an ancient hunting practice mentioned by the Prophet Mohammed. Falconry hunting lodges built in the deserts of Syria and Jordan between AD680-83 by Umayyad caliphs testify to the sport's prestige. Treaties on falconry were written, with Peregrine *Falco peregrinus* and Saker Falcons *Falco cherrug* appearing to be the favoured birds. These continue to be the most favoured today. The history of falconry in The Gulf is little known as it was not, until recently, a written practice. Classically three species were a quarry for falcon hunting:

The Houbara Bustard *Chlamydotis macqueenii*

The Stone Curlew *Burhinus oedicnemus*

The Arabian Hare *Lepus capensis*

The introduction of guns in the 16th c reduced the pressure to hunt with falcons and generally reduced wildlife. Today falconry is no longer what it must have been for originally, which was to obtain food, and is a sport. Wild falcons are trapped during migration between September-November and then trained over the following weeks. In Qatar, captive falcons can be seen in Souq Waqif [PAGE 59] or near the Sealine Hotel south of Doha. There are various pieces of equipment associated with Falconry in The Gulf, the *burqa* (rufter - head hood) used to keep the bird calm; a *wakar* which is the stand on which the bird sits, *subuq* the tethers attached to the ankles, and of course a glove for the man called a *dass*, *kaff* or the more modern *mangaleh*. World Falconry Day is celebrated annually on 16 November. Qatar holds a falconry festival, the Marmi Festival, annually in January. Falcons and Saluki hunting dogs are shown, and hunting demonstrations are held.

Arabic Coffee, as a demonstration of generosity and hospitality, is included in this Intangible Cultural Heritage of Humanity list.

Coffee in Bedouin camp

The Coffee uses green Coffee beans, historically from Yemen. The process of preparing the Coffee was traditionally done in front of guests. The beans are roasted lightly over a fire, pounded with a metal pestle and put in a large copper Coffee pot *dallah al logmah* with water and boiled. To add to the flavour, cardamom, cloves or other spices are added. After the Coffee has been brewed, it is poured into a small Coffee pot *dallah al manzal*, from which it is poured into small cups *finjan*, which look like large thimbles. Usually, the most honoured guest is served first. Arabic Coffee is often accompanied by dates, which are eaten first. When you have had enough Coffee, after two or three cups is polite, return the cup to the person who serves you with a slight shake of the cup in your right hand to signify, enough.

The third of these UNESCO inclusions is the system of holding a *Majlis*, a meeting of people while sitting. A *majlis* is a formal space, either as a specific room in a building or, in *Bedouin* society, it may have been outside. It forms several functions, including a reception for outside guests, a celebration meeting place or as a discussion area. Today a *majlis* is either a physical space within a home or public building or is used as a term to indicate a personal meeting between some people. In traditional society, a *majlis* is a single-sex meeting.

Arabic Coffee in a *majlis* can be a formal occasion with guests often assigned a specific place in relation to the host.

CHAPTER 12
HISTORY OF QATAR

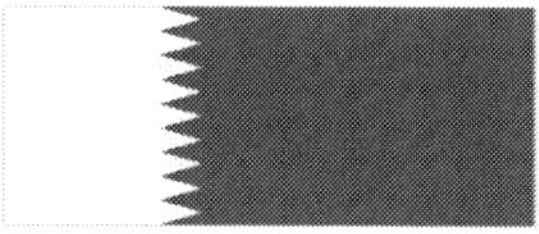

QATAR'S HISTORY IS INTERWOVEN WITH THE surrounding regions and much does have to be inferred from the larger picture of the region.

The archaeological site in central Saudi Arabia on the slopes of Wadi Fatimah at Saffaqah has archaeological remains from the Acheulean Period (1,760,000 - 130,000 years ago). In that period, Saffaqah lay in the headwaters of the major extinct river Wadi Sahba, which flowed east towards what is now The Gulf (Arabian / Persian) in the area of Khor Al Udaid in Qatar. This natural route along a fertile river valley allowed humans to travel very easily during an 'Out of Africa' event into the region of Qatar. The earliest dated evidence of humans found in Qatar has been 'Abbevillian' stone cores (around 600,000-500,000 years ago) found by Dr Julie Scott-Jackson and a University of Oxford team. These cores were found in southwest Qatar (near the Saudi Arabian border) at sites collectively named 'Kapel'.

The Gulf's water size has varied with the increase and decrease of ice cover in northern and southern latitudes over the last 300,000 years. Seawater levels have risen by some 120m during the last 15,000 years. This has covered what must have been an ideal living space used by both animal and human populations in The Gulf. At times the rise in sea levels created swamps to the south of Qatar, effectively making Qatar an island.

As recently as perhaps 7 or 8,000 years ago the area occupied by The Gulf was a historic river flowing through a fertile valley flood plain to the north of Qatar.

On the west coast at Al Daasa, 6km southeast of Dukhan, pottery from the Mesopotamian civilisation of Ubaid 6500-3800 BC has been excavated from a seasonal fishing settlement. Also, from this period, 18 cairn burials have been found on low hills just northwest of Al Khor, north of Doha, with a pit burial covered with slabs of limestone. More recent evidence of human occupation has also been found on nearby Bin Ghannam Island (Al Khor Island), in the lagoon at Al Khor.

Bin Ghannam Island and mangrove

Here fragments of tools, shells and fish have been carbon-dated to between 5610 and 5080. Ceramics from the Dilmun civilisation 2000-1750BC (Bronze Age) have also been found, along with evidence of circular huts and post-holes, stone-lined pits and fire hearths. Kassite pottery (from Mesopotamia) 1530-1160BC were widely distributed over this island. It is this period to which the name 'Purple Island' (Bin Ghannam Island) refers.

The Kassites traded in the dye, 'Tyrian purple' which was colourfast, obtained from a shellfish *Thais savigny*, found at this island [PAGE 114]. Pottery from Sassanid Persia (AD224-651) and pottery from AD1700-1900 have also been excavated on the island. This small island, of less than 17 hectares, was worked on for some 4,000 years.

At another long-established site, Ras Abrouq north of Zekreet on the west coast, Ubaid period (c. 6500–3800 BC), potsherds have been found. Also at Ras Abrouq are some 100 Seleucid (312-63BC) period burial cairns.

Ancient History

The first definitive reference to Qatar in historical records is by Pliny the Elder (AD23-79) in his Natural History when he referred to a tribe the 'Catharrei'.

Qatar became subsumed by the rising power of the new ruling dynasty in Persia, the Sassanids. In AD224 Ardashir I, the Sasanian king, defeated Artabanus V, the Parthian king, and founded the Persian Sassanid Empire, becoming *Shahanshah* (King of Kings). He conducted military excursions around Yamama (south of modern Riyadh) in 240, where he is reputed to have killed the ruler. Farther east, Mazun (modern northern Oman) became a province of the Persian Empire under the Arab Julanda governors. *Shahanshah* Shapur II (309-79) occupied Yamama following ship raids from Arabs into the Persian coast. He set up a buffer kingdom that eventually was ruled by the Arab Lakhmid rulers, who may have been the source of those raiding ships. Shapur II also set up frontier posts along the eastern coast of Arabia running through Qatar to northern Oman and crossed west into the Hijaz and into Syria. In 363, after the Battle of Ctesiphon in the Persian territory of Mesopotamia between Rome and Persia, the Roman Emperor Julian was killed. This marked a high point in the Persian suzerainty of The Gulf region. Following a period where little Persian activity in the region is known, further expansion into Arabia was made during the rule of *Shahanshah* Khosrow I in 532. This expansion by Persia included the Red Sea areas of Hijaz and Yemen, bringing Qatar from the western edge of the Persian Empire towards its geographical centre. However, Arabs again raided into Iran. The new *Shahanshah* Khosrow II occupied northeast Arabia and deposed the Lakhmid dynasty in 600. The buffer client Lakhmid kingdom having been removed, the next wave of Arab invasions into Persia would have unopposed access into the Persian Empire.

Christianity

Christianity was established in Qatar before the middle of the 4th century AD. This establishment of Christianity might have resulted from the relocation of monks after the persecutions carried out by *Shahanshah* Shapur II in Persia. His action may have been a reaction to the Roman Emperor Constantine the Great's support of Christianity after his Edict of Milan in 313. Shapur II may have believed that Christians would be a danger to Persia.

A publication, the 'Vitae Ionae', is the story of a monk who lived during the time of Catholicos Barbashemin (343-346). It mentions a monastery of Rabban Thomas in 'Beth Qatraye', modern Qatar. Beth Qatraye was one of several Christian establishments belonging to the Eastern Church in The Gulf area. These included Sir Bani Yas Island (near Abu Dhabi), Bahrain, Darin Island (on the coast near Dammam Saudi Arabia) and Rew-Ardashir in Fars, northwest Persia that oversaw the others. Rew-Ardashir was under the bishop's administration (later titled Catholicos) of Seleucia-Ctesiphon, the Persian capital in modern Iraq. Beth Qatraye was also the name of the ecclesiastical province that covered the current regions of Kuwait, Eastern Saudi Arabia, Bahrain and Qatar. The neighbouring ecclesiastical province of Beth Mazunaye (the Persian province of Mazun, modern Oman) was noted as attending the Markabta Synod represented by their Bishop Yohannon. In 576, a Bishop mentions a monastery from Beth Qatraye that took part at the Synod of *Mar* Ezekiel, the patriarch of the Eastern Church from 570-581 (*Mar* is an honorific used for Saints and, in this case, Bishops). *Mar* Ezekiel personally visited the region and reported on the Pearl fishing to *Shahanshah* Khosrow I (also known as Chosroes and Anushiruwan the Just). Beth Qatraye hermit monks asked that Patriarch Ishoyahb I (582-95) of Seleucia-

Ctesiphon correspond directly to them, effectively creating their independent role in Qatar. In 613 a man, Ishaq an Naynuwi, was born in Beth Qatraye and was later made Bishop of Nineveh in modern Iraq. After he died in about 700, he became St Isaac of Nineveh. After the establishment of Islam, Beth Qatraye became a tax collector for the Muslim rulers until the end of the 7th Century. During the rise of the Qaramita state, which was based in Bahrain from 899, Beth Qatraye disappeared from records.

The Rise of Islam

Qatar's first contact with Islam came in 628, when the Prophet Mohammed sent an envoy, Abu Al-Alaa Al-Hadrami, to Munzir ibn Sawa Al Tamimi, the Sassanid governor of Qatar. Similar requests were sent to rulers of lands which had contact with the Hijaz, in western Arabia, where the Prophet Mohammed lived. The letter asked for the allegiance of Munzir ibn Sawa Al Tamimi to the Islamic faith, which he and some of his subjects did. After more correspondence, Mohammed advised that those who did not become Muslims should pay *Jizya* (taxation on non-Muslims). After the death of the Prophet Mohammed in 632 a widespread revolt occurred throughout the Islamic world. Abu Al-Alaa Al-Hadrami was sent again to eastern Arabia by the new Caliph, Abu Bakr, to defeat the rebels, in which he succeeded. The next military action by the Caliph in the region was against Persia. The Persian rulers had got rid of the Lakhmid buffer state in the year 600, therefore the Islamic empire had an open door. In 633, the Arab conquest of Persia began, and the Persian capital Ctesiphon (south of modern Baghdad) was occupied in 637. This military action was remarkably done as the Byzantine areas of Palestine and Syria, to the west of Persia were also being conquered by the Caliph; the Islamic war front covered a vast area. After several pauses in military activity in Mesopotamia, by 651, the entire Persian Empire was occupied. The last Sassanid ruler (Yazdegerd III 632-651) was killed by an inhabitant of Merv in central Asia during his long retreat after the occupation of Ctesiphon. Qatar was now firmly within a new Arab Muslim empire.

After the rise of the Islamic Abbasid Caliphate, from 750, the capital of Islam moved to Baghdad in 762. This transfer of power to the region north of Qatar meant a flow of wealth came through The Gulf into the most populous city in the world. Bagdad's splendour was recounted in the One Thousand and One Nights; however, little is known about the history of Qatar during this period.

The only archaeological site dating to this period is what may be the governor's palace at Murwab in northwest Qatar.

The Qarmatians developed a form of Shia Islam from 874. In 899, they took advantage of a rebellion in Basra, Iraq, against Abbasid rule. They seized power in Bahrain, Qatar and Eastern Arabia, periodically controlling as far southeast as the coast of Oman. They became the most powerful force in eastern and central Arabia, exacting tribute and customs until a defeat in 976 by the Abbasid Caliphs. Around 1067 the Qarmatians were finally overpowered. A successor state was ruled by the Uyunid dynasty, who also ruled in eastern and central Arabia; under allegiance to the Abbasids.

The occupation and destruction of Abbasid Bagdad by the Mongol prince, Hulagu Khan, in 1258, ushered in a period of rule of Syria, Iraq and Persia by his various Ilkhanate successors. Qatar was on the periphery of this state, whose capital was in Tabriz, Iran.

Although it is known that from 1253 the Bahrain based Usfurids ruled over eastern Arabia, Qatar was often vassal to the growing power of the Kingdom of Hormuz. This was based on Hormuz Island at the eastern entrance to The Gulf and itself was a nominal vassal to various Persian princes, who often were vassals themselves to empires like the Ilkhanates. It was a complicated power structure that changed often.

The power balance in the region was destroyed with the arrival of the Portuguese in The Gulf in 1507. They quickly defeated the Kingdom of Hormuz and then occupied the island from 1515. Portugal then set up forts in The Gulf, including three on Bahrain.

Portuguese ships Arabian Sea region 1541

A third major power, the Ottoman Turks, appeared in The Gulf region from 1514, They campaigned against Persia's Safavid rulers, and in 1538 the Persian town of Basra (in modern southern Iraq) became an Ottoman town. This gave them a port into The Gulf, where they could campaign against Portugal and Safavid Persia. The 1555 peace treaty between the Ottomans and the Safavids allowed the Ottomans to focus on the Portuguese and the petty states in Arabia. Between 1550 and 1560, there were frequent clashes between the Ottomans and Portugal. The coastal town of Qatif on the eastern Arabian mainland, opposite Bahrain, was occupied by Portugal. Al Ahsa, an inland town 70km west of Qatif was occupied by the Ottomans.

To complicate the power structure around Qatif, Persia's Safavid dynasty ruler Shah Abbas the Great, occupied Bahrain, a few kilometres east of Qatif, in 1602. Subsequently, Bahrain was ruled from Behbahan, a Persian town near the northern end of The Gulf.

Another power had appeared in the region, the English East India Company. In 1622 Persia, joined by an English fleet, defeated Portugal and occupied the island of Hormuz.

Qatar was at the centre of intense competition for territory by four powers - Ottomans, Portuguese, Safavids and the English East India Company. Despite this, it does not seem to have been occupied by any of them. Presumably, however, ships from Qatar's small ports were forced to pay protection and customs duty to those various powers.

By 1670, Qatar came under the rule of the Arab tribe, the Bani Khalid after they had conquered Al Ahsa from the Ottomans. Taking advantage of Persia's increasing weakness following its disastrous defeat in Afghanistan in 1711 Oman occupied Bahrain in 1717. However, by 1736 Persia, under its new ruler Nader Shah Afshar, of the new Afshar dynasty, had reoccupied the island, once again bringing the eastern areas of Arabia under Persian domination.

The Start of Qatar's Modern History

Qatar has a more defined history following these episodes. A series of events also resonate in the region's modern politics. Alliances were made and then broken, with the former allies almost inevitably attacking their previous partners.

In 1732 members of the Al Bin Ali family from Kuwait who were part of a tribal federation, the Utub, are thought to have settled in what would become Al Zubarah [PAGE 122] on the west coast of Qatar. Later the Al Khalifa family, also part of the Utub, moved from Kuwait to Al Zubarah, between 1762-1768, under the leadership of Shaikh Muhammad bin Khalifa.

Al Zubarah grew partly because of the instability elsewhere in the region and the lack of any customs charged by the ruler of the town. The town developed trading links through The Gulf. It attracted traders from Basra to settle in Al Zubarah after they fled Iraq during the Ottoman–Persian wars between 1775/79.

In 1782, a skirmish, one of a series, took place on the island of Bahrain between a group from Al Zubarah and Bahraini merchants. The resulting deaths on both sides escalated the incident. An invasion of Bahrain from Al Zubarah took place, which succeeded in destroying Manama, the main town in Bahrain. Part of the spoils was the ship used by Bahrain's Governor to collect customs. In retaliation, plans were made in Bahrain to invade Al Zubarah with 2,000 soldiers being sent from Persia, who still claimed rule over the island. In May 1783 the Omani Sheikh Nasr Al-Madhkur, was the governor, or probably ruler as vassal, of Bahrain and Busher under the Persian Shah Ali Murad Khan. Sheikh Nasr landed his troops away from the town but was defeated by a combined force from the town and surrounding region. Compounding this defeat was an attack on Bahrain itself, on the same day, by Utub Tribe members from Kuwait who set fire to Manama. By July 1783, Shaikh Ahmad bin Muhammad Al Khalifa captured Bahrain with a force from Al Zubarah. Following that, large numbers of people moved from Al Zubarah to the island of Bahrain.

Al Zubarah came under increasing attacks from 1787. These came from Al Diriyah (near modern Riyadh) led by Amir Abdulaziz ibn Muhammad Al Saud, the ruler of the First Saudi State. Following the Al Saud capture of Al Ahsa (in today's eastern Saudi Arabia), many refugees fled from there and arrived in Al Zubarah in 1795. Al Saud forces, however, exacted taxes from Al Zubarah as a protection payment.

From the death in 1795 of Shaikh Ahmad bin Muhammad Al-Khalifa in Bahrain, two of his sons jointly ruled Bahrain and Al Zubarah. One, Sheikh Abdullah bin Ahmed Al Khalifa, ruled until 1842. In 1797, the Al Khalifa family moved to Bahrain, starting the start of the decline of Al Zubarah.

A series of attacks on Al Zubarah by Omani forces between 1799 and 1802 ended after the Al Khalifa obtained support from the Al Saud family.

Al Zubarah was then a target of a combined attack in 1809 by Al Qassimi forces (from Ras Al Khaimah in the modern UAE) and Al Saud forces. It was occupied by the Al Qassimi/Al Saud forces, giving Britain and Oman, both of which had existing struggles with the Al Qassimi and Al Saud, a new conflict centre to consider. In 1811, a combined British/Omani force attacked Al Zubarah and the Al Qassimi/Al Saud forces, leaving the town in ruins.

British Engagement

The political result of these conflicts was that from 1811 the Al Khalifa family were again the dominant power in Qatar. Britain supported them through various agreements in the following years. Critical was the General Treaty (which also involved Abu Dhabi and Ras Al Khaimah) signed in 1820. A later treaty of Perpetual Truce of Peace and Friendship was signed in 1861.

Britain increased its impact on Qatar in 1821, when an East India Company vessel bombarded the town of Al Bidda, now part of Doha, as retaliation for what was said to be piracy committed by its inhabitants. This action forced between 300 and 400 people to flee, temporally, from Al Bidda.

Al Bidda was involved in a later turning point in Qatar's modern history. A contender for power in Bahrain, Sheikh Abdullah bin Ahmed bin Khalifa, made an alliance with Shaikh Isa Bin Tarif Al Bin Ali of Al Bidda, a leading power in the region and incidentally Sheikh Abdullah's earlier military opponent. They fought a battle at Fuwayrit (often called the Battle of Umm Suwayya) on 17 November 1847 against Sheikh Mohammed bin Khalifa, ruler of Bahrain and Al Zubarah. Shaikh Isa Bin Tarif was killed and his ally, Sheikh Abdullah bin Ahmed, escaped to Persia. Following the battle at Fuwayrit Sheikh Mohammed bin Khalifa attacked and destroyed Shaikh Isa's base of Al Bidda and moved its population to Bahrain.

Rise of the Al Thani

These events created a power vacuum in Qatar. Under the leadership of Sheikh Mohammed bin Thani, the Al Thani family went from Fuwayrit to the growing settlement of Doha, near Al Bidda in 1849 or 50.

The Perpetual Truce of Peace and Friendship, signed in 1861 by Britain with Shaikh Muhammad bin Khalifa Al Khalifa, collapsed in Qatar in 1867 following a series of incidents. After the imprisonment of Sheikh Jassim bin Mohammed Al Thani, by

Sheikh Mohammed bin Khalifa Al Khalifa, there was a battle against Bahraini forces in Qatar, which the Qatari side won. Sheikh Jassim was released in exchange for Bahraini prisoners. Later in the year, 24 boats from Bahrain and 70 ships from Abu Dhabi, with a combined total of 2,700 men, attacked Qatar and destroyed the towns of Al Bidda and Al Wakrah. Despite this, Qatari forces were powerful enough to attack Bahrain, destroy 60 boats and kill 1,000 men. These conflicts resulted in Britain forcing a change of ruler within Bahrain and the confiscation of all his ships. A large fine of $100,000 was levied on Bahrain.

The Leadership of The Al Thani Family

The British Political Resident (Administrator/Minister/Ambassador depending on your viewpoint of Britain's role in the region) in The Gulf, Colonel Lewis Pelly signed a treaty with Sheikh Mohammed bin Thani in 1868. This treaty represents the acknowledgement of Qatar as a separate political entity, rather than a political part of Bahrain, and the Al Thani family as its leaders.

Following a conflict within the Al Saud family, Midhat Pasha, the Ottoman Governor of Bagdad, reoccupied eastern Arabia in 1871 and occupied Qatar. Despite the alarm of Britain, the Ottomans then incorporated Qatar into the *sanjak* (administration area) of Najd (Eastern Arabia) in 1872 as a *Kaza* (small administrative region). Sheikh Mohammed bin Thani was appointed as the *Qaim-makam* (sub-governor), once again supporting his dominant role in Qatar. In 1878 Sheikh Mohammed's son, the future *Qaim-makam* Sheikh Jassim bin Mohammed bin Thani (Al Thani), attacked and defeated the residents of Al Zubarah, who were allies of Shaikh Isa bin Ali Al Khalifa in Bahrain, and captured the nearby Al Murair Fort. In the following years, Bahrain once again tried to regain control of Al Zubarah, probably assuming Britain would support them against the newly confirmed Ottoman *Qaim-makam* Sheikh Jassim bin Mohammed Al Thani; however, Britain did little against Sheikh Jassim.

However, the role of the Ottomans came under pressure because of historical local rivalry. In 1882 Abu Dhabi occupied

Khor Al Udaid in southeast Qatar, at Abu Dhabi's territorial western limits. Sheikh Jassim bin Mohammed Al Thani, the new *Qaim-makam*, was not supported by the Ottomans in regaining it. Sheikh Jassim retaliated against Abu Dhabi's occupation of Khor Al Udaid by raiding 300km southeast of Khor Al Udaid into the Liwa Oasis in the southwest of the modern UAE. This oasis was the original home of the Abu Dhabi Al Nahyan Sheikhs.

A conflict between the Ottomans and Sheikh Jassim bin Mohammed Al Thani followed a simmering dispute after the newly appointed Ottoman Governor of Basra, Mehmed Hafiz Pasha, arrived in Qatar from Al Ahsa, with 340 armed men. Sheikh Jassim bin Mohammed Al Thani relocated to Al Wajbah, 13km west of Doha, with men from several Tribes. After unsuccessful negotiations, the Ottomans captured and imprisoned several men on a ship, the Merrikh. Following this imprisonment, the Battle of Wajbah took place in 1893, with over 4,000 men supporting Sheikh Jassim bin Mohammed Al Thani. Both sides had a substantial loss; however, the Qataris defeated the Ottomans. The result was that Mehmed Hafiz Pasha withdrew to Al Ahsa (the oasis in eastern Arabia) and the Ottoman Sultan then deposed him as governor. This defeat consolidated Sheikh Jassim bin Mohammed Al Thani's position and reduced the ability of the Ottomans to govern.

The Ottomans officially renounced sovereignty over Qatar in 1913 though they stayed in Doha until 1915. On 3rd November 1916, Britain signed a Protectorate treaty with Sheikh Abdullah bin Jassim Al Thani. Qatar gave up independence in foreign affairs in exchange for Britain's support against external threats; similar agreements were previously made throughout The Gulf. Despite this, Britain continued to have little interest in Qatar's internal affairs until first negotiations for oil exploration took place in 1922.

Sheikh Abdullah Bin Jassim Al Thani's fort (now in National Museum)

OIL AND GAS DEVELOPMENT IN QATAR

Oil and natural gas have been a critical part of Qatar's economy for almost 100 years. The Anglo-Persian Oil Company surveyed Qatar in 1926, but no oil was found. After an oil strike in Bahrain in 1933, a Qatari concession was signed on 17th May 1935 with Anglo-Persian representatives for 75 years in return for 400,000 rupees on signature and 150,000 rupees per annum with royalties; Britain agreed to supply enhanced security. In October 1938, the first exploratory oil well was sunk in Dukhan, on Qatar's west coast, and oil was found in late 1939. However, due to 2nd World War, exports did not begin until 1949.

International borders and more

Over this period, the dispute with Bahrain over Al Zubarah continued, and in 1936 it expanded to include the Hawar Islands, just off the Qatari central west coast. A Bahraini police fort was built on the islands, and Bahrain imposed a ban on trade and travel into Qatar. Qatar followed this by building Al Zubarah Fort [PAGE 123], completed in 1938.

Following Britain's announced withdrawal from 'East of Suez' in 1968, The Gulf sheikhdoms future political situation needed to be addressed by them. For many months, it appeared that Qatar would become part of a union that would include

Bahrain and what are now the constituent states of the United Arab Emirates, which includes Abu Dhabi, Qatar's immediate neighbour to its east. Ultimately on 3rd September 1971, Sheikh Khalifa bin Hamad Al Thani, the then Heir Apparent and Prime Minister but soon to be ruler, declared Qatar a separate, independent sovereign state.

In 1971, Qatar discovered the North Dome Gas Field in The Gulf; this field straddles the maritime border between Iran and Qatar as the South Pars/North Dome Gas Field. Production started in 1981, and it eventually turned out to be the largest gas field in the world.

On 27th June 1995, Sheikh Hamad bin Khalifa Al Thani (known since his abdication as The Father Amir), the father of the current ruler Sheikh Tamim, assumed power. During his reign, the State of Qatar saw massive economic, social and cultural development.

The Al Zubarah dispute with Bahrain was settled in March 2001 by a decision by the International Court of Justice. Al Zubarah, Fasht ad Dibal sandbank and Janan Island were confirmed as territory of Qatar, The Hawar Islands and Qitat Jaradah Island were settled as Bahrain's territory.

In 2002, Qatar hosted the United States Central Command, which in 2009 moved to its current base at Al Udeid Air Base, west of Doha. Other USA bases in Qatar have been transferred out of the country.

Sheikh Hamad Bin Khalifa Al Thani abdicated in June 2013 when his son Sheikh Tamim bin Hamad Al Thani, the current Amir of Qatar, became ruler.

From 5th June 2017, Saudi Arabia, the UAE, Bahrain and Egypt instated a political and economic blockade against Qatar. This followed years of disputes that notably included the withdrawal of their ambassadors from Qatar on 5th March 2014. The blockade and resultant focus on self-sufficiency by Qatar has increased the national identity of Qatar. This blockade was officially resolved on 5th January 2021.

Qatar's first general elections were held on 2nd October 2021 for 30 members of a 45-seat Shura Council.

CHAPTER 13
PEARL DIVING

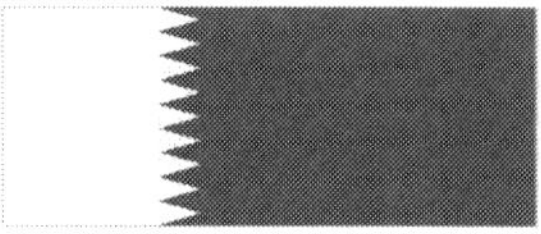

One of the oldest professions in the Gulf region is Pearl diving.

Archaeological evidence dating back to the Late Stone Age in 6000–5000 BC suggest trade and spiritual beliefs within The Gulf included the natural Pearl.

In the early modern era, with increasing stability in the region and its incorporation into international markets, The Gulf's Pearl industry boomed. Divers from Oman's Batinah Coast and the Yemeni island of Socotra, almost 3,000 kilometres away by sea, came to The Gulf to dive for this valuable resource. By around the middle of the 19th century, there could have been few families on the coasts of Eastern Arabia or Western Persia who did not have men working in the Pearl business.

Pearl diver - The Gulf

Historical records illustrate the extent of Pearl diving and the money made. The value of the market in Pearls is estimated to have grown by over 600% between 1790 to 1905. Pearls from The Gulf created an income of about US$1.75 million a year from 1830, rising to US$4 million by the early 20th century.

In the 1829 book Travels in Assyria, Media and Persia, James Silk Buckingham wrote that Pearls from Bahrain brought in approximately £200,000. In the same period, James Wellsted, in his 1838 book 'Travels in Arabia', reported that there were over 4,000 boats engaged in Pearling between Bahrain and Oman.

Pearls from The Gulf were traded to India, the Ottoman Empire, Persia, China, Europe, and North America. Sheikh Mohammed bin Thani of Qatar told William Palgrave in 1877: 'We are all from the highest to the lowest, slaves of one master, Pearl.'

The British Political Resident, John Lorimer, wrote that the Qatar industry was worth £625,933 in 1873/74 and 30 years later in 1904/05 in his Gazetteer of the Persian Gulf £1,076,793. Lorimer also included that there were 350 Pearl boats in Doha.

Two species of Molluscs were sought for their Pearls. The Akoya Pearl oyster *Pinctada imbricata fucata* grows to a shell length of 60–80 mm and creates as a by-product 'Lengeh shells' named after the Iranian port, used for products such as buttons. The second, larger, species *Pinctada margaritifera*, commonly known as the Black-Lip Pearl oyster, grows to 200 mm in length.

Pearl grounds on the western shore of The Gulf run from Kuwait to Musandam in Oman. They also extend on the Persian side of The Gulf, from near Bushehr (opposite Kuwait) to Lengeh (opposite Musandam) in the south.

Pearl diving was a seasonal activity from June to September with two diving periods: the big dive, a 60-day journey, and the small dive, a 40-day trip. Each season dozens of Pearling boats left Doha for coastal banks rich with oysters.

The ship's captain, called the *nakuda*, commanded the whole operation, including the Pearl divers, *ghawas al lulu* (*lulu* is the Arabic for pearl) On the diver's fingers and toes were leather protection, *khabbal,* to protect against sharp rocks, shells and dangerous sea creatures. A wooden nose peg, *fitaam,* stopped seawater drowning the man under deep-water pressure, oil-soaked cotton plugs blocked the ears. They used a knife to cut the shellfish off the rock and a basket, *dadjin,* to put their catch in.

A diver used two ropes to descend which his assistant, the *saib*, held from the ship. The diver would remain underwater for 60 to 90 seconds, going as deep as 20 metres. Each vessel could have up to 40 divers, with each person diving perhaps 40 times a day. A crew could gather 8,000 Pearl oysters a day. In colder waters in The Gulf, some divers greased their body against the chilly water, much as ocean swimmers do today.

These divers lived on credit given to them by their captain, who owned and worked the boats and kept the crew. Many of the divers were slaves – transported from East Africa, typically through Zanzibar and Oman – then into individual towns across Arabia. Pearl merchants, *tawawish,* in turn advanced loans to boat captains in advance of the diving season. The Pearling industry, therefore, functioned on borrowed capital. The captain would collect all the Pearls, and after selling them to the Pearl merchant, he would pay the divers in cash, though despite them risking their lives they received the smallest proportion of the sale, the slaves of course were dependents of their 'owners'. Each season, the system depended on success, with financial ruin for everyone down the chain a possibility.

By 1924, however, the region's Pearling industry was already falling into rapid decline. A primary factor affecting that decline was the development of the cultured (artificially encouraged growth of the Pearl) Pearl industry in Japan from 1916 by the entrepreneur Mikimoto Kokichi.

From then, the number of boats in the Pearl fishing fleets dwindled. The men travelled elsewhere to look for work, perhaps to Baku, Iraq and Persia where oil production had already started.

CHAPTER 14
THE AL THANI FAMILY

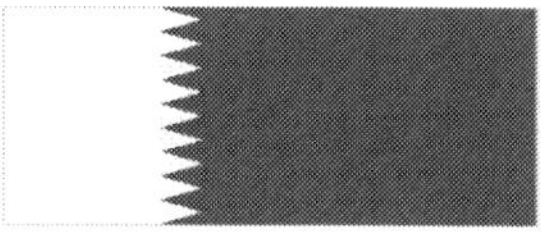

The Al Thani family can be traced back to a branch of the Maadhid Tribe whose eponymous originator, Maadhid bin Musharaf, claims descent from the tribal confederation Banu Tamim, one of the largest in Arabia.

From the 17th century AD, the family lived in Ushayqir, 170km northwest of Riyadh, in present-day Saudi Arabia. At some time around the start of the 18th c, they were settled at Yabrin (Jabrin) oasis 280km southeast of Riyadh. During the 1740s, they moved to Qatar, firstly in the south near Sikak, then Al Zubarah, Fuwayrit and finally, under their leader Sheikh Mohammed bin Thani, the family settled in Doha around 1848. The family takes their name from Thani bin Mohammad bin Thamir, the father of Sheikh Mohammad. Thani died around 1860 and was apparently a 14th generation descendent of Maadhid bin Musharaf who lived in Yabrin oasis. Arabs value their genealogy.

The move into Qatar resulted in the family becoming involved in Pearling and trading, which required families to settle in a permanent base rather than having a nomadic lifestyle. After Sheikh Mohammed's death, his son Sheikh Jassim became the effective ruler of Qatar in 1878. He developed Qatar's Pearl trade and expanded trade links to India and East Africa. Sheikh Jassim's accession date on the 18th November is now the National Day for Qatar.

Sheikh Abdullah Al Thani centre - 1931 by Bertram Thomas

Enhancing the rule of the Al Thani family Sheikh Abdullah Bin Jassim Al Thani, who succeeded his father in 1913, signed the Anglo-Qatari Treaty on 3rd November 1916. This treaty followed the Anglo-Ottoman Convention, which resulted in the withdrawal of the Ottoman Sultanate from Qatar. Under Sheikh Abdullah's rule, the first oil well was drilled in Qatar in 1938.

Sheikh Abdullah abdicated in 1949, and his son Sheikh Ali bin Abdullah became ruler. During this period, oil was first exported from Qatar, and the later flow of money enabled general economic development in Qatar to accelerate and the Al Thani to consolidate their position through economic means. In 1960, Sheikh Ahmad Bin Ali Al Thani became ruler; during his administration, Qatar's independence was declared on 3rd September 1971. Using a coup, his cousin Sheikh Khalifa bin Hamad Al Thani became Amir on 22nd February 1972 and ruled until his own son, H.H. (The Father Amir) Sheikh Hamad bin Khalifa Al Thani took power, again through a coup, on 26th June 1995. During Sheikh Hamad's rule, the economy of Qatar grew dramatically with increased oil revenues and the development of Qatar's vast gas fields. Sheikh Hamad was successful in gaining the 2022 World Cup for Qatar.

Current ruler of Qatar

Sheikh Hamad abdicated on 25th June 2013, and his son His Highness Sheikh Tamim bin Hamad Al Thani became Amir of Qatar (often the spelling Emir is used).

Sheikh Tamim and Ukrainian President

Sheikh Tamim was born on 3rd June 1980 in Doha, Qatar, and after completing secondary school enrolled in the British military academy at Sandhurst, graduating in 1998. Sheikh

Tamim is a multi-linguist, fluent in English and French, in addition to Arabic. The educational role of the Qatar Foundation has grown under his administration.

CHAPTER 15
EXPLORERS OF QATAR

An idea of life in Qatar, before today, is given by some of the travellers who passed through the area.

Lieutenant J.H. Grubb of the Indian Navy (Bombay Marine) in 1822 described Bidda as a 'most miserable place: not a blade of grass nor any kind of vegetation near it; the water good, obtained, they said, at some distance. The anchorage in the inner harbour very good, four fathoms, being about one-eighth of a mile from the shore, surrounded by a reef nearly dry, which forms a complete basin, the entrance to which is very narrow, but deep, and free from danger. Not so in approaching it, as the water is very shoal about seven miles out, there being two and a half fathoms, sand, and a good deal of sea in a north-wester.'

In the 20th Century, the description of Qatar by foreign visitors creates a vivid impression of the country.

In January 1904 Hermann Burchardt, the German explorer and photographer, arrived in Doha after travelling by sea from Kuwait into Al Uqair and overland via Al Ahsa. He went to the Turkish Fort which was found south of the Amiri Diwan (a reception and administration complex for the ruler). This fort was between Al Bidda and Doha, and he was 'quartered with the Commander, a major'. Burchardt described that 'three neighbouring towns are distinguished. Doha, with the garrison, and Al-Bidaa, and As-Solata. The garrison consisted of 1 *tabur* (an armed unit of 250 men appx) with two old cannon. Soldiers, military officers, and administrative officers with their families dwell in miserable mud houses, and the state of health is not good; particularly common are eye diseases. At one time scurvy was also common; better nutrition for the soldiers has eliminated this disease completely'. He continued 'in reality the Turkish influence extends no further than the reach of rifles and canon' from the fort.

Robert Cheesman worked in Iraq from 1920-23 as an assistant to Sir Percy Cox, the High Commissioner of Iraq in the British administration. In 1921 Cheesman travelled through Saudi Arabia and arrived in the small port town of Al Uqair in modern Saudi Arabia. There he used the organisation of Abdul Aziz Al Qusaibi the ship-owner and support of Abdulaziz Al Saud, who ruled the central and eastern areas in what is now Saudi Arabia. Cheesman boarded a '*Baghala*' type of Dhow, in April near Al Uqair and crisscrossed between the western shore of Qatar and the eastern shore of the Saudi coast in the Gulf of Salwa, describing how shallow the water was - as the boat needed to be pushed despite being 1/4 mile (400m) from shore. He wrote, 'Here the Qatar coast is a sandy shore; scrub grows close to the sea and across one to two miles of undulating sand-dunes until the hills are reached, which appear featureless and level-topped, running parallel with the coast and rising from 200 to 300 feet'.

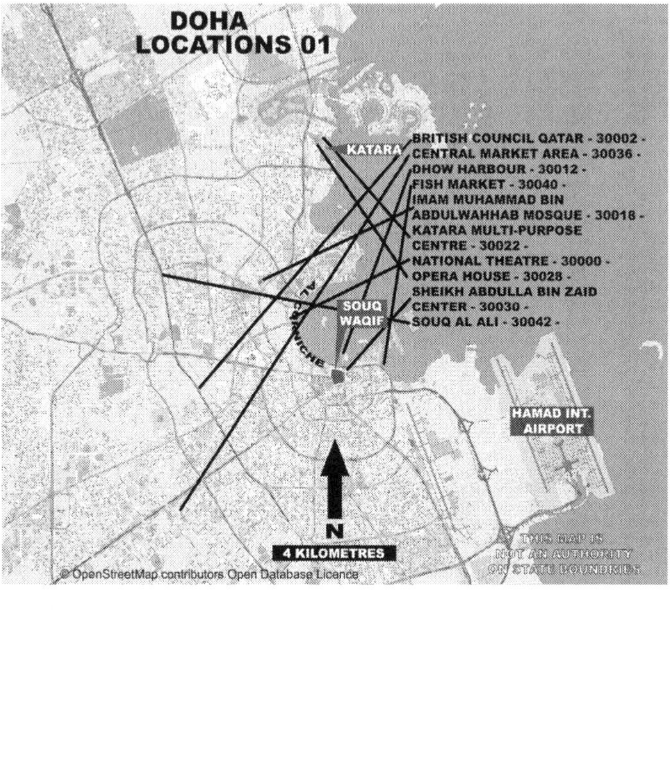
DOHA
LOCATIONS 01
KATARA
BRITISH COUNCIL QATAR - 30002 -
CENTRAL MARKET AREA - 30036 -
DHOW HARBOUR - 30012 -
FISH MARKET - 30040 -
IMAM MUHAMMAD BIN
ABDULWAHHAB MOSQUE - 30018 -
KATARA MULTI-PURPOSE
CENTRE - 30022 -
NATIONAL THEATRE - 30000 -
OPERA HOUSE - 30028 -
SHEIKH ABDULLA BIN ZAID
CENTER - 30030 -
SOUQ AL ALI - 30042 -
SOUQ
WAQIF
AL CORNICHE
HAMAD INT.
AIRPORT
N
4 KILOMETRES
THIS MAP IS
NOT AN AUTHORITY
ON STATE BOUNDRIES
© OpenStreetMap contributors Open Database Licence

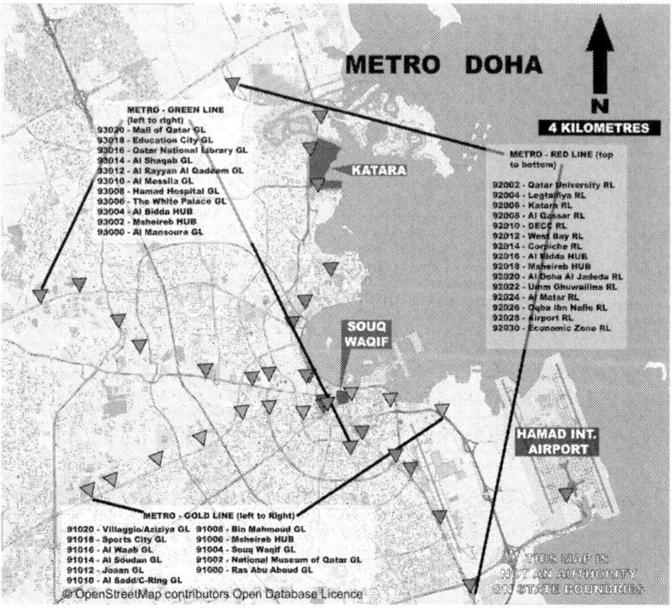
METRO DOHA
N
4 KILOMETRES
METRO - GREEN LINE (left to right)
93020 - Mall of Qatar GL
93018 - Education City GL
93016 - Qatar National Library GL
93014 - Al Shaqab GL
93012 - Al Rayyan Al Qadeem GL
93010 - Al Messila GL
93008 - Hamad Hospital GL
93006 - The White Palace GL
93004 - Al Bidda HUB
93002 - Msheireb HUB
93000 - Al Mansoura GL
KATARA
METRO - RED LINE (top to bottom)
92002 - Qatar University RL
92004 - Legtaifiya RL
92006 - Katara RL
92008 - Al Qassar RL
92010 - DECC RL
92012 - West Bay RL
92014 - Corniche RL
92016 - Al Bidda HUB
92018 - Msheireb HUB
92020 - Al Doha Al Jadeda RL
92022 - Umm Ghuwailina RL
92024 - Al Matar RL
92026 - Oqba Ibn Nafie RL
92028 - Airport RL
92030 - Economic Zone RL
SOUQ WAQIF
HAMAD INT. AIRPORT
METRO - GOLD LINE (left to Right)
91020 - Villaggio/Aziziya GL
91018 - Sports City GL
91016 - Al Waab GL
91014 - Al Soudan GL
91012 - Joaan GL
91010 - Al Sadd/C-Ring GL
91008 - Bin Mahmoud GL
91006 - Msheireb HUB
91004 - Souq Waqif GL
91002 - National Museum of Qatar GL
91000 - Ras Abu Aboud GL
© OpenStreetMap contributors Open Database Licence
THIS MAP IS NOT AN AUTHORITY ON STATE BOUNDRIES

Dhows and Islamic Arts Museum

Printed in Great Britain
by Amazon

52770888R00165